DOMESDAY BOOK

text and translation edited by

JOHN MORRIS

12

Hertfordshire

edited from a draft translation prepared by

Margaret Newman and Sara Wood

PHILLIMORE
Chichester
1976

1976

Published by
PHILLIMORE & CO. LTD.,
London and Chichester

Head Office: Shopwyke Hall,
Chichester, Sussex, England

ISBN 0 85033 137 4 (case)
ISBN 0 85033 138 2 (limp)

Printed in Great Britain by
Titus Wilson & Son Ltd.
Kendal

DOMESDAY BOOK

Hertfordshire

DOMESDAY BOOK

A Survey of the Counties of England

LIBER DE WINTONIA

Compiled by direction of

KING WILLIAM I

Winchester
1086

HERTFORDSHIRE

History from the Sources
General Editor: John Morris

The series aims to publish history
written directly from the sources
for all interested readers, both
specialists and others. The first
priority is to publish important
texts which should be widely
available, but are not.

DOMESDAY BOOK

The contents, with the folio on which each county begins, are:

Domesday Book is termed *Liber de Wintonia* (The Book of Winchester) in column 332c

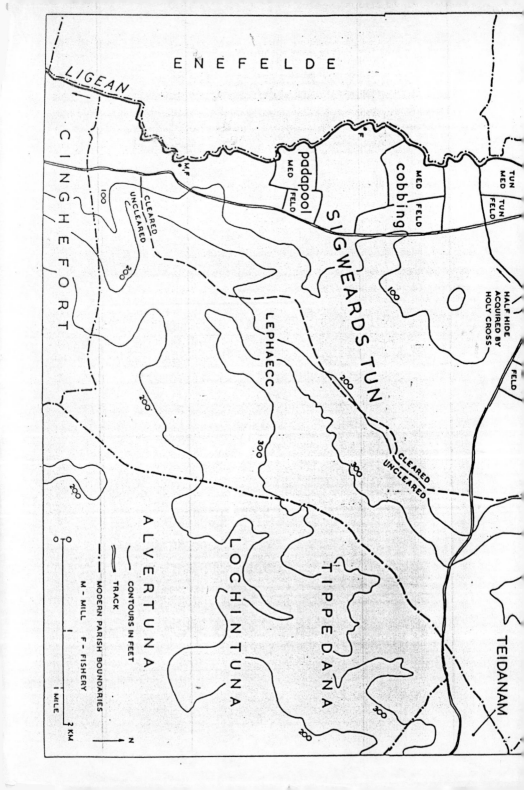

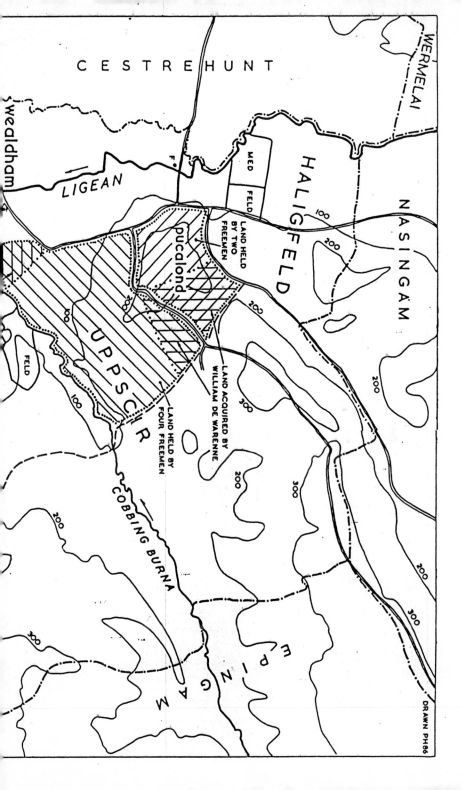

MAP OF WALTHAM (WEALDHAM) circa 1066

CESTREHUNT

WERMELAI

wealdham

LIGEAN

HALIGFELD

NASINGAM

MED

FELD

pucalond

LAND HELD BY TWO FREEMEN

UPPSCIR

LAND ACQUIRED BY WILLIAM DE WARENNE

LAND HELD BY FOUR FREEMEN

FELD

COBBING BURNA

EPINGAM

100
200
200
200
300
200
100
100
200
300
200
300
200
300
100

DRAWN PH86

INTRODUCTION

The Domesday Survey

In 1066 Duke William of Normandy conquered England. He was crowned King, and most of the lands of the English nobility were soon granted to his followers. Domesday Book was compiled 20 years later. The Saxon Chronicle records that in 1085

> at Gloucester at midwinter ... the King had deep speech with his counsellors ... and sent men all over England to each shire ... to find out ... what or how much each landholder held ... in land and livestock, and what it was worth ... The returns were brought to him.[1]

William was thorough. One of his Counsellors reports that he also sent a second set of Commissioners 'to shires they did not know, where they were themselves unknown, to check their predecessors' survey, and report culprits to the King.'[2]

The information was collected at Winchester, corrected, abridged, chiefly by omission of livestock and the 1066 population, and fair-copied by one writer into a single volume. Norfolk, Suffolk and Essex were copied, by several writers, into a second volume, unabridged, which states that 'the Survey was made in 1086'. The surveys of Durham and Northumberland, and of several towns, including London, were not transcribed, and most of Cumberland and Westmorland, not yet in England, was not surveyed. The whole undertaking was completed at speed, in less than 12 months, though the fair-copying of the main volume may have taken a little longer. Both volumes are now preserved at the Public Record Office. Some versions of regional returns also survive. One of them, from Ely Abbey,[3] copies out the Commissioners' brief. They were to ask

> The name of the place. Who held it, before 1066, and now?
> How many *hides*?[4] How many ploughs, both those in lordship and the men's?
> How many villagers, cottagers and slaves, how many free men and Freemen?[5]
> How much woodland, meadow and pasture? How many mills and fishponds?
> How much has been added or taken away? What the total value was and is?
> How much each free man or Freeman had or has? All threefold, before 1066,
>   when King William gave it, and now; and if more can be had than at present?

The Ely volume also describes the procedure. The Commissioners took evidence on oath 'from the Sheriff; from all the barons and their Frenchmen; and from the whole Hundred, the priests, the reeves and six villagers from each village'. It also names four Frenchmen and four Englishmen from each Hundred, who were sworn to verify the detail.

The King wanted to know what he had, and who held it. The Commissioners therefore listed lands in dispute, for Domesday Book was not only a tax-assessment. To the King's grandson, Bishop Henry of Winchester, its purpose was that every 'man should know his right and not usurp another's'; and because it was the final authoritative register of rightful possession 'the natives called it Domesday Book, by analogy

---

[1] Before he left England for the last time, late in 1086. [2] Robert Losinga, Bishop of Hereford 1079-1095 (see *E.H.R.* 22, 1907, 74). [3] *Inquisitio Eliensis,* first paragraph. [4] A land unit, reckoned as 120 acres. [5] *Quot Sochemani.*

from the Day of Judgement'; that was why it was carefully arranged by Counties, and by landholders within Counties, 'numbered consecutively ... for easy reference'.[6]

Domesday Book describes Old English society under new management, in minute statistical detail. Foreign lords had taken over, but little else had yet changed. The chief landholders and those who held from them are named, and the rest of the population was counted. Most of them lived in villages, whose houses might be clustered together, or dispersed among their fields. Villages were grouped in administrative districts called Hundreds, which formed regions within Shires, or Counties, which survive today with minor boundary changes; the recent deformation of some ancient county identities is here disregarded, as are various short-lived modern changes. The local assemblies, though overshadowed by lords great and small, gave men a voice, which the Commissioners heeded. Very many holdings were described by the Norman term *manerium* (manor), greatly varied in size and structure, from tiny farmsteads to vast holdings; and many lords exercised their own jurisdiction and other rights, termed *soca*, whose meaning still eludes exact definition.

The Survey was unmatched in Europe for many centuries, the product of a sophisticated and experienced English administration, fully exploited by the Conqueror's commanding energy. But its unique assemblage of facts and figures has been hard to study, because the text has not been easily available, and abounds in technicalities. Investigation has therefore been chiefly confined to specialists; many questions cannot be tackled adequately without a cheap text and uniform translation available to a wider range of students, including local historians.

Previous Editions
The text has been printed once, in 1783, in an edition by Abraham Farley, probably of 1250 copies, at Government expense, said to have been £38,000; its preparation took 16 years. It was set in a specially designed type, here reproduced photographically, which was destroyed by fire in 1808. In 1811 and 1816 the Records Commissioners added an introduction, indices, and associated texts, edited by Sir Henry Ellis; and in 1861-1863 the Ordnance Survey issued zincograph facsimiles of the whole. Texts of individual counties have appeared since 1673, separate translations in the Victoria County Histories and elsewhere.

This Edition
Farley's text is used, because of its excellence, and because any worthy alternative would prove astronomically expensive. His text has been checked against the facsimile, and discrepancies observed have been verified against the manuscript, by the kindness of Miss Daphne Gifford of the Public Record Office. Farley's few errors are indicated in the notes.

[6] *Dialogus de Scaccario* 1,16.

The editor is responsible for the translation and lay-out. It aims at what the compiler would have written if his language had been modern English; though no translation can be exact, for even a simple word like 'free' nowadays means freedom from different restrictions. Bishop Henry emphasized that his grandfather preferred 'ordinary words'; the nearest ordinary modern English is therefore chosen whenever possible. Words that are now obsolete, or have changed their meaning, are avoided, but measurements have to be transliterated, since their extent is often unknown or arguable, and varied regionally. The terse inventory form of the original has been retained, as have the ambiguities of the Latin.

Modern English commands two main devices unknown to 11th century Latin, standardised punctuation and paragraphs; in the Latin, *ibi* ('there are') often does duty for a modern full stop, *et* ('and') for a comma or semi-colon. The entries normally answer the Commissioners' questions, arranged in five main groups, (i) the place and its holder, its hides, ploughs and lordship; (ii) people; (iii) resources; (iv) value; and (v) additional notes. The groups are usually given as separate paragraphs.

King William numbered chapters 'for easy reference', and sections within chapters are commonly marked, usually by initial capitals, often edged in red. They are here numbered. Maps, indices and an explanation of technical terms are also given. Later, it is hoped to publish analytical and explanatory volumes, and associated texts.

The editor is deeply indebted to the advice of many scholars, too numerous to name, and especially to the Public Record Office, and to the publisher's patience. The draft translations are the work of a team; they have been co-ordinated and corrected by the editor, and each has been checked by several people. It is therefore hoped that mistakes may be fewer than in versions published by single fallible individuals. But it would be Utopian to hope that the translation is altogether free from error; the editor would like to be informed of mistakes observed.

The notes are more extensive than usual. In Hertfordshire it has been possible to combine study of the text with local knowledge. The opportunity has therefore been taken to raise tentatively a few examples of the kind of questions, local and national, that may deserve closer enquiry as more county texts become easily available to local historians and others.

The map was drawn by Jim Hardy.

Conventions

*   refers to a note.
[ ]   enclose words omitted in the MS.   ( )   enclose editorial explanations.

HERFORDSCIRE.

BVRGV̆ HERTFORDE Pro . x . hidis
se defend̄ . T . R . E . 7 modo non facit.
Ibi erant . c . xl . vi . burgenses . in
soca regis Eduuardi.

De his hr̄ m̊ comes Alan⁹ . iii . domos . quæ tc̄
7 modo redd̄ consuetudinē.

Eudo dapifer hr̄ . ii . domos quæ fuer̄ Algari [cochenac.]
7 tc̄ 7 m̊ reddentes c̄suetud̄ . 7 terciā domū
hr̄ isdē Eudo que fuit Vlmari [Etone] . non redd̄ c̄suetud̄.

Goisfrid⁹ de bech . iii . domos . c̄suetud̄ reddent̄.

Hunfrid⁹ de Ansleuile ten̄ sub Eudone . ii.
domos cū uno horto . Harū una accōmodata
fuit cuidā p̄secto regis . 7 altera cū horto fuit
cujdā⁹ burgensis . 7 m̊ reclamant ipsi bur
genses sibi injuste ablatas.

B
1 The Borough of HERTFORD*
answered for 10 hides before 1066, but does not now do
so. There were 146 burgesses in King Edward's jurisdiction.

*2 Of these Count Alan now has 3 houses which paid dues then and now.

3 Eudo the Steward has 2 houses which were Algar of Cokenach's,
which paid dues then and now; Eudo also has a third house,
which was Wulfmer of Eton's, which does not pay dues.

4 Geoffrey of Bec, 3 houses which pay dues.

5 Humphrey of Anneville holds 2 houses with one garden under
Eudo. One of these was leased to a reeve of the King's;
the other, with its garden, was a burgess's, and now the
burgesses claim them back, as wrongfully taken from them.

Alios . xviii . burgenſes hͭ rex . W . qui fueͬ
hͦcs Heraldi 7 Leuuini . oͫs cͳuetuđ redđ.

Petrus de ualongies hͭ . ii . æccłas cū una domo.
quas emit de Vluui de Hatfelde . redđ oͫs
cͳuetudines . Ipſe Vluui 7 dare eas 7 uendͤ poterat.

Goisfriđ de magneuile hͭ occupatū qđđā.
qui fuit Eſgari ſtalri . 7 vii . domos | quæ nullam
cͳuetudinē reddideͬ . niſi geldū regis qͺdo
colligebatur.   cͳuetuđ redđ.

Radulf baniard hͭ . ii . domos . 7 tͨ 7 modo

Harduin de Scalers hͭ . xiiii . domos . qͥs
habuit Achi . T.R.E . nullā cͳuetuđ dabaꝺ
niſi geldū regis . de qͥbͮ aduocat harduin
regem ad ͫtectorem . Adhuc unā domū hͭ
Harduin de dono regis . quæ fuit cujđā burgͤſis.
reddeꝺſ oͫem conſuetudinem.

Hoc ſuburbiū reddit . xxti . liƀ arſas 7 penſatas.
7 iii . molini redđt . x . liƀ ad numerū.
Qͺdo Petrus uicecomes recepꝉ xv . liƀ ad numeͬ.
reddebat . T.R.E.ꝉ vii . liƀ 7 x . ſoł ad numerū.

King William has another 18 burgesses who were Earl Harold's and Earl Leofwin's men, who pay all dues.

Peter of Valognes has 2 churches with 1 house, which he bought from Wulfwy of Hatfield, which pay all dues. Wulfwy could grant and sell them.

Geoffrey de Mandeville has some premises which were Asgar the Constable's, and 7 houses which paid no dues except the King's tax, when it was collected.

Ralph Baynard has 2 houses which paid dues then and now.

Hardwin of Scales has 14 houses which Aki had; before 1066 they gave no dues except the King's tax. Hardwin cites the King as protector for them. Further, Hardwin has one house by the King's gift, which was a burgess's, which pays all dues.

This borough town pays £20, assayed and weighed, and 3 mills pay £10 at face value; when Peter the Sheriff acquired it, it paid £15 at face value; before 1066 £7 10s at face value.

.I. Rex WILLELMVS.

.II. Archieps cantuariensis.

.III. Eps Wintoniensis.

.IIII. Eps Londoniensis.

.V. Eps Baiocensis.

.VI. Eps Lisiacensis.

.VII. Eps Cestrensis.

.VIII Abbas de Elý.

.IX. Abb de Westmonast.

.X. Abb de S Albano.

.XI. Abbatissa de Cetriz.

.XII Canonici de Lundonia.

.XIII Canonici de Waltham.

.XII. Comes moritoniensis.

.XV. Comes Alanus.

.XVI. Comes Eustachius.

.XVII Comes Rogerius.

.XVIII Robtus de Olgi.

.XIX Robtus gernon.

.XX. Robtus de Todeni.

.XXI. Radulf de Todeni.

.XXII Radulf de Limesi.

.XXIII Radulf bainiard.

.XXII. Rannulf fr Ilgerij.

.XXV. Hugo de Grentemaisnil.

.XXVI. Hugo de belcamp.

.XX. Willelmus de Ow.

.XXVII. Willelm de Odburguile.

.XXIX. Walterius Flandrensis.

.XXX. Eudo dapifer.

.XXXI. Eduuard Saresberiensis.

.XXXII. Goisfrid de Manneuile.

.XXXIII Goisfrid de Bech.

.XXXII Goisbertus de beluaco.

.XXXV. Petrus de ualongies.

.XXXVI Harduin de Escalers.

.XXX Edgar.

.XXXVIII. Maigno brito.

.XXX. Gislebtus filius Salomonis.

.XL. Sigar de Cioches.

.XLI. Derman 7 alij Anglici regis.

.XLII. Rothais uxor Ricardi.

.XLIII Adeliz uxor Hugonis.

.XLII. Filia Radulfi tailgebosch.

[LIST OF LANDHOLDERS IN HERTFORDSHIRE]

1	King William		28	William of Eu
2	The Archbishop of Canterbury		29	William of Auberville
3	The Bishop of Winchester		30	Walter the Fleming
4	The Bishop of London		31	Eudo the Steward
5	The Bishop of Bayeux		32	Edward of Salisbury
6	The Bishop of Lisieux		33	Geoffrey de Mandeville
7	The Bishop of Chester		34	Geoffrey of Bec
8	The Abbot of Ely		35	Gosbert of Beauvais
9	The Abbot of Westminster		36	Peter of Valognes
10	The Abbot of St. Albans		37	Hardwin of Scales
*[11	The Abbot of Ramsey]		38	[Prince] Edgar
*12	The Abbess of Chatteris		39	Mainou the Breton
13	The Canons of London		40	Gilbert son of Solomon
14	The Canons of Waltham		41	Sigar of Chocques
15	The Count of Mortain		42	Derman and others of the King's Englishmen
16	Count Alan		42[a]	Rothais wife of Richard [of Tonbridge]
17	Count Eustace		43	Adelaide wife of Hugh [of Grandmesnil]
18	Earl Roger		44	The daughter of Ralph Tallboys
19	Robert d'Oilly			
20	Robert Gernon			
21	Robert of Tosny			
22	Ralph of Tosny			
23	Ralph of Limesy			
24	Ralph Baynard			
25	Ranulf brother of Ilger			
26	Hugh of Grandmesnil			
27	Hugh of Beauchamp			

WILLELM REX ten *WIMVNDESLAI* . p . VIII . hið se defð.

Tra . e̅ . XVIII . car̃ . In dn̅io . II . hidæ 7 dim

7 ibi sunt . III . car̃ . 7 . XXIIII . uilti . 7 un̅

sochs 7 v . borð . 7 v . cot . hn̅t . XV . car̃ . Ibi . VI . serui .

7 I . moliñ de . XX . fol . P̅t̅u̅ . I . car̃ . 7 II . bob . Pasta ad

pecuñ uillæ . Nem̃ ad sepes . Hoc M̃ fuit in dn̅io æcclæ

S̃ MARIÆ . de Cetriz . sed Herald comes abstulit inde

ut tota syra testat . 7 apposuit in hiz manerio suo.

tribz annis ante morte̅ regis Eduuardi.

Rex . W . ten *MENLESDENE* . p . IIII . hið se defð . Tra . e̅

VIII . car̃ . In dn̅io . II . hið 7 II . uirg 7 dim . 7 ibi suñ . III . car̃ .

Pbr cu̅ . VIII . uilłis 7 . II . cot hn̅t . III . car̃ . 7 adhuc . II . poss

fieri . Ibi . VI . serui . p̅t̅u̅ . I . car̃ . Pasta ad pecuñ uillæ.

Silua . XXX . porc̃ . Hoc M̃ jacuit 7 jacet in̅ Hiz . Herald comes

tenuit.

IN DIMIDIO HVNDRET DE HIZ.

Rex WILLELM̃ tenet *HIZ* . p . V . hið se defð.

Tra . e̅ . XXX.IIII . car̃ . In dn̅io . I . hida . 7 ibi suñ

VI . car̃ . 7 XLI . uilłs cu̅ XVII . borð hn̅t . XX . car̃ .

7 VIII . adhuc poss fieri . Ibi . XXII . cot̃ . 7 XII . serui . 7 IIII.

molini de . LIII . fol 7 IIII . den̅ . p̅t̅u̅ . IIII . car̃ . Pastura

ad pecuñ uillæ . Silua sexcent̃ porc̃ . Hoc M̃ tenuit Herald com'

De his . v . hið jacent . II . in monasterio huj uillæ.

Tra . e̅ . IIII . car̃ . In dn̅io . I . hida 7 dim . 7 ibi . e̅ una car̃ .

7 alia pot̃ fieri . 7 ibi . IIII . uilłi hn̅t . II . car̃ . 7 VII . cot ibi.

P̅t̅u̅ . II . bob . Pasta ad pecuñ . Val hæ . II . hidæ . VI . lib.

Qðo recep̃ . XL . fol . T.R.E. . IIII . lib . Hoc M̃ tenuit Herald com̃.

Rex . W . ten *WELEI* . p . II . hið se defð . Tra . e̅ . VII.

car̃ . In dn̅io . I . hida . 7 ibi sunt . II . car̃ . 7 VIII . uilłi cu̅

LAND OF THE KING

In BROADWATER Hundred
King William holds WYMONDLEY. It answers for 8 hides.
Land for 18 ploughs. In lordship 2½ hides; 3 ploughs.
   24 villagers, 1 Freeman, 5 smallholders, and 5 cottagers
      have 15 ploughs. 6 slaves.
   1 mill at 20s; meadow for 1 plough and 2 oxen; pasture for
      the village livestock; wood for fences.
   This manor was in the lordship of St. Mary's Church,
Chatteris, but Earl Harold took it away, as the whole Shire
testifies, and attached it to his manor of Hitchin, three
years before King Edward's death.

King William holds MINSDEN. It answers for 4 hides.
Land for 8 ploughs. In lordship 2 hides and 2½ virgates. 3
ploughs.
   A priest with 8 villagers and 2 cottagers have 3 ploughs;
      a further 2 possible. 6 slaves.
   Meadow for 1 plough; pasture for the village livestock;
      woodland, 30 pigs.
   This manor lay and lies in (the lands of) Hitchin.
   Earl Harold held it.

In the Half-Hundred of HITCHIN   132 c
King William holds HITCHIN. It answers for 5 hides.
Land for 34 ploughs. In lordship 1 hide; 6 ploughs.
   41 villagers with 17 smallholders have 20 ploughs;
      a further 8 possible. 22 cottagers; 12 slaves.
   4 mills at 53s 4d; meadow for 4 ploughs; pasture for the
      village livestock; woodland, 600 pigs.
   Earl Harold held this manor.
   2 of these 5 hides lie in the (lands of the) monastery
of this village. Land for 4 ploughs. In lordship 1½ hides;
   1 plough; another possible.
   4 villagers have 2 ploughs; 7 cottagers.
   Meadow for 2 oxen; pasture for the livestock.
Value of these 2 hides £6; when acquired 40s; before 1066 £4.
   Earl Harold held this manor.

King William holds WAIN*. It answers for 2 hides. Land for 7
ploughs. In lordship 1 hide; 2 ploughs.

v . borđ hñt . iiii . car . 7 v . poť fieri . Ibi . ii . coť . 7 iiii.
ſerui . Paſtá ad peč uillæ . Silua . ccc . porč . Hoc ⋔
tenuit Herald . 7 jacet in Hiz ubi jacuit T.R.E.

Rex . W . ten *WESTONE* . p v . hiđ ſe defđ . Tra . ē
xiiii . car . In dñio . ii . hidæ . 7 ii . car ſunt ibi . 7 xvi.
uiłłi cū . iii . borđ hñt . v . car . 7 adhuc . v . poſſ fieri.
Ibi . iiii . ſerui . Ptū . vii . car . Paſtá ad peč uillæ . Silua
cccc . porč . 7 iii . ſoł . Hoc ⋔ tenuit Herald . 7 jacuit
7 jacet in Hiz . Sed Wara huj ⋔ jacuit in Bedeford
ſcire . T.R.E. in hunđ de Maneheue . 7 ibi . ē ⋔ 7 fuit
ſep . 7 poſt mortē R.E. non ſe adđetauit de gildo regis.

Rex . W . ten *WALDENEI* . p . ii . hiđ ſe defđ . Tra
ē . xx . car . In dñio . ii . uirg . 7 ibi ſunt . ii . car . Pƀr
cū . xiii . uiłłis . 7 iiii . borđ hñt . vi . car . 7 adhuc . ii.
poſſ fieri . Ibi . ii . coť 7 iiii . ſerui . Ptū dim car . Paſtura
ad pecuñ uillæ . Silua . cccc . porč . In totis ualent uał
7 ualuit . viii . liƀ . T.R.E. x . liƀ . Hoc ⋔ tenuit Leueua
de Heraldo . 7 uende potuit abſq̷ ej licentia . In ſerui
tio regis inuen . i . Auerā 7 inwardū . ſed injuſte 7 p ui
ut Scyra teſtat . De his . ii . hiđ ten q̄đ̄ uidua
femina Aſgari . i . hiđ de rege p . i . ⋔ . 7 hƀ ibi . i . car.
7 xvii . uiłłos cū . vii . borđ . hñt . vi . car . 7 iii . poſſ fieri.
Ibi . v . coť . 7 ptū dim car . Silua . cccc . porč . Paſtura
ad pecuñ uillæ . In totis ualent uał 7 ualuit . iiii . liƀ.
T.R.E. viii . liƀ . Eadē femina tenuit hoc ⋔.T.R.E.
de Heraldo . 7 potuit uende abſq̷ ej lictia . 7 injuſte
p uim inuenieƀ . i . Auerā 7 inward in ſeruitio regis.
ut ſcyra teſtat . Hæc . ii . ⋔ appoſuit Ilƀt in Hiz
quando erat uicecomes . teſtante hundret.

8 villagers with 5 smallholders have 4 ploughs; a fifth
   possible. 2 cottagers; 4 slaves.
Pasture for the village livestock; woodland, 300 pigs.
Earl Harold held this manor; it lies in Hitchin, where it
lay before 1066.

King William holds WESTONING. It answers for 5 hides.
Land for 14 ploughs. In lordship 2 hides; 2 ploughs.
   16 villagers with 3 smallholders have 5 ploughs;
      a further 5 possible. 4 slaves.
   Meadow for 7 ploughs; pasture for the village livestock;
      woodland, 400 pigs, and 3s too.
Earl Harold held this manor; it lay and lies in Hitchin; but
the obligations of this manor lay in Bedfordshire before 1066,
in the Hundred of Manshead. It is and always was a manor
there; since 1066 it has not met the King's tax.

King William holds (KING'S) WALDEN. It answers for 2 hides.
Land for 20 ploughs. In lordship 2 virgates; 2 ploughs.
   A priest with 13 villagers and 4 smallholders have 6 ploughs;
      a further 2 possible. 2 cottagers; 4 slaves.
   Meadow for ½ plough; pasture for the village livestock;
      woodland, 400 pigs.
The total value is and was £8; before 1066 £10.
   Leofeva held this manor from Earl Harold; she could sell
without his permission. She found 1 cartage and escort for the
King's service, but wrongfully and by force, as the Shire testifies.
   A widow, Asgar's woman, holds 1 of these 2 hides from the
King as one manor; she has 1 plough.
   17 villagers with 7 smallholders have 6 ploughs;
      (a further) 3 possible. 5 cottagers.
   Meadow for ½ plough; woodland, 400 pigs; pasture for the
      village livestock.
The total value is and was £4; before 1066 £8.
   She also held this manor before 1066 from Earl Harold;
she could sell without his permission. Wrongfully and by
force she found 1 cartage and escort for the King's service,
as the Shire testifies. Ilbert placed these 2 manors in
Hitchin when he was Sheriff, as the Hundred testifies.

Rex.W.ten *WAVEDENE*.p.iii.uirg se defd.

Tra.ē.ii.car 7 vi.bob. 7 ibi funt cū.vi.uitlis.Silua
xl.porc.Hanc trā tenuit Herald in hiz fuo m̄.

7 ibi m̄ jacet.

Rex.W.ten *CERLETONE*.p una uirga fe defd.Tra.ē
.i.car.7 ibi.ē cū.ii.cot.7 i.molin de.xx.den.Val 7 ua
luit fēp.x.fol.Hanc trā tenuer.ii.fochi.de Heraldo
7 uende potuer abfq̗ licentia ej.Soca fuit femp in Hiz.
Ilbt qdo fuit uicecom apposuit in Hiz.

Rex.W.ten *DENESLAI*.p vii.hid fe defd.Tra.ē
xx.car.In dūio.iii.hidæ 7 dim.7 ibi funt.iii.car.
7 xix.uitli.hn̄t.viii.car.7 ix.adhuc pofs fieri.
Ibi.vii.bord.7 vii.cot.7 vi.ferui.7 i.francigena
elemofinari regis.Ibi.ii.molin de xvi.fol.p̄tū.i.car.
Pafta ad pecun uillæ.Silua.cec.porc.In totis ualent
redd p annū.xiiii.lib.arfas 7 penfatas.7 v.lib ad
numerū.Similit T.R.E.7 qdo Petr uicecom recep.

Hoc m̄ tenuer.ii.fochi.p.ii.m̄.de Heraldo.T.R.E.
7 uende potuer.Tam.ii.Aueras 7 ii.inward undfq̗
inuenieb in Hiz.fed p uim 7 injufte ut hund teftat.
Hæc.ii.m̄ tenuit Ilbt p uno m̄.7 inde fuit faifit
p breue regis qdiu uicecom fuit.ut Scyra teftat.
Poftq û dimifit uicecomitatū. Petrus de ualóngies
7 Radulf tailgebofch abftuler ab eo.m̄.7 pofuer
in Hiz.ppt qd nolebat inuenire Auerā uicecomiti.
Goisfr de bech fucceffor Ilbti.reclamat p hoc m̄
mifcdam regis.

Rex.W.ten *OFFELEI*.p.ii.hid fe defd.Tra.ē
ix.car.Quinq̗ fochi tenuer.T.R.E.7 m̄ tene𝔫
de rege.W.Ibi fu𝔫.viii.car.7 ix.pot fieri.

King William holds WANDON. It answers for 3 virgates.
Land for 2 ploughs and 6 oxen; they are there, with
  6 villagers.
  Woodland, 40 pigs.
  Earl Harold held this land in his manor of Hitchin, and
it lies there now.

King William holds CHARLTON. It answers for 1 virgate.
Land for 1 plough; it is there, with
  2 cottagers.
  1 mill at 20d.
The value is and always was 10s.
  2 Freemen held this land from Earl Harold; they could sell
without his permission. The jurisdiction always was in
Hitchin. Ilbert placed it in Hitchin when he was Sheriff.

King William holds (TEMPLE) DINSLEY. It answers for 7 hides.
Land for 20 ploughs. In lordship 3½ hides; 3 ploughs.
  19 villagers have 8 ploughs; a further 9 possible.
    7 smallholders; 7 cottagers; 6 slaves; 1 Frenchman an
    almsman of the King.
  2 mills at 16s; meadow for 1 plough; pasture for the
    village livestock; woodland, 300 pigs.
In total value it pays £14 a year assayed and weighed and £5
at face value; the same before 1066 and when Peter the
Sheriff acquired it.
  2 Freemen held this manor as 2 manors from Earl Harold
before 1066; they could sell. However, each of them found 2
cartages and 2 escorts in Hitchin, but by force and wrongfully,
as the Hundred testifies.
  Ilbert held these 2 manors as 1 manor and was put in
possession thereof through the King's writ, as long as he was
Sheriff, as the Shire testifies. After he relinquished the
sheriffdom, Peter of Valognes and Ralph Tallboys took the
manor from him and placed it in Hitchin because he refused to
find cartage for the Sheriff. Geoffrey of Bec, Ilbert's successor,
claims the King's mercy for this manor.

King William holds (GREAT) OFFLEY. It answers for 2 hides.
Land for 9 ploughs. 5 Freemen held it before 1066; they now
hold from King William. 8 ploughs; a ninth possible.

Ibi . II . uilti 7 XVII . borď . 7 III . cot . 7 III . ſerui . P̃tũ

. I . caŕ . Paſtã ad pecuñ . Silua CXX . porc̃ . Nem̃ ad

ſepes . Int̃ totũ ual 7 ualuit ſẽp . IIII . lib̃ 7 IIII . ſol .

Iſtimet tenueŕ de Heraldo . 7 dare 7 uendẽ potueŕ .

Soca ũ jacuit ſẽp in Hiz . 7 II . Aueras 7 II . inwardos

In caď uilla ten̄ Eduuarď de Periton   ſinueneŕ .

III . uirg . Tra . ẽ . II . caŕ . Ibi . ẽ dimiď . 7 una 7 dim̃

pot fieri . Ibi . ẽ . I . uilts . 7 Nem̃ ad ſepes . Val . V . ſol .

Q̃do recep̃ . VI . ſol 7 VIII . deñ . T . R . E . x . ſol .

De hac t̃ra dimiď hidã tenuit Aluin hõ Stigand

Archiẽpi . 7 uñ hõ Heraldi | . I . uirg̃ habuit . Iſti

7 dare 7 uendẽ t̃rã ſuã potuer . ſoca remanſit in hiz .

In altera Offelei ten̄ uñ ſochs . I . hiď . Tra . ẽ . II .

caŕ . Ibi . ẽ una . 7 alia pot fieri . Ibi uñ uilts . 7 I . borď

7 I . cot . Nem̃ ad ſepes . Val 7 ualuit ſẽp . XXVI . ſol .

ſ 7 VIII . deã .

Iſdẽ qui n̄c ten̄ tenuit T . R . E . de Heraldo . 7 uendẽ

potuit . Soca remanſit in hiz . Auerã 7 inward redď .

H̃c ſochm 7 V . ſupiores de Offelei . appoſuit Ilb̃t

de Hertford in hiz .

In WELLE ten̄ . I . ſochs . I . hiď . Tra . ẽ . V . caŕ . In

dñio . ẽ . I . 7 II . poſſ fieri . Ibi . IIII . borď hn̄t . I . caŕ .

7 alia pot fieri . Paſtã ad pec̃ uillæ . Nem̃ ad ſepes .

Int̃ tot̃ ual XXVI . ſol 7 VIII . deñ . Q̃do | recep̃ . XL . ſol .

T . R . E . LX . ſol . Hanc t̃rã tenuit Leueua de Heraldo

7 uendẽ potuit . Ilb̃t appoſuit in Linlcia ſuo M̃ .

dũ eēt uicecom̃ . Poſtq̃ uicecomitat̃ p̃didit . Petr̃

7 Raduļf tuleŕ ab eo . 7 poſueŕ in Hiz . ut tota ſcy̆ra

teſtat̃ quæ ñ jacuit ibi T . R . E . nec aliquã c̃ſuetuď reddidit .

2 villagers; 17 smallholders; 3 cottagers; 3 slaves.
Meadow for 1 plough; pasture for the livestock;
   woodland, 120 pigs; wood for fences.
In total, the value is and always was £4 4s.

They also held from Earl Harold; they could grant or sell,
but the jurisdiction always lay in Hitchin, and they found 2
cartages and 2 escorts.

In the same village Edward of Pirton holds 3 virgates.
Land for 2 ploughs; ½ there; 1½ possible.
   1 villager.
   Wood for fences.
Value 5s; when acquired 6s 8d; before 1066, 10s.

Alwin, Archbishop Stigand's man, held ½ hide of this land,
and a man of Earl Harold's, named Abo, had 1 virgate; they
could grant and sell their land. The jurisdiction remained
in Hitchin.

1   In the other (LITTLE) OFFLEY 1 Freeman holds 1 hide.
Land for 2 ploughs; 1 there; another possible.
   1 villager; 1 smallholder; 1 cottager.
   Wood for fences.
The value is and always was 26s 8d.

The present holder also held it from Earl Harold before   133 a
1066; he could sell. The jurisdiction remained in Hitchin.
He paid cartage and escort. Ilbert of Hertford placed this
Freeman, and the 5 above from (Great) Offley, in Hitchin.

2   In WELLBURY 1 Freeman holds 1 hide. Land for 5 ploughs.
In lordship 1; 2 possible.
   4 smallholders have 1 plough; another possible.
   Pasture for the village livestock; wood for fences.
In total, value 26s 8d; when Peter acquired it 40s;
before 1066, 60s.

Leofeva held this land from Earl Harold; she could sell.

Ilbert placed it in his manor of Lilley while he was Sheriff. *
After he lost the sheriffdom, Peter of Valognes and Ralph
Tallboys took it from him and placed it in Hitchin, as the
whole Shire testifies; it did not lie there before 1066 nor
did it pay any customary dues.

In Welei ten̄ . i . fochs . i . hid . Tra . ē . ii . car 7 ibi fuꝥ.

Ibi . ii . uilli cū . i . borđ 7 ix . cot . Ptū dim car . Pafta ad

pecun uillæ . Nem̄ ad fepes . Huic træ adjacet filua ad

l . porc . quā inuafit Ofmund de ualle badonis fup

regē . W . 7 jacuit in foca de hiz . T . R . E . ut fcȳra teftat.

Val 7 ualuit H̄ tra . xx . fol . T . R . E . xxx . fol . Hanc

trā tenuit Goduin hō Heraldi . 7 uende potuit.

Hanc pofuit Petr uicecom̄ in Hiz ad firmā . quæ

n̄ fuit ibi T . R . E . neꝗ c̄fuetudinē ibi reddidit.

Quā trā dederat Ilbt cuidā fuo militi dū . eet uicecom̄.

pro qua tra reclamat Gaufrid de bech mifcđam regis.

In Wilei ten̄ . i . fochs dim̄ hid . Tra . ē . i . car . 7 ibi . ē cū

i . cot . Nem̄ ad fepes . Val . x . fol . Qđo recep . v . fol . T . R . E.

xvi . fol . Hanc trā tenuit Edmund hō Heraldi . 7 uende

potuit . Soca remanfit in Hiz . Vnā auerā inuenit.

In Flefmere ten̄ . i . fochs dimid uirg . Tra . ē dim̄ car.

7 ibi . ē cū . iiii . cot . Pafta ad pec . Silua . v . porc . Val

7 ualuit . xl . den . T . R . E . lx . den . Iftemet tenuit T . R . E.

hō Heraldi . 7 potuit uende . Auerā reddidit in Hiz.

In Leglega ten̄ . iii . fochi . i . uirg . Tra . ē . i . car 7 dim̄.

7 ibi fuꝥ cū . iiii . borđ . Silua . xl . porc . Val 7 ualuit

fēp xxvi . fol 7 viii . den . Hanc trā tenuer̄ h̄ō̄c̄s Algari.

non potuer̄ uende ext hiz.

In Hegeftaneftone . ten̄ . i . fochs regis . i . uirg . Tra . ē

dim̄ car . 7 ibi . ē cū . i . uillo . Val 7 ualuit . xx . den . T . R . E.

xl . den . Iftemet ꝗ ten̄ tenuit T . R . E . hō abbis S̄ Albani.

7 uende potuit . Hanc trā appofuit Herald in hiz p ui

7 injufte ut fcȳra teftat. *IN HERTFORD HVND.*

Rex . W . ten̄ *BEGESFORD* . ꝓ . x . hid fe defđ . Tra . ē . xx.

car . In dn̄io . ii . hidæ 7 iii . uirg . 7 ibi funt . iii . car . Pbr

13 In WAIN 1 Freeman holds 1 hide. Land for 2 ploughs; they are there.
2 villagers with 1 smallholder and 9 cottagers.
Meadow for ½ plough; pasture for the village livestock;
wood for fences; attached to this land is woodland for
50 pigs, which Osmund of Vaubadon annexed in King
William's despite. It lay in the jurisdiction of
Hitchin before 1066, as the Shire testifies.
The value of this land is and was 20s; before 1066, 30s.
Godwin, Earl Harold's man, held this land; he could sell.
Peter the Sheriff placed it in Hitchin for the revenue. It
was not there before 1066, nor did it pay customary dues there.
Ilbert gave this land to a man-at-arms of his while he was
Sheriff; Geoffrey of Bec claims the King's mercy for this land.

14 In WAIN 1 Freeman holds ½ hide. Land for 1 plough; it is there, with
1 cottager.
Wood for fences.
Value 10s; when acquired 5s; before 1066, 16s.
Edmund, Earl Harold's man, held this land; he could sell.
The jurisdiction remained in Hitchin. He found 1 cartage.

15 In FLEXMORE 1 Freeman holds ½ virgate. Land for ½ plough;
it is there, with
4 cottagers.
Pasture for the livestock; woodland, 5 pigs.
The value is and was 40d; before 1066, 60d.
He also held it before 1066; he was Earl Harold's man; he
could sell. He paid cartage in Hitchin.

16 In LEY (GREEN) (?) 3 Freemen hold 1 virgate. Land for 1½
ploughs; they are there, with
4 smallholders.
Woodland, 40 pigs.
The value is and always was 26s 8d.
Three of Earl Algar's men held this land; they could not
sell outside Hitchin.

17 In HEXTON 1 of the King's Freemen holds 1 virgate. Land
for ½ plough; it is there, with
1 villager.
The value is and was 20d; before 1066, 40d.
The present holder held it himself before 1066; he was the
Abbot of St. Albans' man; he could sell. Earl Harold placed this
land in Hitchin, by force and wrongfully, as the Shire testifies.

In HERTFORD Hundred
18 King William holds BAYFORD. It answers for 10 hides. Land
for 20 ploughs. In lordship 2 hides and 3 virgates; 3 ploughs.

7 ꝑpofit huj uillæ cū . xxii . uiłłis hnt . xv . car . 7 ii.

adhuc poīs fieri . Ibi . ix . coť . 7 i . feruus . 7 ii . moliɳ

de xxvi . fol . Pťū . xx . car . Paſta ad pec ; 7 ii . fol.

Silua qngent porc . In totis ualent reddit xvi . liƀ

ad numerū . Qdo receꝑ uicecom . viii . liƀ . T.R.E. xx . liƀ.

Hoc M̃ tenuit Tofti com . fed rex E . habebat in dñio.

die quo mortuus . e.

Inť totū reddit *Hiz* p annū . c 7 vi . liƀ arfas

7 penfatas . 7 x . liƀ ad numerū . Qdo receꝑ Petrus.

qt xx . liƀ 7 vi . T . R . E. lx . liƀ de Hiz . 7 de foch ibid

ptinentibʒ . xl . liƀ ad numerū.

.II. TERRA ARCHIEꝔI CANTVAR *IN BRADEWAKE HVND.*

A RCHIEꝔS LANFRANC in Daceuuorde 7 Anfchitil

de eo teɳ . i . hid . Tra . e . ii . car . In dñio . i . car.

7 iii . uiłłi cū . ii . bord . hnt . i . car . Pťū dim boui . Silua

l . porc . Val . xxx . fol . Qdo receꝑ . xx . fol . T.R.E. lx . fol.

Hanc trã tenuit Aluric de aƀƀe Weftmonaſt . T.R.E.

nec poterat eā ab æccła feparare ut hund teftat. fed

pro alijs tris hõ Stigandi archiepi fuit.

I n Watone teɳ Anfchitill de Archiepo . ii . hid 7 dim.

Tra . e vi . car . In dñio . e una . 7 alia poť fieri . Ibi . iiii.

uiłłi cū pƀro 7 ii . bord . hnt . ii . car . 7 aliæ . ii . poīs fieri.

pťū dim car . Silua . c . porc . Paſta ad pec . 7 ii . molini

de . xvii . fol . Val 7 ualuit . l . fol . T.R.E. iiii . liƀ . De

De hac tra tenuit Aluric . ii . hid de aƀƀe Weftmonaſt.

ñ poterat feparare ab æccła . 7 Almær dim hid tenuit

hõ ejdē Alurici . 7 uende potuit.

A priest and the reeve of the village with 22 villagers have
15 ploughs; a further 2 possible; 9 cottagers; 1 slave.
2 mills at 26s; meadow for 20 ploughs; pasture for the
livestock, and 2s too; woodland, 500 pigs.
In total value it pays £16, at face value; when acquired by the
Sheriff £8; before 1066 £20.
Earl Tosti held this manor but King Edward had it in
lordship at his death.

19   In total, Hitchin, with what belongs to it, pays £106 a year,
assayed and weighed, and £10 at face value; when Peter the
Sheriff acquired it, £86; before 1066, £60 from Hitchin, and
from the Freemen belonging thereto, £40 at face value.

2   LAND OF THE ARCHBISHOP OF CANTERBURY

In BROADWATER Hundred
1   Archbishop Lanfranc holds 1 hide in DATCHWORTH and Ansketel
from him. Land for 2 ploughs. In lordship 1 plough.
    3 villagers with 2 smallholders have 1 plough.
    Meadow for ½ ox; woodland, 50 pigs.
Value 30s; when acquired 20s; before 1066, 60s.
    Aelfric Black held this land from the Abbot of Westminster
before 1066 but could not separate it from the Church, as the
Hundred testifies; but for other lands he was Archbishop
Stigand's man.

2   In WATTON Ansketel holds 2½ hides from the Archbishop.
Land for 6 ploughs. In lordship 1; another possible.
    3 villagers with a priest and 2 smallholders have 2 ploughs;
        another 2 possible.
    Meadow for ½ plough; woodland, 100 pigs; pasture for the
        livestock; 2 mills at 17s.
The value is and was 50s; before 1066 £4.
    Aelfric Black held 2 hides of this land from the Abbot of
Westminster; he could not separate it from the Church.
    Aelmer, Aelfric's man, held ½ hide; he could sell.

In Efcepehala . ten Anfchitill de archiepo . ii . hid.

Tra . ē . v . car . In dñio . ē una . 7 alia pot fieri . 7 iii . uilti

hnt . ii . car . 7 iii . pot fieri . Ptū dim car . Silua . xx . porc.

Val . iii . lib . Qdo recep. xl . fol . T.R.E. iiii . lib . Hanc trā

tenuit Aluric hō Stigandi arch : De dñio æcclæ S̄ Albani

fuit . T.R.E. nec potuit uende nec feparare ab æccla.

In Stuterehela ten . i . Anglic de archiepo . ii . acs træ . Val

7 ualuit fep . ii . fol . Ifdē tenuit T.R.E . In uadimonio . potuit

In Stuochāpa ten Anfchitill de archiepo dim uirg ſ uende.

Tra . ē . ii . bob . Val 7 ualuit fep xv . den . Hanc trā tenuit

Aluric hō Stig Archiepi . 7 uende potuit.

<blac>

.III. **TERRA EPI WINTONIENS** *IN ODESEI HVND*

Eps WALCHELIN Winton ten *CHODREI* . p . v . hid fe

defd . Tra . ē . vi . car . In dñio . i . hid 7 dim . 7 ibi . ē una car.

7 xiii . uilti cū vi . bord hnt . v . car . Ibi . i . feruus . Pafta ad

pecun . Silua . c . porc . 7 xii . den . Int totū ual . lx . fol . Qdo

recep. xl . fol . T.R.E. vi . lib . Hoc M jacuit 7 jacet in

dñio æcclæ S̄ Petri Wintonienfis.

133 c

.IIII. **TERRA EPI LVNDONIENSIS.**

Eps LVNDONIENSIS ten 7 Hunfrid de eo . i . hid

7 dim . In Trochinge . Tra . ē . i . car 7 dim . 7 ibi funt cū

ii . uiltis 7 i . bord 7 i . cot . Ptū . i . car . Pafta ad pec . Nem

ad fepes . Val . l.ii . fol . Qdo recep. xxx . fol . T.R.E. xl . fol.

Hanc trā tenuer . ii . frs hoēs Willi epi . de Soca regis fuit.

7 uende potuer . De cfuetud reddider . vi . denar uice

comiti . uel unā Auerā 7 dim . De hac tra . i . uirg fuit

7 ē in uadimonio . Hunfrid adqetat eā de geldo regis.

7 tam n habet . H tra . ē de emptione . W . epi ut dñt

hoēs epi . fed hoēs de Scira non atteftant eis.

3 In SHEPHALL Ansketel holds 2 hides from the Archbishop.
Land for 5 ploughs. In lordship 1; another possible.
 3 villagers have 2 ploughs; a third possible.
 Meadow for ½ plough; woodland, 20 pigs.
Value £3; when acquired 40s; before 1066 £4.
 Aelfric, Archbishop Stigand's man, held this land; it was of
the lordship of St. Albans' Church before 1066; he could
not sell or separate it from the Church.

4 In LIBURY 1 Englishman holds 2 acres of land from the Archbishop.
The value is and always was 2s.
He also held it before 1066, in pledge; he could sell.

5 In SACOMBE Ansketel holds ½ virgate from the Archbishop.
Land for 2 oxen.
The value is and always was 15d.
 Aelfric Black, Archbishop Stigand's man, held this land;
he could sell.

3   LAND OF THE BISHOP OF WINCHESTER

In ODSEY Hundred

1 Bishop Walkelin of Winchester holds COTTERED. It answers
for 5 hides. Land for 6 ploughs. In lordship 1½ hides; 1 plough.
 13 villagers with 6 smallholders have 5 ploughs; 1 slave.
 Pasture for the livestock; woodland, 100 pigs, and 12d too.
Total value 60s; when acquired 40s; before 1066 £6.
 This manor lay and lies in the lordship of St. Peter's Church,
Winchester.

4   LAND OF THE BISHOP OF LONDON   133 c

[In EDWINSTREE Hundred]

*1 The Bishop of London holds 1½ hides in THROCKING, and Humphrey
from him. Land for 1½ ploughs. They are there, with
 2 villagers, 1 smallholder and 1 cottager.
 Meadow for 1 plough; pasture for the livestock; wood for fences.
Value 52s; when acquired 30s; before 1066, 40s.
 Two brothers, Bishop William's men, held this land; it
was of the King's jurisdiction; they could sell. They paid 6d to
the Sheriff in customary dues, or 1½ cartages.
 1 virgate of this land was and is in pledge. Humphrey clears
it from the King's tax; however, he does not have it. This land
is (part) of Bishop William's purchase, as the Bishop's men say, but
the men of the Shire do not confirm them.

Ipſe eps ten *HADAM* . p . vii . hiđ 7 dim ſe defđ.

Tra . e̅ . xxii . car 7 dim . In dn̄io . ii . hidæ . 7 ibi ſuı̄

vi . car . Pbr̄ cu̅ . xxx . v . uiłłis 7 i . milite hn̄t . xv.

car . Ibi . vi . borđ 7 . ii . cot . 7 xii . ſerui . 7 i . molin de

iiii . ſoł . P̊tu̅ . iiii . car . Paſtura ad pec . Silua . cc . porc.

In totis ualet 7 ualuit xx . liƀ . T . R . E . xxiiii . liƀ.

Hoc m̄ fuit 7 eſt de epiſcopatu Lundonienſi.

Ipſe eps ten *WIDEFORD* . p iii . hiđ ſe defđ . Tra . e̅ . v.

car . In dn̄io . ii . hidæ . 7 ibi . ii . ſunt car . 7 v . uiłłi cu̅ . viii.

borđ hn̄t . iii . car . Ibi . i . cot . 7 iii . ſerui . 7 i . molin̄

de . v . ſoł . P̊tu̅ . ii . car . Silua . l . porc . Vał 7 ualuit . c . ſoł.

T . R . E . viii . liƀ . Hoc m̄ tenuit Ełdred teign . R . E . 7 pot

In Wideforde ten Tedƀt de ep̄o . i . hiđ . Tra . e̅ ⌐ uende.

ii . car . Ibi . e̅ una . 7 alia pot fieri . Ibi . viii . borđ . p̊tu̅

dim car . Silua xxx . porc . Vał 7 ualuit . xl . ſoł . T . R . E.

lx . ſoł . Hanc tra̅ tenuit Aluuard hō . S . arch . uende pot.

In Celgdene ten Roderi dim hiđ de ep̄o . Tra . e̅ . ii . car.

Ibi . e̅ una . 7 alia pot fieri . Ibi . i . borđ 7 iiii . ſerui . Silua

l . porc . P̊tu̅ . i . car . Vał 7 ualuit xxx . ſoł . T . R . E . xl . ſoł.

Hanc tra̅ tenuit Æłdred teign . R . E . 7 uende potuit.

Wiłłs ten parua̅ Hada̅ de ep̄o . p . ii . hiđ ſe defđ.

Tra . e̅ . iii . car . In dn̄io ſunt . ii . 7 iiii . borđ cu̅ . i . car.

Ibi . iiii . cot . 7 iii . ſerui . P̊tu̅ . ii . bob . Paſta̅ ad pec.

Silua xxx . porc . Vał 7 ualuit ſep . iiii . liƀ . Hoc m̄ te

nuer̄ . iii . ſochi . Hoꝛ un hō Stig arch ⁊ i . hiđ habuit dim

uirg min . 7 alt hō Roƀti . F . Wimarc . iii . uirg 7 dim habuit.

7 iii . una̅ uirg ſochs . R . E . Hic un den reddeƀ uicecom.

In Hada̅ ten Wiłłs de ep̄o . dim hiđ . Tra ⌐ 7 uende potuer̄.

e̅ . i . car . Ibi . e̅ dimiđ | 7 alia dim pot fieri . Ibi . i . cot.

*2 The Bishop holds HADHAM himself. It answers for 7½ hides.
Land for 22½ ploughs. In lordship 2 hides; 6 ploughs.
   A priest with 35 villagers and 1 man-at-arms have 15
     ploughs. 6 smallholders; 2 cottagers; 12 slaves.
   1 mill at 4s; meadow for 4 ploughs; pasture for the
     livestock; woodland, 200 pigs.
The total value is and was £20; before 1066 £24.
This manor was and is the Bishopric of London's.

3 The Bishop holds WIDFORD himself. It answers for 3 hides.
Land for 5 ploughs. In lordship 2 hides; 2 ploughs.
   5 villagers with 8 smallholders have 3 ploughs;
     1 cottager; 3 slaves.
   1 mill at 5s; meadow for 2 ploughs; woodland, 50 pigs.
The value is and was 100s; before 1066 £8.
   Aldred, a thane of King Edward's , held this manor; he could sell.

4 In WIDFORD Theodbert holds 1 hide from the Bishop.
Land for 2 ploughs; 1 there; another possible.
   8 smallholders.
   Meadow for ½ plough; woodland, 30 pigs.
The value is and was 40s; before 1066, 60s.
   Alfward, Archbishop Stigand's man, held this land; ne
could sell.

*5 In CHALDEAN Rodhere holds ½ hide from the Bishop. Land
for 2 ploughs; 1 there; another possible.
   1 smallholder; 4 slaves.
   Woodland, 50 pigs; meadow for 1 plough.
The value is and was 30s; before 1066, 40s.
   Aldred, a thane of King Edward's, held this land; he could sell.

6 William holds LITTLE HADHAM from the Bishop. It answers for 2
hides. Land for 3 ploughs. In lordship 2.
   4 smallholders with 1 plough; 4 cottagers; 3 slaves.
   Meadow for 2 oxen; pasture for the livestock; woodland, 30 pigs.
The value is and always was £4.
   3 Freemen held this manor. One of them, Archbishop Stigand's
man, had 1 hide less ½ virgate; another, Robert son of Wymarc's
man, had 3½ virgates; the third, a Freeman of King Edward's, 1
virgate, and he paid 1d to the Sheriff; they could sell.

7 In (MUCH) HADHAM William holds ½ hide from the Bishop.
Land for 1 plough; ½ plough there; another ½ possible.
   1 cottager.

Val 7 ual . xv . fol . Edric̊ tenuit hō Afgari . 7 uendẻ pot.

In Leuuareuuiche . ten̋ Wilts de ep̄o . 1 . hiđ . 7 dim̋ . T̊ra . ē

iiii . car̊ . In dñio funt . ii . car̊ . 7 tcia pot fieri . Ibi . iii . uilti

hn̄t . 1 . car̋ . Ibi . ii . coť 7 iiii . ferui . P̊tū . ii . boḃ . Pafta̋ pec

     uillæ.

Nem̋ ad fepes . H̋ tra ual 7 ualuit . L . fol . T . R . E .̕ Lx . fol.

Hoc M̋ tenuit Leuuare de Wilto ep̄o . dim̋ hiđ potuit

uendẻ . fed hiđ n̄ potuit p̊t ej lictiam.

In Hadā . ten̋ Ofbn̋ de ep̄o . 1 . hiđ . T̋ra . ē . ii . car̊ . In dñio

. 1 . car̊ 7 dim̋ . 7 1 . uilts hr̄ dim̋ car̊ . Ibi . vi . coť . 7 1 . feruus.

Val 7 ualuit fep̄ xL . fol . Hanc trā tenuer̋ . ii . fochi . hoᷣ

un hō Algari dim̋ hiđ habuit . 7 alt dim̋ hiđ de foca regis.

ii . denar uicecom̋ reddiđ . Vtriq̢ tam uendẻ potuer̋.

In Patemere ten̋ Balduin̋ de ep̄o . 1 . hiđ 7 y̋ . uirg̋ T̊ra . ē

iiii . car̊ . In dñio funt . ii . 7 ii . uilti hn̄t . 1 . car̊ . 7 alia pot fieri .

Ibi . ii . borđ 7 vi . coť . 7 iii . ferui . P̊tū . ii . boḃ . Silua . Lx . porc̋.

Val 7 ualuit fep̄ . iiii . lib̊ . Hanc trā tenuit Aluuard hō

Algari .̋ 7 uendẻ potuit.

Radulf̋ ten̋ de ep̄o Eldeberie . p̢ . ii . hiđ 7 dim̋ fe defđ.

T̊ra . ē . ix . car̊ . In dñio fuꝗ̆ . ii . 7 vi . uilti 7 ix . borđ hn̄t . vi .

car̊ . 7 . vii . pot fieri . Ibi . iii . coť 7 iii . ferui . P̊tū . ii . boḃᷣ.

Pafta̋ ad pec̊ . Silua . xxx . porc̊ . Val 7 ualuit . vii . lib̊.

T . R . E .̕ viii . lib̊ . Hoc M̋ tenuit Siuurad̋ hō . S . arcħ . 7 uendẻ

In Peleha̅ ten̋ Radulf de ep̄o . 1 . hiđ 7 1 . uirg̋ . T̊ra . ē   pot.

v . car̊ . In dñio fuꝗ̆ . ii . 7 iii . pot fieri . Ibi . ii . uilti 7 iii . borđ

hn̄t . ii . car̋ . Ibi . v . ferui . 7 1 . coť . Pafta̋ ad pec̋ . Silua . xx.

The value is and was 15s.
Edric, Asgar the Constable's man, held it; he could sell.

*8 In LEVERAGE William holds 1½ hides from the Bishop. Land for 4
ploughs. In lordship 2 ploughs; a third possible.
    3 villagers have 1 plough. 2 cottagers; 4 slaves.
    Meadow for 2 oxen; pasture for the village livestock;
        wood for fences.   133 d
The value of this land is and was 50s; before 1066, 60s.
    Leofwara held this manor from Bishop William; she could
sell the ½ hide, but not the hide, without his permission.

*9 In (MUCH) HADHAM Osbern holds 1 hide from the Bishop.
Land for 2 ploughs. In lordship 1½ ploughs.
    1 villager has ½ plough. 6 cottagers; 1 slave.
The value is and always was 40s.
    2 Freemen held this land; one of them, Earl Algar's man,
had ½ hide; the other, ½ hide, of the King's jurisdiction;
he paid 2d to the Sheriff*; however, either could sell.

10 In PATMORE Baldwin holds 1 hide and 3 virgates from the Bishop.
Land for 4 ploughs. In lordship 2.
    2 villagers have 1 plough; another possible. 2 smallholders;
        6 cottagers; 3 slaves.
    Meadow for 2 oxen; woodland, 60 pigs.
The value is and always was £4.
    Alfward, Earl Algar's man, held this land; he could sell.

11 Ralph holds ALBURY from the Bishop. It answers for 2½ hides.
Land for 9 ploughs. In lordship 2.
    6 villagers and 9 smallholders have 6 ploughs; a seventh possible.
        3 cottagers; 3 slaves.
    Meadow for 2 oxen; pasture for the livestock; woodland, 30 pigs.
The value is and was £7; before 1066 £8.
    Siward, Archbishop Stigand's man, held this manor; he could sell. *

12 In PELHAM Ralph holds 1 hide and 1 virgate from the Bishop.
Land for 5 ploughs. In lordship 2; a third possible.
    2 villagers and 3 smallholders have 2 ploughs. 5 slaves;
        1 cottager.
    Pasture for the livestock; woodland, 20 pigs.

porc̄.Val̄ 7 ualuit.iiii.lib̄.T.R.E.⁊v.lib̄.Duo frs tenuer̄

hões Aſgari. 7 uende potuer̄.

In Peleha ten̄ Pagan de epo.i.hid̄.Tra.ē.iii.car̄.In dñio

ſunt.ii.7 i.uilłs h̄t dim̄ car̄.7 dim̄ pot fieri.Ibi.iii.bord̄.

7 iii.cot̄.Silua.vi.porc̄.Val̄ 7 ualuit xl.ſoł.T.R.E.⁊l.ſoł.

Hoc m̄ tenuit Alured hō Aſgari. 7 uende potuit.

In Peleha ten̄ Rannulf de epo.ii.hid̄ 7 dim̄.Tra.ē.viii.

car̄.In dñio ſunt.ii.7 vii.uilłi cū.v.bord̄ hñt.vi.car̄.

Ibi.vi.cot̄ 7 vi.ſerui.p̄tū.i.car̄.Paſta ad pec̄.Silua.xxx.

porc̄.Val̄ 7 ualuit.x.lib̄.T.R.E.⁊xv.lib̄.Hoc m̄ tenuer̄

ii.teigni.Hoꝛ un̄ hō Anſchil 7 alt̄ hō Goduini.uende potuer̄.

In Peleha ten̄ Giſlebt 7 Rannulf de epo.i.hid̄ 7 i.uirḡ.

Tra.ē.iii.car̄.In dñio.ē una.7 i.uilłs cū.iii.bord̄ h̄t

.i.car̄.7 alia pot fieri.Ibi.vii.cot̄.P̄tū dim̄ car̄.Paſta

ad pec̄.Silua.c.porc̄.Val̄ 7 ualuit.xl.ſoł.T.R.E.⁊lx.ſoł.

Duo frs tenuer̄ 7 uende potuer̄.Vn̄ hō Aſgari. 7 alt̄ abbis de Elẏ.

In Peleha ten̄.ii.milites de epo.iii.hid̄ 7 i.uirḡ.Tra.ē

vii.car̄.In dñio ſunt.iii.7 pbr cū vii.uilłis hñt.iiii.car̄.

Ibi.vii.bord̄ 7 vi.cot̄.7 i.ſeruus.p̄tū.ii.car̄ 7 dim̄.

Paſta ad pec̄.Silua.c.porc̄.Val̄ 7 ualuit.v.lib̄.T.R.E.⁊

vi.lib̄.Hoc m̄ tenuer̄.ii.teigni.Un̄ hō Aſchi. 7 alt̄ hō Almari.

7 cū eis.v.ſochi de ſoca regis.E.ii.uirḡ habuer̄. 7 uende potuer̄.

The value is and was £4; before 1066 £5.
2 brothers, Asgar the Constable's men, held it; they could sell.

13 In PELHAM Payne holds 1 hide from the Bishop. Land for 3
ploughs. In lordship 2.
1 villager has ½ plough; ½ possible.
3 smallholders; 3 cottagers.
Woodland, 6 pigs.
The value is and was 40s; before 1066, 50s.
Alfred, Asgar the Constable's man, held this manor;
he could sell.

*14 In PELHAM Ranulf holds 2½ hides from the Bishop. Land
for 8 ploughs. In lordship 2.
7 villagers with 5 smallholders have 6 ploughs. 6 cottagers;
6 slaves.
Meadow for 1 plough; pasture for the livestock;
woodland, 30 pigs.
The value is and was £10; before 1066 £15.
2 thanes held this manor. One of them was Askell of Ware's
man, the other Godwin Benfield's man. They could sell.

15 In PELHAM Gilbert and Ranulf hold 1 hide and 1 virgate from
the Bishop. Land for 3 ploughs. In lordship 1.
1 villager with 3 smallholders has 1 plough;
another possible. 7 cottagers.
Meadow for ½ plough; pasture for the livestock;
woodland, 100 pigs.
The value is and was 40s; before 1066, 60s.
2 brothers held it; they could sell. One was Asgar the
Constable's man, the other the Abbot of Ely's.

*16 In PELHAM 2 men-at-arms hold 3 hides and 1 virgate from the
Bishop. Land for 7 ploughs. In lordship 3.
A priest with 7 villagers have 4 ploughs.
7 smallholders; 6 cottagers; 1 slave.
Meadow for 2½ ploughs; pasture for the livestock;
woodland, 100 pigs.
The value is and was £5; before 1066 £6.
2 thanes held this manor. One was Askell of Ware's man,
the other Aelmer of Bennington's man. With them, 5 Freemen of
King Edward's jurisdiction had 2 virgates; they could sell.

In Meſdone teñ Pagan de eꝑo . i . hiđ . Tra . ē . v . car . In

dñio . ii . car poſs fieri . 7 iii . uilti cū pƀro hñt . iii . car .
Ibi . i . 7 i . ſeruus . p̃tū . iii . car . Paſta ad pec . Silua . cccc .
porc . Val 7 ualuit . xx . ſol . T . R . E . vi . liƀ . Hoc ⋒ tenuit
Aluuard hō Stigandi Archiepi . 7 uende potuit.

In Pelehā . teñ Eldred de eꝑo . i . hiđ . Tra . ē . ii . car . Ibi ē
una 7 dimiđ . 7 dimiđ pot fieri . Ibi . viii . borđ . 7 ii . ſerui .
p̃tū . i . car . Paſta ad pec . Silua xx . porc . Val 7 ualuit
. xx . ſol . T . R . E . xl . ſol . Hanc trā tenuit Aluuin hō Goduin
de Benefelle . 7 uende potuit.

In Pelehā teñ Riculf de eꝑo . ii . hiđ . Tra . ē . iiii . car .
In dñio . ii . car . 7 iiii . uilti cū . iii . borđ hñt . ii . car .
Ibi . x . cot 7 iii . ſerui . p̃tū . i . car . Paſta ad pec . Silua
xl . porc . Val 7 ualuit . c . ſol . T . R . E . v . liƀ 7 x . ſol .
Hoc ⋒ tenuit Wluui hō Goduini de Benedfelle . 7 uende
In Tedriceſhā teñ Wilts 7 Rannulf de eꝑo   potuit.
. i . hiđ 7 dim . Tra . ē . iii . car . In dñio ſunt . ii . 7 ii . uilti
cū . iii . borđ hñt . i . car . Ibi . i . cot . 7 i . ſeruus . Silua
lx . porc . Paſta ad pec . Val 7 ualuit . xl . ſol . T . R . E .
lx . ſol . Hanc tra Wluui hō Aſgari . 7 uende potuit.
Has xxxvi . hiđ teñ eps London 7 ſui milites . 7 cū his
reclamat . iiii . hiđ q̃s teñ aƀƀ de Ely in Hadam.
Storteford teñ iſđ eps . ꝑ vi . hiđ In Brachings hđ .
ſe defđ . Tra . ē . x . car . In dñio . iiii . hidæ 7 dim . 7 ibi ſuꝺ
ii . car . 7 iii . pot fieri . Ibi . vi . uilti cū . viii . borđ hñt
iiii . car . 7 iii . poſs fieri . Ibi pƀr cū . ii . militiƀ . 7 xii .
cot . 7 ii . molenđ de . xxx . ſol . P̃tū . i . car . Silua . ccc .
porc . In totis valent ual 7 ualuit . viii . liƀ . T . R . E .

17 In MEESDEN Payne holds 1 hide from the Bishop. Land for 5
    ploughs. In lordship 2 ploughs possible.   134 a
        3 villagers with a priest have 3 ploughs. 1 [cottager?]; 1 slave.
        Meadow for 3 ploughs; pasture for the livestock;
            woodland, 400 pigs.
    The value is and was 20s; before 1066 £6.
    Alfward, Archbishop Stigand's man, held this manor; he could sell.

18 In PELHAM Aldred holds 1 hide from the Bishop. Land for 2
    ploughs; 1½ there; ½ possible.
        8 smallholders; 2 slaves.
        Meadow for 1 plough; pasture for the livestock; woodland, 20 pigs.
    The value is and was 20s; before 1066, 40s.
    Alwin, Godwin of Benfield's man, held this land; he could sell.

19 In PELHAM Riculf holds 2 hides from the Bishop. Land for 4
    ploughs. In lordship 2 ploughs.
        4 villagers with 3 smallholders have 2 ploughs.
            10 cottagers; 3 slaves,
        Meadow for 1 plough; pasture for the livestock; woodland, 40 pigs.
    The value is and was 100s; before 1066 £5 10s.
    Wulfwy, Godwin of Benfield's man, held this manor; he could sell.

20 In HIXHAM William and Ranulf hold 1½ hides from the Bishop.
    Land for 3 ploughs. In lordship 2.
        2 villagers with 3 smallholders have 1 plough. 1 cottager; 1 slave.
        Woodland, 60 pigs; pasture for the livestock.
    The value is and was 40s; before 1066, 60s.
    Wulfwy, Asgar the Constable's man, (held) this land; he could sell.

21 The Bishop of London and his men-at-arms hold these 36 hides.
    With them he claims 4 hides which the Abbot of Ely holds
    in Hadham.*

    In BRAUGHING Hundred
22 The Bishop also holds STORTFORD. It answers for 6 hides.
    Land for 10 ploughs. In lordship 4½ hides. 2 ploughs there;
    a third possible.
        6 villagers with 8 smallholders have 4 ploughs; 3 possible.
            A priest with 2 men-at-arms; 12 cottagers.
        2 mills at 30s; meadow for 1 plough; woodland, 300 pigs.
    The total value is and was £8; before 1066 £10.

x . lib . Hoc M̃ tenuit Eddeua pulchra . 7 ipſũ eſt de
feudo quẽ emit Wills eps.

In Torlei ten Roderius de epo dim̃ hiđ . Tra . ẽ . I . car̃.
7 ibi . ẽ cũ . II . ſeruis . p̃tũ dim̃ car̃ . Silua . II . porc̃ . Val
7 ualuit . xx̃ . ſol . T.R.E.' xxx . ſol . Hanc trã tenuit
Edzi . hõ Goded . 7 uenđe pot̃ . 7 II . denar̃ reddeb uicecom̃.

In Wichehã ten Hunfrid . II . hiđ 7 xx . acs̃ p̃ uno M̃
de epo . Tra . ẽ . III . car̃ . In dñio ſunt . II . 7 IIII . uilli
cũ . II . borđ hñt . I . car̃ . Ibi . VIII . cot̃ . 7 I . ſeruus . P̃tũ
dim̃ car̃ . Silua . xxx . porc̃ . Val 7 ualuit . XL . ſol.
T.R.E.' LX . ſol . Hanc trã tenuer̃ . IIII . ſochi . 7 uenđe

In Wichehã teñ . II . milites de epo . I . uirg̃ ┌ potuer̃.
7 dim̃ . Tra . ẽ dim̃ car̃ . s; non . ẽ ibi . Silua . xx . porc̃.
7 un̄ uills . Val 7 ualuit . VIII . ſol . T.R.E.' x . ſol.
Hanc trã tenuer̃ . III . ſochi 7 uenđe potuer̃ . Vn̄ eoꝛ
hõ Willi epi . Alt hõ Aſgari . 7 III . hõ Eddeue pulcræ.
Ħ tra . ẽ de feudo epi Willi.

134 b

.V. TERRA EP̃I BAIOCENS̃ . IN ᚱEVINGA HVNĐ.
Eps̃ BAIOCENSIS ten̄ PVTEHÃ . p̃ IIII . hiđ ſe
Rogeri ten̄ de epo . Tra . ẽ . IIII . car̃ . In dñio . ẽ una.
7 alia pot̃ fieri . Ibi . IIII . uilli cũ . II . borđ hñt . II . car̃.
Ibi . IIII . cot̃ . 7 II . ſerui . 7 II . molini de . x . ſol . 7 VIII.
den̄ . p̃tũ . IIII . car̃ . 7 IIII . ſoliđ . Paſta ad pec̃ . Val
LX . ſol . Q̃do recep.' XL . ſol . T.R.E.' IIII . lib . Hoc M̃
tenuit Leuuin̄ comes. IN DANAIS HVNĐ.
In Titeberſt ten̄ Adã de epo dim̃ hiđ . Tra . ẽ . II . bob.

Edeva the Fair held this manor. It is (part) of the Holding which Bishop William bought.

*23 In THORLEY Rodhere holds ½ hide from the Bishop. Land for 1 plough. It is there, with
    2 slaves.
    Meadow for ½ plough; woodland, 2 pigs.
The value is and was 20s; before 1066, 30s.
    Edsi, Godith's man, held this land; he could sell.
He paid 2d to the Sheriff.

24 In WICKHAM Humphrey holds 2 hides and 20 acres as one manor from the Bishop. Land for 3 ploughs. In lordship 2.
    4 villagers with 2 smallholders have 1 plough. 8 cottagers; 1 slave.
    Meadow for ½ plough; woodland, 30 pigs.
The value is and was 40s; before 1066, 60s.
    4 Freemen held this land; they could sell.

25 In WICKHAM 2 men-at-arms hold 1½ virgates from the Bishop. Land for ½ plough, but it is not there.
    Woodland, 20 pigs.
    1 villager.
The value is and was 8s; before 1066, 10s.
    3 Freemen held this land; they could sell. One of them was Bishop William's man, the second Asgar the Constable's man, the third Edeva the Fair's man. This land is (part) of Bishop William's Holding.

5   LAND OF THE BISHOP OF BAYEUX   134 b

In TRING Hundred
*1 The Bishop of Bayeux holds PUTTENHAM. It answers for 4 hides. Roger holds from the Bishop. Land for 4 ploughs. In lordship 1; another possible.
    4 villagers with 2 smallholders have 2 ploughs. 4 cottagers; 2 slaves.
    2 mills at 10s 8d; meadow for 4 ploughs, and 4s too; pasture
       for the livestock.
Value 60s; when acquired 40s; before 1066 £4.
    Earl Leofwin held this manor.

In DACORUM Hundred
*2 In THEOBALD STREET Adam holds ½ hide from the Bishop. Land for 2 oxen.

Ibi . i . borđ . Silua . xx . porc̄ . Val . x . ſol . Q̇do recep̄:

v . ſol . 7 tn̄tđ T.R.E. Hanc trā tenuit Aluuard

de abƀe S̅ Albani . n̄ potuit uendẻ p̄t ej lictiā.   ⌐ HD̅.

Iſdē Adā ten̄ de eṗo Lāpeth . p dim̄ hiđ *IN ALBANESTOV*

Tra . ē . i . car̄ . ſed ibi n̄ eſt . Silua . L . porc̄ . Val . x . ſol.

Q̇do recep̄: v . ſol . T.R.E: xx . ſol . Hanc trā tenuit

Alnod Grutt . 7 uendẻ potuit .   *IN BRADEWATRE HD̅.*

In Grauelai ten̄ Adā de eṗo . i . hiđ 7 dim̄ 7 x . ac̄s.

Tra . ē . iii . car̄ . In dn̄io . ē una . 7 alia pot̄ fieri . Ibi

iiii . uiłłi cū . iii . borđ hn̄t . i . car̄ . Ibi . ii . ſerui . Nem⁹

ad ſepes . Paſtā ad pec̄ . Val . xx . ſol . Q̇do recep̄:

L . ſol . 7 tn̄tđ . T.R.E. De hac trā tenuit Alnod

. i . hiđ 7 dim̄ 7 Bruning . x . ac̄s . ambo uendẻ potueř.

Hic tam̄ reddeƀ de conſuetuđ dimiđ den̄ uicec̄.

In Almeſhou ten̄ Adā de eṗo . i . hiđ . Tra . ē . i . car̄.

7 ibi . ē cū . iii . borđ . Silua . Lx . porc̄ . Val xx . ſol.

Q̇do recep̄: x . ſol . T.R.E: xxx . ſol . Hanc trā tenuit

Edmund hō⁹ Heraldi . 7 uendẻ potuit.

In Wimundeſlai ten̄ Adā de eṗo . i . hiđ 7 i . uirḡ.

Tra . ē . i . car̄ . 7 ibi . ē cū . iii . borđ . P̄tū dim̄ car̄.

Val 7 ualuit . x . ſol . T.R.E: xx . ſol . Hanc trā te

nuit Alflet de Roƀto . f . Wimarc̄ . n̄ poterat

uendẻ p̄ter ej lictiā ut Scira teſtatur.

In Boxe ten̄ Oſbern⁹ de eṗo dimiđ hiđ . Tra . ē . i . car̄.

7 ibi un̄ borđ . Val 7 ualuit ſep̄ . x . ſol . Samar hō⁹ Alnod

tenuit eā . 7 uendẻ potuit.

1 smallholder.
Woodland, 20 pigs.
Value 10s; when acquired 5s; before 1066, as much.
Alfward held this land from the Abbot of St. Albans; he
could not sell without his permission.

In CASHIO Hundred
*3 Adam also holds *LAMPETH* from the Bishop for ½ hide. Land for 1
plough, but it is not there.
Woodland, 50 pigs.
Value 10s; when acquired 5s; before 1066, 20s.
Alnoth Grutt held this land; he could sell.

In BROADWATER Hundred
4 In GRAVELEY Adam holds 1½ hides and 10 acres from the Bishop.
Land for 3 ploughs. In lordship 1; another possible.
4 villagers with 3 smallholders have 1 plough. 2 slaves.
Wood for fences; pasture for the livestock.
Value 20s; when acquired 50s; before 1066 as much.
Alnoth held 1½ hides of this land and Browning 10 acres;
both could sell. However, the latter paid ½d to the Sheriff in
customary dues.

5 In ALMSHOE Adam holds 1 hide from the Bishop. Land for 1
plough. It is there, with
3 smallholders.
Woodland, 60 pigs.
Value 20s; when acquired 10s; before 1066, 30s.
Edmund, Earl Harold's man, held this land; he could sell.

6 In WYMONDLEY Adam holds 1 hide and 1 virgate from the Bishop.
Land for 1 plough. It is there, with
3 smallholders.
Meadow for ½ plough.
The value is and was 10s; before 1066, 20s.
Aelfled held this land from Robert son of Wymarc; she
could not sell without his permission, as the Shire testifies.

7 In BOX Osbern holds ½ hide from the Bishop. Land for 1 plough.
1 smallholder.
The value is and always was 10s.
Saemer, Alnoth's man, held it; he could sell.

Ipfe eps ten *ESTONE* . p x . hid fe defd . Tra . e xv . car.

In dnio . 1111 . hidæ . 7 ibi . 1111 . car . 7 v . pot fieri . Ibi pbr

7 xı . uilti cu . v . bord hnt v . car . 7 aliæ . v . poff fieri.

Ibi . vı . cot 7 1111 . ferui . Ptu . 11 . car . Pafta ad pec . Silua

cc . porc . In totis ualent ual . xvııı . lib . Qdo recep. xıııı .

lib . T . R . E. xx . lib . Hoc ⋒ tenuer . 111 . hoes Stigandi

archiepi . 7 uende potuer.

In Sutrefhele ten Petrus de epo . 1 . hid 7 una uirg.

7 x . acs . Tra . e . 1 . car . 7 ibi . e cu . 11 . uiltis . 7 qda francig.

Silua . xxx . porc . Val x . fot . Qdo recep. vıı . fot . T . R . E.

xx . fot . Hanc tra tenuer . 11 . fochi hoes Leuuini . de foca

regis . E . 7 uende potuer . 7 inuenieb uicecom regis . 1 . auera

t . v . denar 7 unu quadrante p annu.

In ead uilla ten eps . 11 . hid 7 1 . uirg 7 ıx . acs . Tra . e . 11 . car.

134 c

fed nulla . e ibi . In dnio . 11 . hide 7 ıx . acræ . 7 111 .

bord . 7 1 . molin de xvı . den . Ptu . 11 . bob . Silua

lv . porc . Val 7 ualuit . xx . fot . T . R . E. xl . fot.

Hanc tra tenuer 111 . hoes Stigandi archiepi . 7 uen

dere potuer . 7 1 . ho Leuuini dim hid habuit.

7 uende potuit . Inuenieb dimid Auera t . 11 . den uice

In ead uilla ten Turftin de epo . 11 . hid . comiti.

Tra . e . 11 . car . fed n funt ibi . nifi . 11 . cot . 7 1 . molin

de . 1111 . fot . Ptu . 11 . bob . Silua . c . porc . Val 7 ua

luit . xxx . fot . T . R . E. lx . fot . Hanc tra tenuit

Almar de foca regis ho Afgari . uende potuit.

11 . Aueras t vııı . den reddeb uicecomiti.

In ead uilla ten ipfe eps . xı . acs . Val 7 ualuer

fep . xı . den . Aluuard tenuit de . S . archiepo.

8 The Bishop holds ASTON himself. It answers for 10 hides.
Land for 15 ploughs. In lordship 4 hides; 4 ploughs there;
a fifth possible.
    A priest and 11 villagers with 5 smallholders have 5 ploughs;
        another 5 possible; 6 cottagers; 4 slaves.
    Meadow for 2 ploughs; pasture for the livestock; woodland, 200 pigs.
    Total value £18; when acquired £14; before 1066 £20.
    3 of Archbishop Stigand's men held this manor; they could sell.

9 In LIBURY Peter holds 1 hide, 1 virgate and 10 acres from the
Bishop. Land for 1 plough. It is there, with
    2 villagers and a Frenchman.
    Woodland, 30 pigs.
Value 10s; when acquired 7s; before 1066, 20s.
    2 Freemen, Earl Leofwin's men, of King Edward's jurisdiction,*
held this land; they could sell. They found 1 cartage, or 5¼d a
year for the King's Sheriff.

10 In the same village the Bishop holds 2 hides, 1 virgate and 9 acres.
Land for 2 ploughs, but none is there. In lordship 2 hides   134 c
and 9 acres.
    3 smallholders.
    1 mill at 16d; meadow for 2 oxen; woodland, 55 pigs.
The value is and was 20s; before 1066, 40s.
3 men of Archbishop Stigand's held this land; they could sell.
    Scova, a man of Leofwin's, had ½ hide; he could sell. He
found ½ cartage, or 2d for the Sheriff.

*11 In the same village Thurstan holds 2 hides from the Bishop.
Land for 2 ploughs, but they are not there; only
    2 cottagers.
    1 mill at 4s; meadow for 2 oxen; woodland, 100 pigs.
The value is and was 30s; before 1066, 60s.
    Aelmer, of the King's jurisdiction, Asgar the Constable's man,
held this land; he could sell. He paid 2 cartages or 8d to the Sheriff.

12 In the same village the Bishop holds 11 acres himself.
The value is and always was 11d.
    Alfward held it from Archbishop Stigand.

In Lufenhate ten Ofbn de epo . *In Odesei Hvnd.*

ii . hid 7 dim . Tra . e̅ . v . car . In dñio . iii . car .

7 iii . bord cu̅ . iii . uittis hn̅t . ii . car . Ibi . iiii . cot

7 iiii . ferui . Nem ad fepes . Val 7 ualuit . xl . fot .

T . R . E. lx . fot . Hanc tra̅ tenue̅r . iii . fochi . Duo

ho̗ hoẽs . S . archiepi . i . hid 7 dim habue̅r . 7 uende

potue̅r . 7 tcius ho̅ Almari de belintone . i . hid

habuit . 7 uende potuit . Vna̅ Auera̅ l . iiii . den redd .

In Cladhele . ten Ofbn de epo . vii . hid 7 iii .

uirg 7 dim . Tra . e̅ . x . car . In dñio funt . ii . 7 iii .

pot fieri . Ibi . viii . uitti cu̅ . xii . bord hn̅t . vii .

car . Ibi . iii . cot 7 iiii . ferui . Nem ad fepes . Pafta

ad pec . In totis ualent uat . vii . lib . Q̅do recep .

v . lib . T . R . E. x . lib . Hoc m̅ tenuit Alnod grud

ho̅ . S . archiepi . 7 uende potuit . 7 de hac tra . iii .

fochi hoẽs . S . archiepi . ii . hid 7 iii . uirg habue̅r .

qui ibi n̅ fue̅r . T . R . E . fed poft morte̅ ej huic m̅

appofiti funt . 7 uende tra̅ fua̅ potue̅r . 7 de c̅fu

etudine reddeb . xi . denar uicecomiti p annu̅ .

7 alij . ii . fochi hoẽs . S . archiepi ten 7 tenue̅r dim

uirg . 7 dare 7 uende potue̅r .

In Orduuelle ten Ofbn de epo dim hid . Tra . e̅

. i . car . 7 ibi . e̅ cu̅ . ii . uitis . Val 7 ualuit fep . xv .

fot . Hanc tra̅ tenue̅r . iii . hoes . S . archiepi . 7 uende

In Retth ten Ofbn de epo . i . hid .   potue̅r .

Tra . e̅ . iii . car . In dñio . e̅ . una . 7 alia pot fieri .

Ibi . vi . bord hn̅t . i . car . Val . xl . fot . Q̅do recep .

In ODSEY Hundred

*13 In LUFFENHALL Osbern holds 2½ hides from the Bishop. Land
for 5 ploughs. In lordship 3 ploughs.
    3 smallholders with 3 villagers have 2 ploughs. 4 cottagers; 4 slaves.
    Wood for fences.
The value is and was 40s; before 1066, 60s.
    3 Freemen held this land. Two of them, Archbishop Stigand's
men, had 1½ hides and could sell; the third, Aelmer of Bennington's
man, had 1 hide and could sell. He paid 1 cartage, or 4d.

14 In CLOTHALL Osbern holds 7 hides and 3½ virgates from the
Bishop. Land for 10 ploughs. In lordship 2; a third possible.
    8 villagers with 12 smallholders have 7 ploughs. 3 cottagers; 4 slaves.
    Wood for fences; pasture for the livestock.
Total value £7; when acquired £5; before 1066 £10.
    Alnoth Grutt, Archbishop Stigand's man, held this manor; he
could sell. 3 Freemen, Archbishop Stigand's men, had 2 hides
and 3 virgates of this land. They were not there in King Edward's
time, but they were placed in this manor after his death; they could
sell their land, and paid 11d a year to the Sheriff in customary dues.
2 other Freemen, Archbishop Stigand's men, hold and held ½ virgate;
they could grant and sell.

*15 In ORWELL Osbern holds ½ hide from the Bishop.
Land for 1 plough. It is there, with
    2 villagers.
The value is and always was 15s.
    3 men of Archbishop Stigand's held this land; they could sell.

16 In REED Osbern holds 1 hide from the Bishop. Land for 3
ploughs. In lordship 1; another possible.
    6 smallholders have 1 plough.
Value 40s; when acquired 60s; before 1066 as much.

LX.fol.7 tntď.T.R.E.Hanc trā tenuit Eddeua

puella teftante hund. hō.S.archiepi fuit.7 uendě

In Radéuuelle ten Adā fub epo.IIII.hiđ Ⱶpotuit.

Tra.ē.VII.caꝛ.In dñio funt.II.7 aliæ.II.poſſ.ee.

Ibi.VIII.uilli cū.IIII.borđ hñt.III.caꝛ.Ibi.IIII.

ferui.7 I.moliñ de.VIII.fol.p̃tū dim caꝛ.Paſtă

ad pec.Val.c.fol.Qdo recep̃⁏xL.fol.T.R.E.

x.liɓ.Hoc M̃ tenuit Alnod hō Stig arcĥ.7 uendě

HVND.In Berlai ten Adā de epo IN EDWINESKEV Ⱶpot.

.I.hiđ 7 dim.Tra.ē.II.caꝛ.Ibi.ē una.7 alia pot fieri.

134 d

Ibi.III.uilli.7 II.ferui.Val.xx.fol.Qdo recep̃⁏xII.fol.

T.R.E.⁏xL.fol.Hanc trā tenuit de Stig arcĥ.7 uendě

In Haflehangra ten Adā de epo tciā partē Ⱶpotuit.

unius hidæ.Tra.ē dim caꝛ.Val.IIII.fol.Qdo recep̃⁏

II.fol.T.R.E.⁏x.fol.Hanc trā tenuit Leflet de Stig

archiepo.7 uendě potuit.

Ofɓn ten de epo Bochelande.p.III.hiđ 7 III.uirg

fe defđ.Tra.ē.VI.caꝛ.In dñio.II.caꝛ.7 III.pot fieri.

Ibi pɓr 7 VIII.uilli 7 VI.borđ hñt.III.caꝛ.Ibi.VIII.cot.

7 IIII.ferui.P̃tū.I.caꝛ.Paſtă ad pec.Silua.xL.porc.

De paftura 7 filua.x.fol.In totis ualent ual.VI.liɓ.

Qdo recep̃⁏VIII.liɓ.T.R.E.⁏x.liɓ.Hoc M̃ tenuit

Sailt hō Leuuini.7 uendě potuit.

In Odenhou ten Ofɓn de epo.I.hiđ 7 dim uirg.

Tra.ē.II.caꝛ 7 dim.7 ibi funt.cū.III.uillis.7 VI.borđ.

7 uno francig.Val.xL.fol.Qdo recep̃⁏xxx.fol.

T.R.E.⁏Lx.fol.Hanc trā tenueꝛ.IIII.fochi.Hoꝛ.III.

hōꝰ Stig arcĥ fueꝛ.7 IIII.hō Algari.7 uendě potueꝛ.

Edeva, a girl, as the Hundred testifies, held this land; she
was Archbishop Stigand's man;* she could sell.

17 In RADWELL Adam holds 4 hides under the Bishop. Land for 7
ploughs. In lordship 2; another 2 possible.
    8 villagers with 4 smallholders have 3 ploughs. 4 slaves.
    1 mill at 8s; meadow for ½ plough; pasture for the livestock.
Value 100s; when acquired 40s; before 1066 £10.
    Alnoth, Archbishop Stigand's man, held this manor; he could sell.

In EDWINSTREE Hundred

18 In BARLEY Adam holds 1½ hides from the Bishop. Land for 2
ploughs; 1 there; another possible.
    3 villagers; 2 slaves.   134 d
Value 20s; when acquired 12s; before 1066, 40s.
    ... held this land from Archbishop Stigand; he could sell.*

19 In 'HAZELHANGER' Adam holds the third part of 1 hide from the
Bishop. Land for ½ plough.
Value 4s; when acquired 2s; before 1066, 10s.
    Leofled held this land from Archbishop Stigand; she could sell.

20 Osbern holds BUCKLAND from the Bishop. It answers for 3 hides
and 3 virgates. Land for 6 ploughs. In lordship 2 ploughs; a
third possible.
    A priest, 8 villagers and 6 smallholders have 3 ploughs.
    8 cottagers; 4 slaves.
    Meadow for 1 plough; pasture for the livestock; woodland, 40 pigs;
    from pasture and woodland 10s.
Total value £6; when acquired £8; before 1066 £10.
    Saehild, Earl Leofwin's man, held this manor; she could sell.

21 In HODENHOE Osbern holds 1 hide and ½ virgate from the Bishop.
Land for 2½ ploughs. They are there, with
    3 villagers, 6 smallholders and 1 Frenchman.
Value 40s; when acquired 30s; before 1066, 60s.
    4 Freemen held this land; 3 of them were Archbishop Stigand's
men, the fourth Earl Algar's man; they could sell.

In Trochinge ten Ofbn de epo.xii.acs.Tra.e̅.i.boui.
Val 7 ualuit fep.ii.fol.Aluric fcoua tenuit.7 uende pot.
In Ichetone ten Ofbn de epo.i.hid.Tra.e̅.ii.car 7 dim̅.
In dn̅io.e̅ una.7 ii.uilti cu̅.ii.bord hn̅t.i.car 7 dim
pot fieri.Ibi.i.cot 7 iiii.ferui.P̊tu̅.i.car̅.Pafta ad pec.
Silua.x.porc.Val.xl.fol.Q̊do recep̅.xxx.fol.T.R.E.
lx.fol.Hanc tr̅a tenuer̅.iiii.fochi.Vn eo₂ ho̅ Stig arch.
fuit 7.ii.hoes regis.E.de c̅fuetud.ii.den reddider̅.
7 iiii.ho̅ Heraldi fuit.Om̅s hi tr̅a fua̅ uende potuer̅.

Radulf ten de epo Kamintone IN DIMID HVND DE HIZ.
p.iiii.hid fe defd.Tra.e̅ x.car̅.In dn̅io funt.ii.7 iii.
pot fieri.Ibi.ii.francig 7 xii.uilti cu̅.ii.bord.hn̅t
vii.car̅.Ibi.iii.cot 7 v.ferui.P̊tu̅.vi.bob.Silua
octingent porc̅.7 i.molin de.viii.fol.In totis ualent
ual 7 ualuit.xii.lib.T.R.E.xv.lib.Hoc M̅ tenuit
Ælueua mat Morcari. IN BRACHINGS HVND.
In EIA ten Petrus de epo dim̅ hid.Tra.e̅ dim̅ car̅.fed
non.e̅ ibi.Vnu̅ mol de.iii.fol.De gurgitib̅.cc.anguilt.
p̊tu̅ dim̅ car̅.7 de feno.x.fol.H̅ tra ual.xx.fol.
Q̊do recep̅.x.fol.T.R.E.xxx.fol.Suen tenuit ho̅
Heraldi.7 uende potuit.

In Torinch ten Hugo de grentmaifnil.i.hid de epo.
Tra.e̅.iiii.car̅.In dn̅io.e̅ una.7 alia pot fieri.Ibi.iiii.
uilti cu̅.iii.bord hn̅t.ii.car̅.Ibi.ii.ferui.7 i.molin de
.v.fol.P̊tu̅.iiii. Silua.xvi.porc.H̅ tra ual.xxx.fol.
Q̊do recep̅.xl.fol.T.R.E.c.fol.Hoc M̅ tenuit Alnod
ho̅ Stig archiep̅i.7 uende potuit.

22 In THROCKING Osbern holds 12 acres from the Bishop. Land for 1 ox.
The value is and always was 2s.
    Aelfric Scova held it; he could sell.

23 In BUNTINGFORD* Osbern holds 1 hide from the Bishop. Land
for 2½ ploughs. In lordship 1.
    2 villagers with 2 smallholders have 1 plough; ½ possible.
        1 cottager; 4 slaves.
    Meadow for 1 plough; pasture for the livestock; woodland, 10 pigs.
    Value 40s; when acquired 30s; before 1066, 60s.
    4 Freemen held this land. One of them was Archbishop Stigand's
    man; two were King Edward's men; they paid 2d in customary dues;
    the fourth was Earl Harold's man; all of them could sell their land.

In the Half-Hundred of HITCHIN

24 Ralph holds KIMPTON from the Bishop. It answers for 4 hides.
Land for 10 ploughs. In lordship 2; a third possible.
    2 Frenchmen and 12 villagers with 2 smallholders have 7
        ploughs. 3 cottagers; 5 slaves.
    Meadow for 6 oxen; woodland, 800 pigs; 1 mill at 8s.
    The total value is and was £12; before 1066 £15.
    Aelfeva, mother of Earl Morcar, held this manor.

In BRAUGHING Hundred

25 In RYE Peter holds ½ hide from the Bishop. Land for ½
plough, but it is not there.
        1 mill at 3s; from weirs, 200 eels; meadow for ½ plough;
            from hay 10s.
    Value of this land, 20s; when acquired 10s; before 1066, 30s.
    Swein, Earl Harold's man, held it; he could sell.

26 In THUNDRIDGE Hugh of Grandmesnil holds 1 hide from the Bishop.
Land for 4 ploughs. In lordship 1; another possible.
        4 villagers with 3 smallholders have 2 ploughs. 2 slaves.
        1 mill at 5s; meadow for 4...; woodland, 16 pigs.
    Value of this land, 30s; when acquired 40s; before 1066, 100s.
    Alnoth, Archbishop Stigand's man, held this manor; he could sell.

TERRA EPI LISIACENSIS. *IN DANEIS HVND.*

Eps LISIACENSIS in Redborne ht . 1 . uirg træ.

Wigot ten de eo . Tra . e dim car . 7 ibi . e cu . 1 . bord.

Val . VIII . fol . Qdo recep̄ . II . fol . T.R.E. x . fol . Aluuin

uenator hō Leuuini com tenuit . 7 uende potuit.

135 a

.VII

TERRA ROBERTI EPI DE CESTRE. *IN DANAIS HVND.*

Eps de CESTRE ten *MIMMINE* . p VIII . hid 7 1 . uirg fe

defd T.R.E. 7 m̄ p VIII . hid . Tra . e . XIII . car . In dnio . IIII . hidæ.

7 ibi funt . II . car . 7 III cia . pot fieri . Ibi . XVII . uilli cu . VIII to . bord

hnt . x . car . Ibi . III . cot 7 1 . feruus . Pafta ad pec . Silua . cccc .

porc . In totis ualent ual 7 ualuit . VIII . liƀ . T.R.E. x . liƀ.

Hoc m̄ tenuer . III . teigni hōes reginæ Eddid . 7 uende potuer.

Hoc m̄ non . e de epifcopatu . fed fuit Raynerij patris Roƀti epi.

Ipfe eps ten *BIGRAVE* . p . v . hid fe defd . *IN ODESEI HVND.*

Tra . e . XII . car . In dnio . II . hidæ . 7 ibi funt . III . car . Prƀr

7 II . fochi cu . x . uillis 7 IX . bord hnt . IX . car . Ibi . VI . cot .

7 VII . ferui . 7 1 . molin de . x . fol . In totis ualent ual x . liƀ.

Qdo recep̄ . VIII . liƀ . T.R.E. XII . liƀ . Hoc m̄ tenuit Lemar

hō Stig Arch . 7 uende potuit . 7 II . fochi qui ibid funt . III . uirg

tenuer . fʒ p̄t lictia archiepi uende non potuer.

In Bradefella ten ifd eps . 1 . uirg træ . Tra . e . III . boƀ.

Ibi . e un feruus . Val 7 ualuit . III . fol . T.R.E . v . fol . Lædmær

tenuit hō Stig archiepi . 7 uende potuit . *IN BRADEWATRE HD.*

In Wilge ten ifd eps dim hid . Tra . e dim car . Val

7 ualuit fep . III . fol . H tra jacet in Bigrave m̄ ejd epi.

Stigand archieps ea tenuit.

6   LAND OF THE BISHOP OF LISIEUX

In DACORUM Hundred
1   The Bishop of Lisieux has 1 virgate of land in REDBOURN.
   Wigot holds from him. Land for ½ plough; it is there, with
      1 smallholder.
   Value 8s; when acquired 2s; before 1066, 10s.
      Alwin Hunter, Earl Leofwin's man, held it; he could sell.

7   LAND OF BISHOP ROBERT OF CHESTER   135 a

In DACORUM Hundred
1   The Bishop of Chester holds (NORTH) MIMMS. Before 1066 it
   answered for 8 hides and 1 virgate; now for 8 hides.
   Land for 13 ploughs. In lordship 4 hides; 2 ploughs there;
   a third possible.
      17 villagers with 8 smallholders have 10 ploughs.
        3 cottagers; 1 slave.
   Pasture for the livestock; woodland, 400 pigs.
   The total value is and was £8; before 1066 £10.
      3 thanes, Queen Edith's men, held this manor; they could sell.
      This manor is not the Bishopric's; but was Rayner's,
   Bishop Robert's father's.

In ODSEY Hundred
2   The Bishop holds BYGRAVE himself. It answers for 5 hides. Land
   for 12 ploughs. In lordship 2 hides; 3 ploughs there.
      A priest and 2 Freemen with 10 villagers and 9 smallholders
        have 9 ploughs. 6 cottagers; 7 slaves.
      1 mill at 10s.
   Total value £10; when acquired £8; before 1066 £12.
      Ledmer, Archbishop Stigand's man, held this manor; he
   could sell. 2 Freemen, who are also there, held 3 virgates; but
   they could not sell without the Archbishop's permission.

3   In BROADFIELD the Bishop also holds 1 virgate of land. Land
   for 3 oxen.
      1 slave.
   The value is and was 3s; before 1066, 5s.
      Ledmer, Archbishop Stigand's man, held it; he could sell.

In BROADWATER Hundred
*4   In WELWYN the Bishop also holds ½ hide. Land for ½ plough.
   The value is and always was 3s.
      This land lies in (the lands of) Bygrave, the Bishop's manor.
   Archbishop Stigand held it.

TERRA ABBATIS DE ELẎ *IN BRADEWATRE HVND.*

.VIII. ABBAS de ELẎ ten *HETFELLE* . p̄ XL . hid se defd.

Tra . ē . xxx . caŕ . In dñio . xx . hidæ . 7 ibi sunt . II . caŕ.

7 III . adhuc poſſ fieri . Ibi p̄br cū xVIII . uiłłis 7 xVIII.

bord hñt xx . caŕ . 7 adhuc . v . caŕ poſſ fieri . Ibi . xII.

cot 7 vI . serui . 7 IIII . moł de . xLVII . soł 7 ĩĩĩ . or . den.

P̄tū . x . caŕ . Pastura ad peć . Silua . ĩĩ . mił porc̄ . 7 de

c̄suetud siluæ 7 pastǽ . x . soł . In totis ualent uał 7 ualuit

xxv . liƀ . T.R.E. xxx . liƀ . Hoc M̄ jacuit 7 jacet in

dñio æccłæ de Elẏ . *IN ODESEI HVND.*

Ipse aƀƀ ten *CHELESELLE* . p̄ . v . hid se defd . Tra . ē

x . caŕ . In dñio . II . hidæ . 7 ibi sunt . III . caŕ . 7 ĩĩĩĩ ta . pot

fieri . Ibi xII . uiłłi cū . Ix . bord hñt . vI . caŕ . Ibi . vII . serui.

P̄tū . I . caŕ . Pastá ad peć . Int totū uał 7 ualuit sēp

x . liƀ . Hoc M̄ jacuit 7 jacet in dñio æccłæ de Elẏ.

Ipse aƀƀ ten *HADAM* . p̄ IIII . hid *IN EDWINESTREV HVND.*

se defd . Tra . ē . xIII . caŕ . In dñio . II . hidæ . 7 ibi sunt . III . caŕ.

7 IIII ta . pot fieri . Ibi . xv . uiłłi hñt . vIII to . caŕ . 7 Ix na . pot fieri.

Ibi . xv . bord 7 vII . serui . P̄tū . II . caŕ . Pastá ad peć . Silua

c . porc̄ . In totis ualent uał 7 ualuit . xv . liƀ . T.R.E. xII . liƀ.

Hoc M̄ jacuit 7 jacet in dñio æccłæ de Elẏ . 7 ibi jacuit die

qua rex . E . fuit uiuus 7 mortuus . ut tota Scira testat̄.

135 b

.IX. A TERRA ABBATIÆ DE WESTMON *IN DANAIS HVND.*

ABBAS de WESTMONAST S̄ PETRI . tenet

WATAMESTEDE . p̄ x . hid se defd . Tra . ē . x . caŕ.

In dñio . v . hide . 7 ibi sunt . III . caŕ . 7 adhuc . ĩĩ æ . poſſ

fieri . Ibi p̄br cū xv . uiłłis hñt . v . caŕ . Ibi . xII . bord.

7 Ix . cot . 7 IIII . moł de xL . soł . P̄tū . IIII . caŕ . Pastá

ad peć . Silua . cccc . porc̄ . In totis ualent uał 7 ua

LAND OF THE ABBOT OF ELY*

In BROADWATER Hundred

*1 The Abbot of Ely holds HATFIELD. It answers for 40 hides.
Land for 30 ploughs. In lordship 20 hides; 2 ploughs there;
a further 3 possible.
   A priest with 18 villagers and 18 smallholders have 20 ploughs;
      a further 5 ploughs possible. 12 cottagers; 6 slaves.
   4 mills at 47s 4d; meadow for 10 ploughs; pasture for the
      livestock; woodland, 2000 pigs; from the customary dues
      of the woodland and pasture, 10s.
The total value is and was £25; before 1066 £30.
This manor lay and lies in the lordship of the Church of Ely.

In ODSEY Hundred

*2 The Abbot holds KELSHALL himself. It answers for 5 hides. Land for 10
ploughs. In lordship 2 hides; 3 ploughs there; a fourth possible.
   12 villagers with 9 smallholders have 6 ploughs. 7 slaves.
   Meadow for 1 plough; pasture for the livestock.
In total, the value is and always was £10.
This manor lay and lies in the lordship of the Church of Ely.

In EDWINSTREE Hundred

*3 The Abbot holds HADHAM himself. It answers for 4 hides. Land for 13
ploughs. In lordship 2 hides; 3 ploughs there; a fourth possible.
   15 villagers have 8 ploughs; a ninth possible.
   15 smallholders; 7 slaves.
   Meadow for 2 ploughs; pasture for the livestock; woodland, 100 pigs.
The total value is and was £15; before 1066 £12.
This manor lay and lies in the lordship of the Church of Ely;
it lay there in 1066, as the whole Shire testifies.

LAND OF WESTMINSTER ABBEY

In DACORUM Hundred

1 The Abbot of St. Peter's of Westminster holds WHEATHAMSTEAD.
It answers for 10 hides. Land for 10 ploughs. In lordship 5
hides; 3 ploughs there; a further 2 possible.
   A priest with 15 villagers have 5 ploughs.
   12 smallholders; 9 cottagers.
   4 mills at 40s; meadow for 4 ploughs; pasture for the
      livestock; woodland, 400 pigs.

luit . xvi . lib . T . R . E. xxx . lib . Hoc M jacuit 7 jacet
in dnio æcclæ S PETRI.

In Titebersth ten isd abb . i . hid . Tra . e dim car.
Silua . xl . porc. Val 7 ualuit . x . sol . T . R . E. xiii . sol
In ead uilla ten Goisfr de magneuilæ ⌐ 7 iiii . den.
iii . uirg . de abbe . Tra . e dim car . Silua . xii . porc.
Val 7 ualuit . vi . sol 7 viii . den . T . R . E. x . sol.
In ELDEHA ten isd abb . ix . hid . Tra . e . vi . car.
In dnio . iiii . hide . 7 ibi . e una car . 7 alta pot fieri.
Pposit cu . viii . uittis hnt iii . car . 7 iiii . pot fieri.
Ibi . v . cot . 7 ii . serui . 7 i . molin de . v . sol . Ptu . i . car.
Pastura ad pec . Silua octing porc . Val 7 ualuit
iii . lib . T . R . E. viii . lib . Hoc M jacuit 7 jacet in dnio
æcclæ S PETRI . de Westmon. *IN BRADEWATRE HVND.*
Ipse abb ten *STIGENACE* . p viii . hid se defd.
Tra . e . x . car . In dnio . iiii . hidæ . 7 ibi sunt . ii . car.
Ibi xvi . uitti cu . viii . bord hnt . vii . car 7 viii.
pot fieri . Ibi . iiii . serui . Pasta ad pec . Silua . l . porc.
In totis ualent ual 7 ualuit xii . lib . T . R . E. xiii . lib.
Hoc M jacuit 7 jacet in dnio æcclæ S PETRI.
Ipse abb ten Theunge . p . ii . hid 7 dim se defd.
Tra . e . i . car . 7 ibi . e in dnio . cu . ii . cot . Ptu . i . car.
Pasta ad pec . Silua . l . porc . H tra . e Harduich
de Stigenace . 7 est appciata cu ea.
In Daceuuorde . ten isd abb . iii . hid 7 una uirg.
Tra . e . iii . car . In dnio . ii . hide . 7 ibi . e . i . car . 7 vi.
uitti hnt . ii . car . Ibi . ii . cot . ptu dim car . Pasta
ad pec . Silua . l . porc . Val 7 ualuit xl . sol.
T . R . E. lx . sol . Hoc M jacuit 7 jacet in dnio æcclæ S Petri.

The total value is and was £16; before 1066 £30.
This manor lay and lies in the lordship of St. Peter's Church.

2   In THEOBALD STREET the Abbot also holds 1 hide. Land for ½ plough.
Woodland, 40 pigs.
The value is and was 10s; before 1066, 13s 4d.

3   In the same village Geoffrey de Mandeville holds 3 virgates from
the Abbot. Land for ½ plough.
Woodland, 12 pigs.
The value is and was 6s 8d; before 1066, 10s.

*4 In ALDENHAM the Abbot also holds 9 hides. Land for 6 ploughs.
In lordship 4 hides; 1 plough there; a second possible.
    A reeve with 8 villagers have 3 ploughs; a fourth possible.
        5 cottagers; 2 slaves.
    1 mill at 5s; meadow for 1 plough; pasture for the livestock;
        woodland, 800 pigs.
The value is and was £3; before 1066 £8.
    This manor lay and lies in the lordship of St. Peter's Church,
Westminster.

In BROADWATER Hundred
5   The Abbot holds STEVENAGE himself. It answers for 8 hides.
Land for 10 ploughs. In lordship 4 hides; 2 ploughs there.
    16 villagers with 8 smallholders have 7 ploughs; an eighth possible.
        4 slaves.
    Pasture for the livestock; woodland, 50 pigs.
The total value is and was £12; before 1066 £13.
    This manor lay and lies in the lordship of St. Peter's Church.

*6 The Abbot holds TEWIN himself. It answers for 2½ hides. Land
for 1 plough; it is there, in lordship, with
    2 cottagers.
    Meadow for 1 plough; pasture for the livestock; woodland, 50 pigs.
This land is a ranch of Stevenage and is assessed with it.

7   In DATCHWORTH the Abbot also holds 3 hides and 1 virgate. Land
for 3 ploughs. In lordship 2 hides; 1 plough there.
    6 villagers have 2 ploughs. 2 cottagers.
    Meadow for ½ plough; pasture for the livestock; woodland,
        50 pigs.
The value is and was 40s; before 1066, 60s.
    This manor lay and lies in the lordship of St. Peter's Church.

In Watone . ten iſd abb . I . hiđ . Tra . e̅ . II . car.

In dn̅io . e̅ una . 7 IIII . borđ hn̅t . I . car. Ibi . II . cot.

7 I . mol de . II . ſol. Paſta ad pec̄ . Silua . c . porc̄. Val

7 . . luit . x . ſol . T . R . E: xx . ſol. H̅ tra jacuit in æcła S̄ Petri.

In Aiete , ten Goisfr de abbe . II . hiđ 7 dim̄ . Tra . e̅

VII . car. In dn̅io . e̅ una . 7 alia pot fieri . Ibi XIII.

uilłi cu̅ . IIII . borđ hn̅t . v . car. Ibi . v . cot̄ . 7 I . molin̅

de . VI . ſol 7 VIII . den̄ . P̊tu̅ . I . car. Silua . xxIIII . porc̄.

Val in̅t tot̄ . lx . ſol. Q̊do recep: xx . ſol . T . R . E: c . ſol.

Hoc M̃ tenuit Aluuin teign̄ . R . E . 7 uende̅ potuit.

De hoc M̃ reuocat abb . W . rege̅ ſibi c̅ceſſiſſe

Ipſe abb ten̄ *ESCEWELLE* . p . VI . hiđ ſe deſđ.

135 c

Tra . e̅ . xII . car. In dn̅io . II . hidæ 7 dim̄ . 7 ibi ſu̅ɴ . II .

car. Pbr cu̅ xVI . uilłis 7 IX . borđ hn̅t . v . car̄ . aliæ

æ . car̄ poſs fieri . Ibi . xIIII . burgſes 7 IX . cot̄ . De

theloneo 7 de alijs c̅ſuetuđ burgi . xL . IX . ſol 7 IIII.

den̄. Ibi . IIII . ſerui . 7 II . molin̅ de . xIIII . ſol . P̊tu̅ . VI.

car̄. Paſtura ad pec̄ . Silua . c . porc̄. In totis ualent

ual 7 ualuit . x̊x . lib . T . R . E: xx . II . lib. De hac tra

ten̄ Petrus uiceco̅ de abbe dim̄ hiđ . 7 Goisfriđ

de manneuile . I . uirg 7 I . molin̅ de . x . ſol. Hoc M̃

jacuit 7 jacet in dn̅io æccłæ S̄ PETRI Weſtmon̄.

8   In WATTON the Abbot also holds 1 hide. Land for 2 ploughs. In lordship 1.

4 smallholders have 1 plough. 2 cottagers.

1 mill at 2s; pasture for the livestock; woodland, 100 pigs.

The value is and was 10s; before 1066, 20s.

This land lay in (the lands of) St. Peter's Church.

*9   In AYOT (ST. LAWRENCE) Geoffrey holds 2½ hides from the Abbot.
Land for 7 ploughs. In lordship 1; another possible.

13 villagers with 4 smallholders have 5 ploughs. 5 cottagers.

1 mill at 6s 8d; meadow for 1 plough; woodland, 24 pigs.

In total, value 60s; when acquired 20s; before 1066, 100s.

Alwin, a thane of King Edward's, held this manor; he could sell.
Of this manor, the Abbot of Westminster avouches that the King assigned it to him.

In ODSEY Hundred

*10   The Abbot holds ASHWELL himself. It answers for 6 hides.
Land for 12 ploughs. In lordship 2½ hides; 2 ploughs there.   135 c

A priest with 16 villagers and 9 smallholders have 5 ploughs;
another 5 ploughs possible. 14 burgesses; 9 cottagers.

From tolls and other customary dues of the Borough, 49s 4d.
4 slaves.

2 mills at 14s; meadow for 6 ploughs; pasture for the livestock;
woodland, 100 pigs.

The total value is and was £20; before 1066 £22.

Peter the Sheriff holds ½ hide of this land from the Abbot;
Geoffrey de Mandeville, 1 virgate, and 1 mill at 10s. This manor
lay and lies in the lordship of St. Peter's Church, Westminster.

TERRA ECCLE SCĪ ALBANI. *IN ALBANESTOV HD.*

Abbas Scī Albani. ten *HENAMESTEDA.*

p̄ xx. hiđ se defđ. Tra. ē. xx. car̄. In dn̄io. vi. hidæ.
7 ibi sunt. iii. car̄. 7 iiii. pot fieri. Ibi xxvi. uilti cū.iiii.
francig hn̄t. xiii. car̄. 7 adhuc. iii. poss fieri. Ibi.iii.
borđ 7 i. seruus. 7 ii. moł de. xx. soł. p̄tū. iii. car̄. 7 xiii.
soł. Pastura ad pec̄. Silua miłł porc̄. In totis ualent
uał ĺ.xxii. lib̄ 7 x. soł. T.R.E. xxv. lib̄. Hoc m̄ jacuit
7 jacet in dn̄io æcclæ Ŝ albani.

Ipse abb̄ ten *SCENLAI* .p̄. vi. hiđ se defđ. Tra. ē. viii.
car̄. In dn̄io.ii.hidæ. 7 ibi sunt.ii. car̄. Ibi.xi. uilti cū
uno francig hn̄t.v. car̄. 7 vi. pot fieri. Ibi.iii. cot.
p̄tū dim̄ car̄. Pastura ad pec̄. Silua.cccc. porc̄.
In totis ualent uał. xii. lib̄. Qdo recep̄: vi. lib̄. 7 tn̄tđ.T.R.E.
Hoc m̄ jacuit 7 jacet in dn̄io æcclæ Ŝ albani.

Ipse abb̄ ten *SANDRIGE*. p̄ x. hiđ se defđ. Tra. ē
xiii. car̄. In dn̄io. iii. hide. 7 ibi sunt.ii. car̄. 7 tcia
pot fieri. Ibi.xxvi. uilti hn̄t. x. car̄. Ibi.ii. cot. 7 un̄
seruus. 7 i. molin̄ de. x. soł. P̄tū.ii. car̄. Pastura
ad pec̄. Silua.ccc. porc̄. In totis ualent uał. xviii.
lib̄. Qdo recep̄: xii. lib̄. 7 tn̄tđ T.R.E. Hoc m̄ jacuit
7 jacet in dn̄io æcclæ Ŝ Albani.

Ipse abb̄ ten *WALDENE* .p̄ x. hiđ se defđ. Tra. ē
xiiii. car̄. In dn̄io.iii. hide. 7 ibi sunt. ii. car̄. 7 tcia
pot fieri. Ibi xvii. uilti cū uno francig hn̄t. x. car̄.
7 adhuc. i. pot fieri. Ibi.ix. borđ 7 iii. serui. 7 ii. mo
lenđ de.xv. soł. P̄tū. i. car̄. Pastura pecun̄. Nem̄ ad
sepes 7 domos. In totis ualent uał 7 ualuit. xviii.
7 x. soł. T.R.E. xx.lib̄ 7 x. soł. Hoc m̄ jacuit 7 jacet
in dn̄io æcclæ Ŝ Albani.

0   **LAND OF ST. ALBANS CHURCH**

In CASHIO Hundred

1   The Abbot of St. Albans holds HANSTEAD. It answers for 20 hides.
Land for 20 ploughs. In lordship 6 hides; 3 ploughs there; a
fourth possible.
   26 villagers with 4 Frenchmen have 13 ploughs; a further 3
      possible. 3 smallholders; 1 slave.
   2 mills at 20s; meadow for 3 ploughs, and 13s too; pasture
      for the livestock; woodland, 1000 pigs.
The total value is and was £22 10s; before 1066 £25.
   This manor lay and lies in the lordship of St. Albans Church.

2   The Abbot holds SHENLEY himself. It answers for 6 hides.
Land for 8 ploughs. In lordship 2 hides; 2 ploughs there.
   11 villagers with 1 Frenchman have 5 ploughs; a sixth possible.
   3 cottagers.
   Meadow for ½ plough; pasture for the livestock; woodland, 400 pigs.
Total value £12; when acquired £6; before 1066 as much.
   This manor lay and lies in the lordship of St. Albans Church.

3   The Abbot holds SANDRIDGE himself. It answers for 10 hides.
Land for 13 ploughs. In lordship 3 hides; 2 ploughs there; a
third possible.
   26 villagers have 10 ploughs. 2 cottagers; 1 slave.
   1 mill at 10s; meadow for 2 ploughs; pasture for the livestock;
      woodland, 300 pigs.
Total value £18; when acquired £12; before 1066 as much.
   This manor lay and lies in the lordship of St. Albans Church.

*4 The Abbot holds (ST. PAUL'S) WALDEN himself. It answers for 10
hides. Land for 14 ploughs. In lordship 3 hides; 2 ploughs there;
a third possible.
   17 villagers with 1 Frenchman have 10 ploughs; a further 1
      possible. 9 smallholders; 3 slaves.
   2 mills at 15s; meadow for 1 plough; pasture for the livestock;
      wood for fences and houses.
The total value is and was [£] 18 10s; before 1066 £20 10s.
   This manor lay and lies in the lordship of St. Albans Church.

Villa S̅ *ALBANI* ꝑ.x. hiđ ſe defđ. Tra.e̅.xvi.caꝛ.

Tra.e̅.xvi.caꝛ. In d̅nio.iii. hidæ. 7 ibi ſunt.ii̊. caꝛ. 7 tcia

pot fieri. Ibi.iiii. franciǵ 7 xvi. uiłłi. cu̅.xiii. borđ

h̅nt.xiii. caꝛ. Ibi.xlvi. burgſes. de theloneo 7 de

alijs redditis uillæ.xi. liƀ 7 xiiii. ſoł. ꝑ annu̅. 7 iii.

molenđ de. xl. ſoł. p̊tu̅.ii. caꝛ. Silua miłł porc̅.

7 vii. ſoł. In totis ualent uał. xx. liƀ. Qꝺo recep̅.

xii. liƀ.T.R.E.́xxiiii liƀ. In eađ uilla ſuꞂ adhuc

xii.cot. 7 uꝺ parcus ibi. e̅ beſtiaru̅ ſiluaticarum.

7 unu̅ uiuariu̅ piſciu̅. Ᵽdicti burgſes dim̅ hiđ h̅nt.

CODICOTE 7 *OXEẂICHE*. *IN BRADEẂATRE HVND*.

duo m̅ fueꝛ.T.R.E. 7 m̅ eſt unu̅. ꝑ.viii. hiđ ſe

defđ.Tra.e̅.xii. caꝛ. In d̅nio.iiiͤͤ. hidæ 7 i.uirga.

7 ibi.iiii. caꝛ. Ibi.xvi. uiłłi h̅nt.vii. caꝛ. 7 viii. pot

⌐ fieri.

135 d

Ibi uꝺ franciǵ 7 iii.cot.7 iiii.ſerui. 7 ii. molenđ de.xii.

ſoł. p̊tu̅.ii. caꝛ. Paſtura ad pec̅. Silua.cc. porc̅. In totis

ualent uał.vi. liƀ. Qꝺo recep̅.́v. liƀ.T.R.E.́xii.liƀ.

H̅ duo m̅ jacueꝛ in æccła S̅ Albani.T.R.E. Ibi A̷łuuin ᵍᵒᵗᵒⁿᵉ ꝯ

tenuit.iii. hiđ ſub abƀe. n̅ potuit ab æccła ſeparare.

De hac tra.xv.acs inuaſeꝛ ho̅es comitis morit ſup

abƀem. ut ho̅es de hunđ teſtant̅.

Iꝑſe abƀ ten̅ *NORTONE*. ꝑ.iiii. hiđ ſe defđ. Tra.e̅ x. caꝛ.

In d̅nio.ii. hidæ.7 ibi ſunt.iii. caꝛ. Ibi pƀr 7 q̷đa̅ fran

cigena cu̅.xiiii. uiłłis h̅nt.vii. caꝛ. Ibi.v. cot. 7 i. ſeruus.

7 ii. molenđ de.xvi. ſoł. Ᵽtu̅.ii. caꝛ. Paſtura ad pec̅.

In totis ualent uał 7 ualuit xvi. liƀ. T.R.E.́xvii. liƀ.

Hoc m̅ tenuit 7 tenet S̅ Albaꝺ in d̅nio.

*5 The town of ST. ALBANS answers for 10 hides. Land for 16 ploughs.
In lordship 3 hides; 2 ploughs there; a third possible.
   4 Frenchmen and 16 villagers with 13 smallholders have 13
      ploughs. 46 burgesses.
   From tolls and other payments of the town, £11 14s a year;
      3 mills at 40s; meadow for 2 ploughs; woodland, 1000
      pigs, and 7s too.
Total value £20; when acquired £12; before 1066 £24.
   In this town there are a further 12 cottagers, a park for
woodland beasts, and a pond for fish. The said burgesses have ½ hide.

In BROADWATER Hundred
   CODICOTE and 'OXWICK' were two manors before 1066 and are now one.
It answers for 8 hides. Land for 12 ploughs. In lordship 3 hides
and 1 virgate; 4 ploughs there.
   16 villagers have 7 ploughs; an eighth possible. *
      1 Frenchman; 3 cottagers; 4 slaves.   135d
   2 mills at 12s; meadow for 2 ploughs; pasture for the
      livestock; woodland, 200 pigs.
Total value £6; when acquired £5; before 1066 £12.
   These two manors lay in (the lands of) St. Albans Church before
1066. Alwin Gotton held 3 hides under the Abbot; he could not
separate them from the Church. The Count of Mortain's men
annexed 15 acres of this land in the Abbot's despite, as the men
of the Hundred testify.

7 The Abbot holds NORTON himself. It answers for 4 hides. Land
   for 10 ploughs. In lordship 2 hides; 3 ploughs there.
      A priest and a Frenchman with 14 villagers have 7 ploughs.
         5 cottagers; 1 slave.
      2 mills at 16s; meadow for 2 ploughs; pasture for the livestock.
   The total value is and was £16; before 1066 £17.
      St. Albans held and holds this manor in lordship.

Ipſe abb ten̄ *ESCEPEHALE* . III . hiđ . Tra . ē . v . caŕ . In

dn̄io . I . hida 7 dim̄ . 7 ibi . ē una caŕ . 7 altera pot fieri.

Ibi . VIII . uiłłi hn̄t . III . caŕ . Ibi . II . cot 7 I . ſeruus . p̄tū . I . caŕ.

Paſtura ad pec̄ . Silua . x . porc̄ . Int tot ual . IIII . liƀ.

Q̄do recep̄ .́ III . liƀ . T . R . E .́ IIII . liƀ . Hoc m̄ jacuit 7 jacet

in dn̄io æcclæ ᛋ Albani.　　*IN DANAIS HVND.*

Ipſe abb ten̄ *LANGELAI* . ꝓ v̄ . hiđ ſe defđ 7 dimiđ . T . R . E.

7 modo ꝓ . III . hiđ . Tra . ē . xv . caŕ . In dn̄io . II . hide 7 dim̄.

7 ibi ſunt . IIII . caŕ . 7 v̄ta . pot fieri . Ibi p̄br 7 un̄ francig

cū . x . uiłłis hn̄t . x . caŕ . Ibi . v . borđ 7 II . ſerui . 7 II . molđ

de . xx . ſoł . P̄tū . v . caŕ . Paſtura ad pec̄ . Silua . ccc . porc̄.

De hac tra hƀ un̄ miles dimiđ hiđ . In totis ualent

ual x . liƀ . Q̄do recep̄ .́ xII . liƀ . T . R . E .́ xv . liƀ . Hoc m̄

jacuit 7 jacet in æccła ᛋ Albani . De hoc m̄ tulit 7 oc

cupauit Herbt fili Iuonis . I . hiđ int boſcū 7 planū.

t̄p̄r Baiocenſis ep̄i . Ipſa hida jaceƀ in æccła ᛋ Albani.

die qua rex . E . fuit uiuus 7 mortuus . modo ten̄ Comes morit́.

In *REDBORNE* ten̄ iſđ abb . VII . hiđ 7 I . uirǵ . Tra eſt

xvi . caŕ . In dn̄io . III . hidæ 7 I . uirga . 7 ibi . IIII . caŕ.

Ibi . xvi . uiłłi hn̄t . xII . caŕ . Ibi . I . ſeruus . 7 II . molenđ

de . xxvi . ſoł . P̄tū . I . caŕ 7 dim̄ . Paſtura ad pec̄ . Silua

ccc . porc̄ . In totis ualent ual . xxx . liƀ . Q̄do recep̄ .́

xv . liƀ . T . R . E .́ xvi . liƀ . Hoc m̄ jacuit 7 jacet in æccła

ᛋ Albani . Stig archieps teneƀ die mortis . R . E . ſed

ab æccła ſeparare non poterat.

Ipſe abb ten̄ *ABSA* . ꝓ . III . hiđ ſe defđ T . R . E . 7 modo

ꝓ dim̄ hida . Tra . ē . IIII . caŕ . In dn̄io . II . hidæ 7 dimiđ.

7 ibi ſunt . II . caŕ . 7 II . uiłłi cū . IIII or . borđ hn̄t . II . caŕ.

8   The Abbot holds SHEPHALL himself. 3 hides. Land for 5
ploughs. In lordship 1½ hides; 1 plough there; a second possible.
   8 villagers have 3 ploughs. 2 cottagers; 1 slave.
   Meadow for 1 plough; pasture for the livestock; woodland, 10 pigs.
In total, value £4; when acquired £3; before 1066 £4.
   This manor lay and lies in the lordship of St. Albans Church.

   In DACORUM Hundred

9   The Abbot holds (ABBOT'S) LANGLEY himself. It answered for 5½
hides before 1066; now for 3 hides. Land for 15 ploughs.
In lordship 2½ hides; 4 ploughs there; a fifth possible.
   A priest and a Frenchman with 10 villagers have 10 ploughs.
      5 smallholders; 2 slaves.
   2 mills at 20s; meadow for 5 ploughs; pasture for the
      livestock; woodland, 300 pigs.
   A man-at-arms has ½ hide of this land.
Total value £10; when acquired £12; before 1066 £15.
   This manor lay and lies in (the lands of) St. Albans Church.
   Herbert, son of Ivo, took and appropriated 1 hide of scrub
and open land from this manor in the time of the Bishop of
Bayeux. This hide lay in (the lands of) St. Albans Church in 1066;
now the Count of Mortain holds it.

10   In REDBOURN the Abbot also holds 7 hides and 1 virgate.
Land for 16 ploughs. In lordship 3 hides and 1 virgate;
4 ploughs there.
   16 villagers have 12 ploughs. 1 slave.
   2 mills at 26s; meadow for 1½ ploughs; pasture for the
      livestock; woodland, 300 pigs.
Total value £30; when acquired £15; before 1066 £16.
   This manor lay and lies in (the lands of) St. Albans Church.
Archbishop Stigand held it in 1066, but he could not separate it
from the Church.

11   The Abbot holds NAPSBURY himself. It answered for 3 hides before
1066; now for ½ hide. Land for 4 ploughs. In lordship 2½
hides; 2 ploughs there.
   2 villagers with 4 smallholders have 2 ploughs. 2 slaves.

Ibi .II. ſerui. 7 I.molend de .x. ſol. P̃tū .I. car̃. Paſtura
ad pec̃. Silua .ccc. porc̃. Val hoc M̃ .LX.ſol. Q̃do
recep̃. xx. ſol. T.R.E. IIII. lib̃. Hoc M̃ tenuit Godric
hō Stig arch̃ .n̄ potuit mittere ext̃ æcclam S Albani.
In Wenrige ten̄ Goisfr̃ de bech .I. hid 7 dim̃ de
abbe. Tra .ē. II. car̃. In dñio .ē una. 7 v. uilti cū .II.
bord hn̄t .I. car̃. Paſtura ad pec̃. Silua .ccc. porc̃.
Val xL. ſol. Q̃do recep̃. T.R.E. L. ſol. Hanc tr̃a
tenuit Oſbn̄ monach 7 Goding hō ej̃ .n̄ potuer̃
ſeparare ab æccla ut hund̃ teſtatur.
In Titeberſth ten̄ Goisfr̃ de abbe dim̃ hid. Val
7 ualuit ſemp .vi. ſol. Quida̅ ſochs tenuit T.R.E.
hō abbis S Albani. n̄ potuit uende̅ ext̃ æcclam.
136 a
In Redborne ten̄ Amelger de abbe .III. uirg̃ 7 dim̃.
Tra .ē. II. car̃. 7 ibi ſunt cū .II. uiltis. 7 II. cot. Silua
cc. porc̃. Val .xxx.ſol. Q̃do recep̃. xx. ſol. T.R.E.
xL. ſol. Hanc tr̃a tenuit 7 tenet S Albanus.

HD.
Ipſe abb ten̄ *PRICHEMAREWORDE.* *IN ALBANESTOV*
p xv. hid ſe defd̃. Tra .ē. xx. car̃. In dñio. v. hide.
7 ibi ſunt .III. car̃. 7 adhuc .II. poſſ fieri. Ibi .IIII.
francig̃ 7 xxII. uilti cū .Ix. bord hn̄t xIIII. car̃.
7 adhuc .I. pot fieri. Ibi .v. cot 7 v. ſerui. 7 I. moliñ
de .v. ſol 7 IIII. den̄. p̃tū .IIII. car̃. De piſcib̃ .IIII.ſol.
Paſtura ad pec̃. Silua. mille 7 .cc. porc̃. In totis
ualent ual xx. lib̃ 7 x. ſol. Q̃do recep̃. xII. lib̃.
T.R.E. xx. lib̃. Hoc M̃ tenuit 7 ten̄ in dñio S Alban̄.
Ipſe abb ten̄ *CAISSOV.* p.xx. hid ſe defd̃.
De his ten̄ abb xIx. Tra .ē. xxII. car̃. In dñio
vI. hidæ. 7 ibi ſunt .v. car̃. 7 vI. pot fieri. Ibi

1 mill at 10s; meadow for 1 plough; pasture for the
   livestock; woodland, 300 pigs.
Value of this manor 60s; when acquired 20s; before 1066 £4.
   Godric, Archbishop Stigand's man, held this manor;
he could not dispose of it outside St. Albans Church.

12 In WINDRIDGE Geoffrey of Bec holds 1½ hides from the Abbot.
   Land for 2 ploughs. In lordship 1.
      5 villagers with 2 smallholders have 1 plough.
      Pasture for the livestock; woodland, 300 pigs.
   Value 40s; when acquired ....; before 1066, 50s.
      The monk Osbern and Goding, his man, held this land;
   they could not separate it from the Church, as the Hundred testifies.

13 In THEOBALD STREET Geoffrey holds ½ hide from the Abbot.
   The value is and always was 6s.
      A Freeman, the Abbot of St. Albans' man, held it before
   1066; he could not sell outside the Church.

14 In REDBOURN Amalgar holds 3½ virgates from the Abbot.   136 a
   Land for 2 ploughs; they are there, with
      2 villagers and 2 cottagers.
   Woodland, 200 pigs.
   Value 30s; when acquired 20s; before 1066, 40s.
      St. Albans held and holds this land.

   In CASHIO Hundred
15 The Abbot holds RICKMANSWORTH himself. It answers for 15 hides.
   Land for 20 ploughs. In lordship 5 hides; 3 ploughs there; a
   further 2 possible.
      4 Frenchmen and 22 villagers with 9 smallholders have 14 ploughs;
      a further 1 possible. 5 cottagers; 5 slaves.
      1 mill at 5s 4d; meadow for 4 ploughs; from fish, 4s;
      pasture for the livestock; woodland, 1200 pigs.
   Total value £20 10s; when acquired £12; before 1066 £20.
      St. Albans held and holds this manor in lordship.

16 The Abbot holds CASSIO himself. It answers for 20 hides. The
   Abbot holds 19 of them. Land for 22 ploughs.
   In lordship 6 hides; 5 ploughs there; a sixth possible.

III. francig 7 xxxvi. uilli cū. viii. borđ hn̄t. xv.
car̄. 7 adhuc una pot fieri. Ibi. iii. borđ adhuc
7 ii. serui. 7 iiii. molenđ de. xxvi. sol̄ 7 viii. den̄.
Ptū xx.ii. car̄. pastura ad pec̄. Silua. mille
porc̄. In totis ualent ual xxviii. lib̄. Q̊do recep̄:
xxiiii. lib̄, T.R.E: xxx. lib̄. Hoc M̃ tenuit 7 ten̄
S Albaṇ in dn̄io.

In Eldehā. ten̄ Goisfriđ de bech sub abbe. i. hiđ.
Tra. ē. i. car̄. sed deest car̄. Ibi. ii. cot̄. Silua
c. porc̄. Val 7 ualuit. xii. sol̄. T.R.E: xx. solid̄.
Hanc trā tenuit Blache hō S Albani. n̄ pot uende.
Ipse abb ten̄ *Nevhā.*   *In Odesei Hđ.*
p. iii. hiđ 7 iii. uirḡ se defđ. Tra. ē. viii. car̄. In
dn̄io. i. hida. 7 iii. uirḡ. 7 ibi sunt. ii. car̄. Ibi. x. uilli
cū. viii. borđ hn̄t. iiii. car̄. 7 adhuc. ii. fieri possuɴ.
Ibi. iii. cot̄. p̊tū. i. car̄. Pastura ad pec̄. In totis
ualent ual 7 ualuit. ix. lib̄. T.R.E: x. lib̄. Hoc M̃
jacuit 7 jacet in dn̄io æcclæ S Albani.   *In Dimidio*
In Hegæstaneftone ten̄ isđ abb   *T Hvnđ de Hiz.*
viii. hiđ 7 iii. uirḡ. Tra. ē. xii. car̄. In dn̄io. iiii. hidæ.
7 ibi. iiii. car̄. 7 v. pot fieri. Ibi xiii. uilli cū. iii.
borđ hn̄t. iii. car̄. 7 adhuc. iiii. possunt fieri. Ibi
iii. cot̄. 7 iiii. serui. 7 Goisfr̄ de bech ten̄ ibi dim̄
hiđ sub abbe. Ibi. ii. molđ de. iii. sol̄ 7 iiii. den̄.
p̊tū. ii. car̄. pastura ad pec̄. In totis ualentijs
ual xvii. lib̄ 7 x. sol̄. Q̊do recep̄: xii. lib̄. T.R.E:
xvi. lib̄. Hoc M̃ jacuit 7 jacet in dn̄io æcclæ S Albani.
De hac trā ten̄ un anglicus. iii. hiđ sub abbe.

3 Frenchmen and 36 villagers with 8 smallholders have 15 ploughs;
a further 1 possible. A further 3 smallholders; 2 slaves.
4 mills at 26s 8d; meadow for 22 ploughs; pasture for the
livestock; woodland, 1000 pigs.
Total value £28; when acquired £24; before 1066 £30.
St. Albans held and holds this manor in lordship.

*17 In ALDENHAM Geoffrey of Bec holds 1 hide under the Abbot.
Land for 1 plough, but the plough is missing.
2 cottagers.
Woodland, 100 pigs.
The value is and was 12s; before 1066, 20s.
Black, St. Albans' man, held this land; he could not sell.

In ODSEY Hundred
18 The Abbot holds NEWNHAM himself. It answers for 3 hides and 3
virgates. Land for 8 ploughs. In lordship 1 hide and 3
virgates; 2 ploughs there.
10 villagers with 8 smallholders have 4 ploughs;
a further 2 possible. 3 cottagers.
Meadow for 1 plough; pasture for the livestock.
The total value is and was £9; before 1066 £10.
This manor lay and lies in the lordship of St Albans Church.

In the Half-Hundred of HITCHIN
19 In HEXTON the Abbot also holds 8 hides and 3 virgates. Land
for 12 ploughs. In lordship 4 hides; 4 ploughs there; a fifth possible.
13 villagers with 3 smallholders have 3 ploughs; a further
4 possible. 3 cottagers; 4 slaves.
Geoffrey of Bec holds ½ hide there under the Abbot.
2 mills at 3s 4d; meadow for 2 ploughs; pasture for the livestock.
Total value £17 10s; when acquired £12; before 1066 £16.
This manor lay and lies in the lordship of St. Albans Church.
An Englishman holds 3 hides of this land under the Abbot.

Ipſe abb ten̄ *BENEDIS* . ᵱ una hida ſe defđ . Tra
ē . ıı . cař. 7 ibi ſunt cū . ıııı . uiłłis ꝗ ten̄ hanc trā.
Ibi . ıı . cot̄. Nem⁹ ad ſepes. p̄tū dim̄ cař. Paſtura
ad pec̄ uillæ. Vał 7 ualuit . L . ſoł . T . R . E .꞉ xL . ſoł.
H̄ tr̄a jacuit 7 jacet in dn̄io æcclæ S Albani.

136 b

.XI.   TERRA SC̄I BENEĐ DE RAMESY. *IN ODESEI HVNĐ.*

ABBAS de RAMESY ten̄ in Furreuuelde . x . hiđ
7 ı . uirg. Tra . ē . ᵗⁱxx . cař. In dn̄io . ıı . hide 7 dim̄.
7 ibi ſunt . ıı̈ . cař 7 dim̄ . 7 adhuc dim̄ pot̄ fieri.
Ibi . xxvıı . uiłłi 7 p̄b̄ro 7 uno francig h̄n̄t . xı . cař.
7 adhuc . vı . poſſunt fieri. Ibi . xıııı . cot̄ 7 ıııı.
ſerui . Paſtura ad pec̄. Silua . xx . porc̄. In totis
ualent uał xı . lib̄. Q̄do recep̄ ꞉ x . lib̄ . T . R . E .꞉ xıı . lib̄.
Hoc M̄ jacuit 7 jacet in dn̄io æcclæ S Benedicti.

.XII.   TERRA ÆCCLÆ DE CETRIZ. *IN EDWNESTREV HĐ.*

ABBATISSA de CETRIZ ten̄ in *BERLAI* . ıı . hiđ
7 dim̄ . ᵱ uno M̄ . Tra . ē . ıııı . cař. In dn̄io una hida
7 dimiđ. 7 adhuc dim̄ pot̄ fieri. Ibi . vııı.
liberi hōes h̄n̄t . ıı . cař 7 dimiđ. Ibi . vı . borđ . 7 ıı.
ſerui. Silua . xx . porc̄. Int totū uał 7 ualuit
Lxx . ſoł . T . R . E .꞉ ıııı . lib̄. Hoc M̄ jacuit 7 jacet
in dn̄io ſc̄e MARIÆ dē Cetriz æcclæ.

.XIII   TERRA SC̄I PAVLI LVNDON̄. *IN DANAIS HVNĐ.*

CANONICI Lundonienſes . ten̄ *CANESWORDE.*
ᵱ . x . hiđ ſe defđ . Tra . ē . x . cař. In dn̄io . v . hidæ.
7 ibi ſunt . ıı . cař. 7 adhuc . ııı . poſſunt fieri. Ibi
vıı̄ . uiłłi cū . ııı . borđ h̄n̄t . ıı . cař. 7 adhuc . ııı.

136 a, b

20 The Abbot holds BENDISH himself. It answers for 1 hide.
Land for 2 ploughs; they are there, with
    4 villagers, who hold this land. 2 cottagers.
    Wood for fences; meadow for ½ plough; pasture for the
      village livestock.
The value is and was 50s; before 1066, 40s.
This land lay and lies in the lordship of St. Albans Church.

11   LAND OF ST. BENEDICT'S OF RAMSEY   136 b

In ODSEY Hundred

1 The Abbot of Ramsey holds 10 hides and 1 virgate in THERFIELD.
Land for 20 ploughs. In lordship 3½ hides; 2½ ploughs there;
a further ½ possible.
    27 villagers with a priest and a Frenchman have 11 ploughs;
      a further 6 possible. 14 cottagers; 4 slaves.
    Pasture for the livestock; woodland, 20 pigs.
Total value £11; when acquired £10; before 1066 £12.
This manor lay and lies in the lordship of St. Benedict's Church.

12   LAND OF CHATTERIS CHURCH

In EDWINSTREE Hundred

*1 The Abbess of Chatteris holds 3½ hides in BARLEY as one manor.
Land for 4 ploughs. In lordship 1½ hides; [1 plough there];
a further ½ possible.
    8 free men have 2½ ploughs. 6 smallholders; 2 slaves.
    Woodland, 20 pigs.
The total value is and was 70s; before 1066 £4.
    This manor lay and lies in the lordship of St. Mary's Church,
Chatteris.

13   LAND OF ST. PAUL'S, LONDON

In DACORUM Hundred

*1 The Canons of London hold KENSWORTH. It anwers for 10 hides.
Land for 10 ploughs. In lordship 5 hides; 2 ploughs there;
a further 3 possible.
    8 villagers with 3 smallholders have 2 ploughs; a further
      3 possible. 3 slaves.

possunt fieri. Ibi .iii. serui. Paſtura ad pec̅. Silua
c. porc̅. 7 de reddita ſiluæ. ii. ſol. In totis ualent
ual .lxx. ſol. Q̆do recep̅. c. ſol. 7 tntd̅ T.R.E. Hoc M̅
tenuit Leuuin cilt de rege .E.

Ipſi Canonici ten̅ *CADENDONE*. p x. hid̅ ſe defd̅.
Tra .e̅. x. car̅. In dn̅io .iiii. hide. 7 ibi .e̅ una car̅.
7 adhuc .iii. poſſ. ee. Ibi. xxii. uilli hn̅t. vi. car̅.
Ibi. v. bord̅ 7 ii. ſerui. Paſtura ad pec̅. Silua .c. porc̅.
7 ii. ſolid̅. In totis ualent ual. cx. ſol. Q̆do recep̅.
vi. lib̅. 7 tntd̅. T.R.E. Hoc M̅ tenuit Leuuin de rege.E.

Ipſi canonici ten̅ *ERDELEI*. *IN ODESEI HVND*.
p vi. hid̅ ſe defd̅. Tra. e̅ x. car̅. In dn̅io .iii. hide.
7 ibi ſunt .ii. car̅. 7 tcia pot fieri. Ibi xii. uilli hn̅t
vii. car̅. Ibi. vi. bord̅ 7 ii. cot̅. 7 iiii. ſerui. p̅tu. ii. bob̅.
Paſtura ad pec̅. Silua. cc. porc̅. In totis ualent ual
7 ualuit. vii. lib̅. T.R.E. x. lib̅. Hoc M̅ jacuit 7 jacet
in æccla S̅ Pavli.

In Lufenelle ten̅ canonici .ii. hid̅. Tra. e̅. ii. car̅.
In dn̅io .i. hida 7 dim̅. 7 ibi. e̅. i. car̅. 7 i. uills cu̅. ii.
bord̅ h̅t dim̅ car̅. 7 adhuc dim̅ pot fieri. Ibi un̅
ſeruus. Paſtura ad pec̅. Nem̅ ad ſepes. Val 7 ualuit
xx. ſol. T.R.E. xl. ſol. Hoc M̅ tenuit S̅ Paulus. T.R.E.

Ipſi canonici ten̅ *SANDONE*. p x. hid̅ ſe defd̅.
Tra. e̅ xx. car̅. In dn̅io. v. hidæ. 7 ibi ſunt. vi. car̅.
Ibi p̅br cu̅. xxiiii. uillis hn̅t .xiii. car̅. 7 adhuc una
pot fieri. Ibi. xii. bord̅ 7 xvi. cot̅. 7 xi. ſerui. p̅tu
ii. car̅. Paſtura ad pec̅. Silua. cl. porc̅. In totis
ualent ual 7 ualuit xvi. lib̅. T.R.E. xx. lib̅.
Hoc M̅ jacuit 7 jacet in æccla S̅ PAVLI.

Pasture for the livestock; woodland, 100 pigs, and from the
payments of the woodland 2s.
Total value 70s; when acquired 100s; before 1066 as much.
Young Leofwin held this manor from King Edward.

*2 The Canons hold CADDINGTON themselves. It answers for 10 hides.
Land for 10 ploughs. In lordship 4 hides; 1 plough there;
a further 3 possible.
22 villagers have 6 ploughs. 5 smallholders; 2 slaves.
Pasture for the livestock; woodland, 100 pigs, and 2s too.
Total value 110s; when acquired £6; b⁻ᶠɔre 1066 as much.
Leofwin held this manor from King Edward.

In ODSEY Hundred
3 The Canons hold ARDELEY themselves. It answers for 6 hides.
Land for 10 ploughs. In lordship 3 hides; 2 ploughs there;
a third possible.
12 villagers have 7 ploughs. 6 smallholders; 2 cottagers; 4 slaves.
Meadow for 2 oxen; pasture for the livestock; woodland, 200 pigs.
The total value is and was £7; before 1066 £10.
This manor lay and lies in (the lands of) St. Paul's Church.

4 In LUFFENHALL the Canons hold 2 hides. Land for 2 ploughs.
In lordship 1½ hides; 1 plough there.
1 villager with 2 smallholders has ½ plough; a further ½
possible. 1 slave.
Pasture for the livestock; wood for fences.
The value is and was 20s; before 1066, 40s.
St. Paul's held this manor before 1066.

*5 The Canons hold SANDON themselves. It answers for 10 hides.
Land for 20 ploughs. In lordship 5 hides; 6 ploughs there.
A priest with 24 villagers have 13 ploughs; a further 1
possible. 12 smallholders; 16 cottagers; 11 slaves.
Meadow for 2 ploughs; pasture for the livestock;
woodland, 150 pigs.
The total value is and was £16; before 1066 £20.
This manor lay and lies in (the lands of) St. Paul's Church.

.XIIII. CTERRA CANONIC̄ DE WALTHĀ *In Hertford* HD̄.

Canonici S̄ crvcis de walthā. teneſ

Wermelai. ꝑ v. hid̄ ſe defđ. Tra̅ .ē. iiii. car̄.

In dn̄io. iii. hidæ. 7 ii. uirg 7 dim̄. 7 ibi.ē una car̄.

7 alia poꞇ fieri. Ibi. v. uiłłi hn̄t. ii. car̄. Ibi. iiii.

borđ. 7 iii. cot. 7 ii. ſerui. P̊tū. iiii. car̄. P̊tū. iiii.

car̄. Paſtura ad pec̄. Silua. ccc. porc̄. In totis ua

lentijs uał 7 ualuit. iiii. lib̄. T.R.E. c. ſoł. Hoc M̄

jacuit 7 jacet in æccła S̄ crvcis de Waltham.

Ipſi canonici teñ *Brichendone.* ꝑ v. hiđ ſe defđ.

Tra̅ .ē. viii. car̄. In dn̄io. iii. hide 7 dimiđ. 7 ibi ſunt

ii. car̄. 7 tcia poꞇ fieri. Ibi. ix. uiłłi hn̄t. iiii. car̄.

7 v̊ᵗᵃ. poꞇ fieri. Ibi. ix. borđ 7 xxiiii. cot. 7 ii. ſerui.

7 i. molđ de. viii. ſoł. P̊tū. ii. car̄. Paſtura ad

pec̄ uille. 7 ii. ſoł. Silua. cc. porc̄. In totis ualent

uał 7 ualuit. c. ſoł. T.R.E. viii. lib̄. Hoc M̄ jacuit

7 jacet in æccła S̄ crvcis de Waltham.

.XV. CTERRA COMITIS MORITON. *In Ϝevng Hvnđ.*

Comes Moriton teñ *Berchehastede.* ꝑ xiii.

hiđ ſe defđ. Tra̅ .ē. xxvi. car̄. In dn̄io. vi. hidæ.

7 ibi ſunt. iii. car̄. 7 aliæ. iii. poſſunt fieri. Ibi ꝑbr

cū. xiiii. uiłłis 7 xv. borđ hn̄t. xii. car̄. 7 adhuc

viii. poſſunt fieri. Ibi. vi. ſerui. 7 q̇đā foſſarius

hab̄ dim̄ hiđ. 7 Rannulꝼ. i. uirg ſeruieꝕ comit.

In Burbio huꝯ uillæ. lii. burgenſes. q̇ reddunt

de theloneo. iiii. lib̄. 7 hn̄t dim̄ hidā. 7 ii. moliñ

de. xx. ſoł. Ibi. ii. arpenđ uineæ. P̊tū. viii. car̄.

Paſtura ad pec̄ uillæ. Silua mille porc̄. 7 v. ſoł.

In totis ualent uał. xvi. lib̄. Q̇do recep̄. xx. lib̄.

T.R.E. xxiiii. lib̄. Hoc M̄ tenuit Edmarus

teignus Heraldi comitis.

LAND OF THE CANONS OF WALTHAM

In HERTFORD Hundred

*1 The Canons of Holy Cross of Waltham hold WORMLEY. It answers
for 5 hides. Land for 4 ploughs. In lordship 3 hides and
2½ virgates; 1 plough there; another possible.
    5 villagers have 2 ploughs. 4 smallholders; 3 cottagers;
    2 slaves.
    Meadow for 4 ploughs; meadow for 4 ploughs; pasture
        for the livestock; woodland, 300 pigs.
The total value is and was £4; before 1066, 100s.
    This manor lay and lies in (the lands of) the Church of Holy
Cross of Waltham.

2 The Canons hold BRICKENDON themselves. It answers for 5 hides.
Land for 8 ploughs. In lordship 3½ hides; 2 ploughs there;
a third possible.
    9 villagers have 4 ploughs; a fifth possible.
        9 smallholders; 24 cottagers; 2 slaves.
    1 mill at 8s; meadow for 2 ploughs; pasture for the village
        livestock, and 2s too; woodland, 200 pigs.
The total value is and was 100s; before 1066 £8.
    This manor lay and lies in (the lands of) the Church of Holy
Cross of Waltham.

15   LAND OF THE COUNT OF MORTAIN

In TRING Hundred

*1 The Count of Mortain holds BERKHAMSTED. It answers for 13
hides. Land for 26 ploughs. In lordship 6 hides; 3 ploughs
there; another 3 possible.
    A priest with 14 villagers and 15 smallholders have 12 ploughs;
        a further 8 possible. 6 slaves. A dyke builder has ½
        hide and Ranulf, a Servant of the Count, 1 virgate.
    In the borough of this town, 52 burgesses, who pay £4 from
        tolls, have ½ hide.
    2 mills at 20s; 2 *arpents* of vines; meadow for 8
        ploughs; pasture for the village livestock; woodland,
        1000 pigs, and 5s too.
Total value £16; when acquired £20; before 1066 £24.
    Edmer, a thane of Earl Harold's, held this manor.

Rannulf ten de comite *SCENLEI*. p . I . hida ſe defd.

Tra . ē . II . car. Ibi . ē una. 7 alta pot fieri. Ibi . II.

bord . Paſta ad pec. Silua . c . ſol. Int totū ual . v . ſol.

Qdo recep. III . lib . T.R.E. IIII . lib. Hanc trā tenuer

II . ſochi. Vn huſcarl . R.E. 7 alt hō Leuuini . comitis uende

Ipſe comes ten *ALDEBERIE* . p x . hid ſe defd. potuer.

Tra . ē . VII . car. In dnio . VI . hidæ . 7 ibi ſunt . III . car.

7 VIII . uilti cū . I . ſocho 7 I . francig hnt . IIII . car.

Ibi . I . bord. 7 IIII . ſerui . ptū dim hid. Silua qngent

porc. In totis ualent ual . cx . ſol. Qdo recep. VIII.

lib. 7 tntd T.R.E. Hoc M tenuit Aluuin teign . R.E.

In Pentlai ten ipſe com. II . hid . Tra . ē . II . car. Ibi . I.

uilts cū . VI . bord hnt . I . car. 7 alia pot fieri . ptū . I.

car 7 dim. Val . xxx . ſol. Qdo recep. xx . ſol . T.R.E.

XL . ſol. Hanc trā tenuit Eddeua moniat de Ingelrico.

n potuit dare. He . II . hidæ ſunt de VII . hid quas

ſupſit com moriton in Treunge.

Hunfrid ten de comite *WIGENTONE* . p VII . hid

7 dim. 7 tcia parte dim hidæ ſe defd . Tra . ē . v . car.

In dnio eſt una. 7 alia pot fieri. Ibi . v . uilti hnt . II . car.

7 tcia pot fieri. Ibi . VI . cot. 7 I . ſeruus. 7 I . molin de . v.

ſol . Ptū . I . car. Silua . c . porc. In totis ualent ual . IIII . lib.

136 d

Qdo recep. XL . ſol . T.R.E. VI . lib. De hoc M tenuit Briſtric

III . hid 7 dim. hō Eddid reginæ. 7 Goduin hō Engelrici habuit

III . hid 7 tciā part dimid hidæ. n potuit dare nec uende

ext Tredunga. 7 Hæ ſunt de . VII . hid quas ſupſit comes

moriton de Tredunga. 7 Leuric hō Oſulfi tenuit dim

hidā. 7 potuit uende. 7 alia dim hida jacuit in Berchāſtede.

*2 Ranulf holds SHENLEY from the Count. It answers for 1 hide.
Land for 2 ploughs; 1 plough there; a second possible.
2 smallholders.
Pasture for the livestock; woodland, 100 [pigs and ..] s. *
In total, value 5s; when acquired £3; before 1066 £4.
2 Freemen held this land; one was a Guard of King Edward's; the
second was Earl Leofwin's man; they could sell.

*3 The Count holds ALDBURY himself. It answers for 10 hides. Land
for 7 ploughs. In lordship 6 hides; 3 ploughs there.
8 villagers with 1 Freeman and 1 Frenchman have 4 ploughs.
1 smallholder; 4 slaves.
Meadow, ½ hide *(? plough)*; woodland, 500 pigs.
Total value 110s; when acquired £8; before 1066 as much.
Alwin, a thane of King Edward's, held this manor.

*4 In PENDLEY the Count holds 2 hides himself. Land for 2 ploughs.
1 villager with 6 smallholders have 1 plough; another possible.
Meadow for 1½ ploughs.
Value 30s; when acquired 20s; before 1066, 40s.
The nun Edeva held this land from Engelric; she could not
grant it. These 2 hides are of the 7 hides which the Count of
Mortain took in Tring. *

5 Humphrey holds WIGGINGTON from the Count. It answers for
7½ hides and the third part of ½ hide. Land for 5 ploughs.
In lordship 1; another possible.
5 villagers have 2 ploughs; a third possible. 6 cottagers;
1 slave.
1 mill at 5s; meadow for 1 plough; woodland, 100 pigs.
Total value £4; when acquired 40s; before 1066 £6.   136d
Brictric, Queen Edith's man, held 3½ hides of this
manor and Godwin, Engelric's man, had 3 hides and the third part of
½ hide; he could not grant or sell outside Tring. These are of
the 7 hides which the Count of Mortain took from Tring. Leofric,
Oswulf's man, held ½ hide; he could sell. Another ½ hide
lay in (the lands of) Berkhamsted.

Fulcold ten̄ Bublecote de comite. p̄ una hida 7 dim̄
ſe defđ. Tra . ē . ı . car̄ 7 dim̄. In dn̄io eſt car̄. 7 ııı . uiłłi lūt
dimiđ. Ibi . ıı . borđ 7 ı . molin̄ de xıı . ſoł 7 ıııı . den̄. p̊tū
ıı . car̄. Vał 7 ualuit . xxx . ſoł . T . R . E .˙ xl . ſoł. Hanc trā
tenuit Eddeua de Ingelrico. n̄ potuit mittere ext̄ Tredung.
Ħ tra . ē de . vıı . hiđ quas ſupſit com̄ morit de Tredung.
In Miſſeuuelle ten̄ Radułf de comite dim̄ hidā . Tra . ē
dim̄ car̄. p̊tū dim̄ car̄. Vał 7 ualuit . ıııı . ſoł . T . R . E .˙ x . ſoł.
Hanc tram tenuit Wiga hō Oſulfi filij Frane . uendė pot.
Leuuin̄ ten̄ de comite Bvre. p̄ una hida 7 dim̄ ſe defđ.
Tra . ē . ı . car̄. 7 ibi . ē in dn̄io. 7 ıııı . cot̄. p̊tū dim̄ car̄. Valet
xx . ſoł 7 ıx . den̄. Q̊do recep̄ .˙ x . ſoł . T . R . E .˙ xx . ſoł 7 ıx . den̄.
Hanc trā tenuit iſđ Leuuin̄ de rege . E. 7 uendė potuit.
Modo ten̄ ad firmā de comite.
In Daneſlai ten̄ quedā uidua de comite tc̄iā part dimiđ
hide . Tra . ē . ı . boui. Vał 7 ualuit ſēp xıı . den̄. Hanc trā
tenuit Ingelric̊ de tra . vıı . hidarū de Tredunge . quā
ſupſit comes.
Ipſe com̄ ten̄. Hamelamestede. p̄ x . hiđ ſe defđ. Tra . ē
xxx . car̄. In dn̄io . ııı . hidæ . 7 ibi . ıııı . car̄. 7 adhuc . ıı . car̄
poſſunt fieri. Ibi . ıı . francig̊. cū xııı . borđ . hn̄t . xx . car̄.
7 adhuc . ıııı . poſſunt fieri. Ibi . vııı . ſerui. 7 ıııı . molđ
de . xxxvıı . ſoł 7 ıııı . den̄. 7 ccc . anguillis . xxv . minus.
p̊tū . ıııı . car̄. paſtura ad pec̄. 7 ıı . ſoł. Silua mille . 7 cc .
porc̄. In totis ualent uał xxıı . lib̄. Q̊do recep̄ .˙ xxv . lib̄.
7 tn̄tđ T . R . E. Hoc Ϻ tenuer̄ . ıı . frs hōes Leuuini . fuer̄.

6 Fulcwold holds GUBBLECOT from the Count. It answers for 1½
hides. Land for 1½ ploughs. In lordship [1] plough, and
   3 villagers have ½. 2 smallholders.
   1 mill at 12s 4d; meadow for 2 ploughs.
The value is and was 30s; before 1066, 40s.
   Edeva held this land from Engelric; she could not put it
outside Tring. This land is of the 7 hides which the Count of
Mortain took from Tring.

7 In MISWELL Ralph holds ½ hide from the Count. Land for ½ plough.
   Meadow for ½ plough.
The value is and was 4s; before 1066, 10s.
   Wicga, Oswulf son of Fran's man, held this land; he could sell.

8 Leofwin holds BOARSCROFT from the Count. It answers for 1½ hides.
Land for 1 plough; it is there in lordship.
   4 cottagers.
   Meadow for ½ plough.
Value 20s 9d; when acquired 10s; before 1066, 20s 9d.
   Leofwin also held this land from King Edward; he could sell.
Now he holds it at a revenue from the Count.

9 In DUNSLEY a widow holds the third part of ½ hide from the Count.
Land for 1 ox.
The value is and always was 12d.
   Engelric held this land; (it was) of the 7 hides of land which the
Count took from Tring.

   [In DACORUM Hundred?*]
10 The Count holds HEMEL HEMPSTEAD himself. It answers
for 10 hides. Land for 30 ploughs. In lordship 3 hides;
4 ploughs there; a further 2 ploughs possible.
   2 Frenchmen with 13 smallholders have 20 ploughs; a further
     4 possible. 8 slaves.
   4 mills at 37s 4d; 300 eels less 25; meadow for 4 ploughs;
     pasture for the livestock, and 2s too; woodland, 1200 pigs.
Total value £22; when acquired £25; before 1066 as much.
   Two brothers held this manor; they were Earl Leofwin's men.

Radulf ten *LANGELEI* de comite. p una hida 7 dimid

se defd. Tra . e . xvi . car. In dnio nulla . e . sed . ii . pois fieri.

Ibi un francig cu . iiii . uittis 7 v . bord . hnt . ii . car. 7 xii .

car possunt fieri. Ibi . ii . molini . de xvi . sot . 7 ii . serui.

ptu . iii . car. Pastura ad pec. Silua . cc . porc. 7 xl . In totis

ualent uat . xl . sot. Qdo recep. iiii . lib . T.R.E. viii . lib.

Hoc M tenuer . ii . hoes Leuuini . Thuri 7 Seric.

Hunfrid ten de comite *GATESDENE* . p v . hid se defd.

Tra . e . iii . car. In dnio . e una . 7 v . uitti cu . ii . bord hnt

ii . car. Ibi un seruus. Pastura ad pec. Silua . l . porc.

In totis ualent uat . xl . sot. Qdo recep. lx . sot. T.R.E.

iiii . lib. Hoc M tenuit Edmer. 7 fuit Bereuuick in Berchastede.

In Redborne ten Rannulf de comite dim hid.

Tra . e . i . car. sed n est ibi . nisi . ii . bord . Ptu . i . car. Pasta

ad pec. Vat xvii . sot . 7 iiii . den. Qdo recep. xx . sot.

T . R . E . xl. sot. Siuuard tenuit sochs . R . E . 7 uende pot.

.XVI. CTERRA ALANI COMITIS *IN BRADEWATRE HVND.*

COMES ALANVS ten in Watone . i . hid 7 dim. Go

duin ten de eo. Tra . e . iiii . car. In dnio pois . ii . fieri.

Ibi . iii . bord 7 ii . cot hnt . ii . car. Ptu . ii . boby . pastura

ad pec. Vat 7 ualuit . xx . sot. T . R . E . xxx . sot. Hanc

tra tenuit Goduin de æccta S Petri . n poterat uende.

sed post morte ej debebat ad æcctam redire ut

137 a

hund testat. Sed uxor ej cu hac tra uertit se p uim ad

Eddeua pulchra . 7 tenebat ea die qua rex . E . fuit uiuus

7 mortuus. De hac tra suptæ sunt . xvi . acræ post adventu

regis . W . quas m tenet Anschitillus de ros sub Archiepo.

7 tam comes Alan adqetat eas de geldo regis.

11 Ralph holds (KING'S) LANGLEY from the Count. It answers for 1½
    hides. Land for 16 ploughs. In lordship none, but 2 possible.
        1 Frenchman with 4 villagers and 5 smallholders have 2
           ploughs; 12 ploughs possible.
        2 mills at 16s; 2 slaves; meadow for 3 ploughs; pasture for the
           livestock; woodland, 240 pigs.
    Total value 40s; when acquired £4; before 1066 £8.
    Thorir and Seric, two of Earl Leofwin's men, held this manor.

*12 Humphrey holds (LITTLE) GADDESDEN from the Count. It answers for
    5 hides. Land for 3 ploughs. In lordship 1.
        5 villagers with 2 smallholders have 2 ploughs. 1 slave.
        Pasture for the livestock; woodland, 50 pigs.
    Total value 40s; when acquired 60s; before 1066 £4.
    Edmer Ator held this manor; it was an outlier in Berkhamsted.

13 In REDBOURN Ranulf holds ½ hide from the Count. Land for 1 plough,
    but it is not there; only
        2 smallholders.
        Meadow for 1 plough; pasture for the livestock.
    Value 17s 4d; when acquired 20s; before 1066, 40s.
    Siward, a Freeman of King Edward's, held it; he could sell.

16   LAND OF COUNT ALAN

In BROADWATER Hundred
1 Count Alan holds 1½ hides in WATTON. Godwin holds from him.
    Land for 4 ploughs. In lordship, 2 possible.
        3 smallholders and 2 cottagers have 2 ploughs.
        Meadow for 2 oxen; pasture for the livestock.
    The value is and was 20s; before 1066, 30s.
        Godwin held this land from St. Peter's Church (Westminster);
    he could not sell, but after his death it was to return to the
    Church, as the Hundred testifies. But his wife turned with   137a
    this land to Edeva the Fair, by force, and held it in 1066. 16
    acres were taken from this land after 1066; Ansketel of Rots
    now holds them under the Archbishop; however Count Alan
    clears them for the King's tax.

Ⓜ Ipſe comes ten' *MVNDENE* . ꝑ VII . hiđ 7 dim | ſe defđ

T.R.E. Tra . ē . XIIII . ca�r . In dñio . IIII . hidæ 7 I . uirg.

7 ibi ſunt . IIII . caꝛ . Ibi XVI . uilti cū . VI . borđ ħnt . x . caꝛ.

Ibi . I . cot' 7 II . ſerui . 7 I . moliñ de . x . ſot . Silua . CL . porč.

7 Alterā ſiluā unde . cc . porč paſcerent' de hoc Ⓜ

Roger de mucelgros abſtulit poſtꝗ comes Radulf

foriſfecit . ut tota ſcẏra teſtat.' In totis ualent ual

XVI . liɓ . Qdo recep' XII . liɓ . T.R.E.' XVI . liɓ . Hoc Ⓜ

tenuit Eddeua pulchra. *IN ODESEI HVND.*

In Cladhele ten' Leuiet' de comite . I . uirg' . Tra . ē . I . caꝛ.

7 ibi . ē . Val 7 ualuit ſēp . xx . ſot . Hanc tenuit Oſgot

ħo Eddeue . 7 potuit uende' . Modo jacet in Mundene.

ubi ñ fuit . T.R.E.

In Wallingtone ten' Wimund de comite . II . hiđ decē

acs miñ . Tra . ē . II . caꝛ . Ibi . ē una . 7 alia pot' fieri . Ibi

un uilts 7 II . cot' 7 II . ſerui . Paſtura ad pec . Val . xxx . ſot.

Qdo recep' x . ſot . T.R.E.' LX . ſot . Hanc trā tenueꝛ . II.

ſocħi hoēs Eddeue . 7 uende' potueꝛ.

In Rete . ten' Harđ de comite . I . hiđ . Tra . ē . III . caꝛ.

Vna . ē . ibi . 7 duæ poſſ fieri . Ibi . ē uñ uilts . 7 nem ad ſepes.

Val xx . ſot . Qdo recep' x . ſot . T.R.E.' LX . ſot . Hanc

trā tenu Leuing pɓr ħo Eddeue . 7 potuit uendere.

In Retth . ten' Aluuard de comite . I . hiđ . Tra . III . caꝛ.

Vna . ē ibi . 7 II . poſſunt fieri . Ibi . VI . cot' . Val 7 ualuit

xx . ſot . T.R.E.' LX . ſot . Hanc trā tenuit Turɓnus ħo

Eddeue . 7 potuit uendere. *IN EDWINESTREV HĐ.*

In Wachelei . ten' Radulf de com' XL . acs træ . Tra . ē

.I . caꝛ . Ibi . ē uñ ſocħs 7 uñ ſeru . Ꝑtū . II . boɔ . Val 7 ua

luit . x . ſot . T.R.E.' xx . ſot . Hoc Ⓜ tenuit Eddeua pulc.'

*2 M.The Count holds MUNDEN himself. It answered for 7½ hides
and [1] virgate before 1066. Land for 14 ploughs. In lordship
4 hides and 1 virgate; 4 ploughs there.
    16 villagers with 6 smallholders have 10 ploughs.
        1 cottager; 2 slaves.
    1 mill at 10s; woodland, 150 pigs; Roger of Mussegros took
        away a second woodland where 200 pigs could pasture from
        this manor after Earl Ralph's forfeiture, as the whole
        Shire testifies.
Total value £16; when acquired £12; before 1066 £16.
    Edeva the Fair held this manor.

In ODSEY Hundred

3   In CLOTHALL Leofgeat holds 1 virgate from the Count.
Land for 1 plough; it is there.
The value is and always was 20s.
    Osgot, Edeva's man, held it; he could sell. Now it lies in
(the lands of) Munden; it was not there before 1066.

4   In WALLINGTON Wimund holds 2 hides less 10 acres from the Count.
Land for 2 ploughs; 1 there; another possible.
    1 villager; 2 cottagers; 2 slaves.
    Pasture for the livestock.
Value 30s; when acquired 10s; before 1066, 60s.
    2 Freemen, Edeva's men, held this land; they could sell.

*5   In REED Hardwin holds 1 hide from the Count. Land for 3 ploughs;
1 there; 2 possible.
    1 villager.
    Wood for fences.
Value 20s; when acquired 10s; before 1066, 60s.
    Leofing the priest, Edeva's man, held this land; he could sell.

6   In REED Alfward holds 1 hide from the Count. Land for 3 ploughs;
1 there; 2 possible.
    6 cottagers.
The value is and was 20s; before 1066, 60s.
    Thorbern, Edeva's man, held this land; he could sell.

In EDWINSTREE Hundred

7   In WAKELEY Ralph holds 40 acres of land from the Count. Land
for 1 plough.
    1 Freeman; 1 slave.
    Meadow for 2 oxen.
The value is and was 10s; before 1066, 20s.
    Edeva the Fair held this manor.

In Langeport ten Roger de com dim hiđ. Traₑ.ē dim
car̃.7 ibi.ē cū.ɪ.cot 7 ɪɪ.feruis. Val.x.fol.Q̃do recep̃.
v.fol.T.R.E.⁚ xɪɪɪ.fol. Hanc trā tenuit Alric hō Stig
Archiep̃i.7 uende potuit.   *IN HERFORT HVND̄.*

Ipfe com̃ ten̄ *CESTREHVNT.* p̃ xx. hiđ fe defđ.Traₑ.ē
xxxɪɪɪ.car̃. In dñio.x.hidæ.7 ibi funt.ɪɪɪɪ.car̃.7 ɪɪ.
adhuc poffunt fieri. Ibi.xL.ɪ.uilti cū p̃bro 7 xɪɪ.borđ
hñt.xvɪɪ.car̃.Ibi.x.mercatores redđ.x.fol.de con
fuetuđ.Ibi.vɪɪɪ.cot 7 vɪ.ferui.7 ɪ.molin de.x.fol.
De gurgite.xvɪ.den. P̃tū.xxɪɪɪ.car̃.7 ad dñicos eq̃s.
Paftura ad pec̃. Silua mille.cc.porc̃.7 xL.denar̃.

Ipfe com̃ ten̄ Hodefdone.p̃.ɪɪ.hiđ 7 ɪɪɪ.uirg̃ fe defđ.
Bereuuich̃ ē de Ceftrehont. Traₑ.ē.ɪɪɪɪ.car̃. In dñio
ɪɪ.hidæ.7 ibi funt.ɪɪ.car̃.7 ɪɪ.uilti cū.vɪɪɪ.borđ hñt
ɪɪ.car̃.Ibi.un̄ feru.7 p̃tū.ɪɪɪɪ.car̃. Pafta ad pecun̄.
Silua.cc.Lx.porc̃. De gurgite⁚ c.Anguilt.
In totis ualent ual Ⓜ cū *BER* xx.ɪɪɪɪ.lib̃. Q̃do recep̃⁚ xxɪɪ.
lib̃.T.R.E.⁚ xxx.lib̃. Hoc Ⓜ tenuit Eddeua pulchra.7 ibi
fuit 7 eft.ɪ.fochs hñs dimiđ hidā.potuit uende.T.R.R.
WERMELAI ten̄ Wimund̄ de comite.p̃ ɪ.hiđ 7 dim̃
fe defđ.Traₑ.ē.ɪɪ.car̃. In dñio.ē una.7 vɪ.borđ cū.ɪ.cot
hñt.ɪ.car̃. P̃tū.ɪɪ.car̃. Paftura ad pec̃. Silua.c.L.porc̃.
De dimiđ gurgite⁚ L.anguilt. Val 7 ualuit xL.fol.T.R.E.⁚
Lx.fol.Hoc Ⓜ tenuit Alfi hō Eddeuæ.7 potuit uende.

⌐H̃ trā jacet in Ceftrehunt.

In Belingehou ten̄ comes.ɪ.uirg̃.Traₑ.ē dim̃ car̃.p̃tū
ɪɪ.bob₂. Val 7 ualuit fep̃.v.fol. Hanc trā tenuit Snerri
hō Eddeue pulchræ.7 potuit uendere.

*8   In HARE STREET Roger holds ½ hide from the Count. Land for ½
plough; it is there, with
1 cottager and 2 slaves.
Value 10s; when acquired 5s; before 1066, 13s.
Alric, Archbishop Stigand's man, held this land; he could sell.

In HERTFORD Hundred
*9 M. The Count holds CHESHUNT himself. It answers for 20 hides.
Land for 33 (23?) ploughs. In lordship 10 hides; 4 ploughs there;
a further 2 possible.
41 villagers with a priest and 12 smallholders have 17 ploughs.
10 merchants pay 10s in customary dues. 8 cottagers; 6 slaves.
1 mill at 10s; from a weir, 16d; meadow for 23 ploughs, and for
the lord's horses; pasture for the livestock; woodland,
1200 pigs, and 40d too.

*10   The Count holds HODDESDON himself. It answers for 2 hides and 3
virgates. It is an outlier of Cheshunt. Land for 4 ploughs.
In lordship 2 hides; 2 ploughs there.
2 villagers with 8 smallholders have 2 ploughs. 1 slave.
Meadow for 4 ploughs; pasture for the livestock; woodland,
260 pigs; from a weir, 100 eels.
Total value of the manor with the outlier £24; when acquired £22;
before 1066 £30.
Edeva the Fair held this manor. 1 Freeman was and is there,
who has ½ hide; he could sell before 1066.

11   Wimund holds WORMLEY from the Count. It answers for 1½ hides.
Land for 2 ploughs. In lordship 1.
6 smallholders with 1 cottager have 1 plough.
Meadow for 2 ploughs; pasture for the livestock; woodland,
150 pigs; from ½ weir, 50 eels.
The value is and was 40s; before 1066, 60s.
Alfsi, Edeva's man, held this manor; he could sell.
This land lies in Cheshunt.

12   In BENGEO the Count holds 1 virgate. Land for ½ plough.   137b
Meadow for 2 oxen.
The value is and always was 5s.
Snerri, Edeva the Fair's man, held this land; he could sell.

CTERRA COMITIS EVSTACHII.

COMES EVSTACHIVS teñ *KEVNGE* . p̄ xxxix . hid
se defd T.R.E. 7 modo p̄ . v . hid 7 una uirg . Tra . e
xx . car . In dñio . xii . hidæ . 7 ibi sunt . iii . car . 7 adhuc
pos̄s fieri duæ . Ibi . xxi . uilłs cū . vi . bord 7 xvi . cot . 7 iii .
sochis hñt . ix . car . 7 adhuc pos̄s . vi . fieri . Ibi . viii . serui .
7 ii . molin de . ix . sot . P̄tū . x . car . Pastura ad pec̄ uillæ .
7 iii . sot . Silua . mille porc̄ . In hac uilla . e Bereuuicha
ubi sedent . viii . uilłi hñtes . ii . car . 7 tcia pot̄ fieri .
In totis ualent̄ ual . xxii . lib . de alb̄ denar ad pensū
huj⁹ comitis . Q̄do recep̄ ꞌ xx . lib . T.R.E. ꞌ xxv . lib . Hoc ᴍ̄
tenuit Engelri . T.R.E. 7 ibi fuer̄ . ii . sochi hōes Osulfi filij
Frani . ii . hid tenuer̄ 7 uende potuer̄ . Hos sochos appo
suit isd Engelric⁹ huic ᴍ̄ post aduentū . R.W. ut hōes
de hund testant̄ ꞌ 7 un⁹ hō abb̄is de Ramesy̆g . v . hid
de hoc ᴍ̄ habuit . ad eund modū . Iste n̄ potuit dare
ł uende tra suā ext̄ æcclam S̄ Benedicti . Que Engelri
apposuit huic ᴍ̄ post aduentū regis . W . qui n̄ fuit
ibi . T.R.E. ut hund testatur . Illi p̄dicti . iii . sochi qui
adhuc ibi suꝗ . i . hid hñtes hōes Engelrici fuer̄ . 7 tra
suā uendere potuer̄ .   *IN ODESEI HVND.*
In Retth . teñ Rob̄tus fili⁹ Rozelini de comite . iiii . hid
7 i . uirg 7 dim̄ . Tra . e . v.. car . In dñio sunt . ii . 7 vii . uilłi
cū . ii . bord hñt . iii . car . Ibi . iiii . serui . P̄tū dim̄ car .
Pastura ad pec̄ . Val . iiii . lib . Q̄do recep̄ ꞌ l . sot . T.R.E. ꞌ
iiii . lib . Hoc ᴍ̄ tenuit Aluuard hō Heraldi . 7 uende pot̄ .
Ipse com̄ teñ *ANESTIGE* . p̄ v . hid se defd . Tra . e . x .
car . In dñio . iii . hide . 7 ibi sunt . ii . car . 7 tcia pot̄ fieri .
Ibi . viii . uilłi cū pb̄ro 7 vi . bord hñt . v . car . 7 adhuc
possunt . ii . fieri . Ibi . v . cot̄ 7 vi . serui . P̄tū dim̄ car .

[In TRING Hundred]
1 Count Eustace holds TRING. It answered for 39 hides before 1066;
   now for 5 hides and 1 virgate. Land for 20 ploughs. In lordship
   12 hides; 3 ploughs there; a further 2 possible.
       21 villagers with 6 smallholders, 16 cottagers and 3 Freemen
       have 9 ploughs; a further 6 possible. 8 slaves.
       2 mills at 9s; meadow for 10 ploughs; pasture for the village
       livestock, and 3s too; woodland, 1000 pigs.
   In this village is an outlier where 8 villagers reside who have
       2 ploughs; a third possible.
   Total value £22 of white pence, at this Count's weights;
   when acquired £20; before 1066 £25.
       Engelric held this manor before 1066; 2 Freemen, Oswulf
   son of Fran's men, were there; they held 2 hides; they could sell.
   Engelric placed these Freemen in this manor after 1066, as the
   men of the Hundred testify.
       A man of the Abbot of Ramsey's had 5 hides of this manor in
   the same way; he could not grant or sell his land outside St.
   Benedict's Church. Engelric placed him in this manor after 1066;
   he was not there before 1066, as the Hundred testifies. The said
   3 Freemen, who are still there, and who have 1 hide, were
   Engelric's men; they could sell their land.

   In ODSEY Hundred
2 In REED Robert son of Rozelin holds 4 hides and 1½ virgates from
   the Count. Land for 5 ploughs. In lordship 2.
       7 villagers with 2 smallholders have 3 ploughs. 4 slaves.
       Meadow for ½ plough; pasture for the livestock.
   Value £4; when acquired 50s; before 1066 £4.
       Alfward,Earl Harold's man, held this manor; he could sell.

   [In EDWINSTREE Hundred] *
3 The Count holds ANSTEY himself. It answers for 5 hides. Land
   for 10 ploughs. In lordship 3 hides; 2 ploughs there; a
   third possible.
       8 villagers with a priest and 6 smallholders have 5 ploughs;
       a further 2 possible. 5 cottagers; 6 slaves.

Paſtura ad pec̚ . Silua . L . porc̚ . In totis ualent̚ ual

7 ualuit . xIIII . liɓ . T . R . E .⁷ xv . liɓ . Hoc m̄ tenuit

Aluuard teign⁹ Heraldi . uende̚ potuit . *IN EDWINESKEV HD.*

In Cornei ten⁷ Roɓt de comite . I . hidā . Tr̄a . e̅ . I . car̄ .

7 ibi eſt cū . IIII . borð 7 IIII . cot 7 II . ſeruis . P̊tū dim̄ car̄ .

Paſtura ad pec̚ . Silua . x . porc̚ . Int totū ual . xIII .

ſol . 7 IIII . den̚ . Q̥do recep̚⁷ x . ſol . T . R . E .⁷ xx . ſol . De hac

tr̄a tenuit Aluuard hō Heraldi . I . uirg̚ . 7 uende̚ potuit .

7 Gode hō regis . E . habuit . III . uirg̚ . uende̚ potuit .

De c̄ſuetuð reddeɓ uicecom̚ . III . den̚ . aut . III .es̚ . part̚ uni⁹ Aueræ .

In Trochinge ten̚ Rumold⁹ de comite xvIII . ac̄s .

Tr̄a . e̅ . II . boḃ₂ . Val 7 ualuit ſep̄ . II . ſol . Hanc tram̚

tenuit Alric hō Stigand archiep̄i .

In Ichetone ten̚ Rumold de com̚ dim̄ hidā . Tr̄a . e̅

. I . car̄ . Ibi . e̅ un⁹ borð . Val xx . ſol . Q̥do recep̚⁷ xL . ſol .

7 tntð T . R . E . Hanc tr̄a tenuit Godid hō Aſgari staɪrɪ . uende̚

In ead̚ úilla ten . II . milites de comite ⌐ potuit .

xx . ac̄s . Tr̄a . e̅ . II . boḃ . 7 ibi ſunt . Val 7 ualuit ſep̄ . III .

ſol . Hanc tr̄a tenuit Godid hō Aſgari staɪrɪ . 7 uende̚ pot .

In Berchedene ten̚ Roɓt⁹ de comite . I . hið ⍬ uno m̄ .

Tr̄a . e̅ . IIII . car̄ . In dn̄io ſunt . II . 7 II . uiłłi cū pɓro 7 v . borð

hn̄t . II . car̄ . Ibi . vI . ſerui . P̊tū dim̄ car̄ . Nem̚ ad ſepes .

7 xxx . porc̚ . 7 I . mol de . II . ſol 7 vIII . den̚ . Int totū ual . III . liɓ .

137 c

Q̥do recep̚⁷ xL . ſol . T . R . E .⁷ c . ſol . Hoc m̄ te

nuit Aluuard hō Heraldi ᐧcomitisᐧ ; 7 uende̚ potuit .

In Wachelei ten̚ Roɓt⁹ de com̚ . xL . ac̄s . Tr̄a . e̅

. I . car̄ . P̊tū . II . boḃ₂ . Nem̚⁹ ad ſepes . Val 7 ualuit

Meadow for ½ plough; pasture for the livestock; woodland,
50 pigs.
The total value is and was £14; before 1066 £15.
Alfward, a thane* of Earl Harold's, held this manor;
he could sell. In EDWINSTREE Hundred.

4 In CORNEY Robert holds 1 hide from the Count. Land for 1 plough;
it is there, with
4 smallholders; 4 cottagers; 2 slaves.
Meadow for ½ plough; pasture for the livestock; woodland, 10 pigs.
In total, value 13s 4d; when acquired 10s; before 1066, 20s.
Alfward, Harold's man, held 1 virgate of this land; he
could sell. Gode, King Edward's man, had 3 virgates; she
could sell. She paid 3d to the Sheriff in customary dues, or
3 parts of one cartage.

5 In THROCKING Rumold holds 18 acres from the Count. Land for 2 oxen.
The value is and always was 2s.
Alric, Archbishop Stigand's man, held this land.

6 In BUNTINGFORD Rumold holds ½ hide from the Count. Land for
1 plough.
1 smallholder.
Value 20s; when acquired 40s; before 1066 as much.
Godith, Asgar the Constable's man, held this land; she could sell.

7 In the same village 2 men-at-arms hold 20 acres from the Count.
Land for 2 oxen; they are there.
The value is and always was 3s.
Godith, Asgar the Constable's man, held this land; she could sell.

*8 In BERKESDEN Robert holds 1 hide from the Count as one manor.
Land for 4 ploughs. In lordship 2.
2 villagers with a priest and 5 smallholders have 2 ploughs.
6 slaves.
Meadow for ½ plough; wood for fences, and 30 pigs. 1 mill at 2s 8d.
In total, value £3; when acquired 40s; before 1066, 100s.   137c
Alfward, Earl Harold's man, held this manor, he could sell.

9 In WAKELY Robert holds 40 acres from the Count. Land for 1 plough.
Meadow for 2 oxen; wood for fences.

sep . v . sol . Hanc trā tenuit Aluuard⁹ hō Heraldi

In Alfledauuicha teñ Rumold ⌐ 7 uende potuit.
de comite . ii . hid . Tra . ē . ii . car . 7 ibi sunt cū
vii . bord . 7 ii . seruis . Ibi . i . molin de . ii . sol . Ptū
ii . bobz . Pastura ad pec . Silua . xx . porc . Val
xxx . sol . Qdo receṗ. xl . sol . 7 tntd T.R.E.
Hanc trā tenuit Godid hō Asgari . 7 uende pot.

In Horemede . teñ . ii . Angli de comite . iii . hid
7 i . uirg . Tra . ē . iii . car 7 dim . In dñio sunt . ii .
7 pbr cū . ii . cot ht . i . car 7 dim . ptū . i . car.
Silua . xii . porc . Int totū ual . iii . lib . Qdo
receṗ. iiii . lib . T.R.E. c . sol . Hoc ᛗ tenuit
Wluuard hō Asgari stalri . 7 uende potuit.

In Bordesdene teñ com . i . hid 7 i . uirg | Tra . ē
iii . car . In dñio . iii . uirg . 7 ibi . ē . i . car . 7 xi .
uitti cū pbro hñt . ii . car . Ibi . ii . serui . ptū dim
car . Pastura ad pec . Silua . xx . porc . Int tot
ual 7 ualuit . iii . lib . T.R.E. iiii . lib . Hanc trā
tenuer . ix . sochi Asgari . 7 uende potuer.

Ipse comes teñ COCHEHAMESTEDE . p . ii . hid
se defd . Tra . ē . vi . car . In dñio . iii . uirg . 7 ibi est
una car . Ibi . v . uitti cū . iii . bord hñt . v . car.
Ibi . i . cot 7 iiii . serui . ptū . i . car . Pasta ad pec.
Silua . x . porc . In totis ualent ual 7 ualuit
sep . vii . lib . Hoc ᛗ tenuit Gouti teigñ Heraldi

In Hodesdone teñ canonici ⌐ 7 uende pot.
S̃ Martini London . i . hid de comite . Tra . ē . i . car.
7 ibi . ē cū . iii . bord . ptū . i . car . Pastura ad pec.
Silua . l . porc . De gurgite. xxi . Anguitt . Val
xv . sol . Qdo receṗ . v . sol . T.R.E. xl . sol . Hanc
trā tenuit Godid hō Asgari . 7 uende potuit.

The value is and always was 5s.

Alfward, Earl Harold's man, held this land; he could sell.

10 In BEAUCHAMPS Rumold holds 2 hides from the Count. Land for 2
ploughs; they are there, with
7 smallholders and 2 slaves.
1 mill at 2s; meadow for 2 oxen; pasture for the livestock;
woodland, 20 pigs.
Value 30s; when acquired 40s; before 1066 as much.

Godith, Asgar's man, held this land; she could sell.

11 In HORMEAD 2 Englishmen hold 3 hides and 1 virgate from the Count.
Land for 3½ ploughs. In lordship 2.
A priest with 2 cottagers has 1½ ploughs.
Meadow for 1 plough; woodland, 12 pigs.
In total, value £3; when acquired £4; before 1066, 100s.

Wulfward, Asgar the Constable's man, held this manor; he
could sell.

12 In BOZEN the Count holds 1 hide, 1 virgate and 4 acres.
Land for 3 ploughs. In lordship 3 virgates; 1 plough there.
11 villagers with a priest have 2 ploughs. 2 slaves.
Meadow for ½ plough; pasture for the livestock; woodland, 20 pigs.
In total, the value is and was £3; before 1066 £4.

9 Freemen, Asgar the Constable's [men], held this land; they could sell.

*13 The Count holds COCKHAMSTEAD himself. It answers for 2 hides.
Land for 6 ploughs. In lordship 3 virgates; 1 plough there.
5 villagers with 3 smallholders have 5 ploughs.
1 cottager; 4 slaves.
Meadow for 1 plough; pasture for the livestock; woodland, 10 pigs.
The total value is and always was £7.

Gauti, a thane of Earl Harold's, held this manor; he could sell.

[In HERTFORD Hundred]
14 In HODDESDON the Canons of St. Martin's, London, hold 1 hide
from the Count. Land for 1 plough; it is there, with
3 smallholders.
Meadow for 1 plough; pasture for the livestock; woodland,
50 pigs; from weirs, 21 eels.
Value 15s; when acquired 5s; before 1066, 40s.

Godith, Asgar the Constable's man, held this land; she could sell.

Ⓜ Ipſe comes ten̄ *Brachinges*. *In Brachinges* hd̄.

p̄.v.hid ſe deſd.Tra.ē.xi.car̄. In dn̄io.iii.hidæ.

7 ibi ſunt.iii.car̄. Ibi.x.uilli cū p̄bro 7 ix.bord

hn̄t.viii.car̄. Ibi.iii.cot 7 vi.ſerui. 7 i.molin̄

de.xii.den̄.p̄tū.iii.car̄. Paſtura ad pec̄ uillæ.

Silua.vi.porc̄. In totis ualent ual 7 ualuit.xvi.

lib̄.T.R.E.́xx.lib̄. Hoc Ⓜ tenuer̄.ii.teigni.

Hoꝛ un̄ hō.R.E. habuit.iiii.hid. 7 alter hō

Aſgari.i.hid habuit. Vend̄ n̄ potuer̄.quia

ſemp̄ jacuer̄ iɳ elemoſina.R.E. tp̄r. 7 om̄ium

anteceſſoꝛ ſuoꝛ.ut ſcȳra teſtatur.

.XVIII. **Terra Rogerij Comitis**. *In Odesei hi̅nd̄*.

Comes Rogeri9 ten̄ In Bradefelle dim̄ hidā.

Tra.ē dim̄ car̄.s; non.ē ibi. Silua.xl.porc̄.

Val 7 ualuit.v.ſol̄.T.R.E.́x.ſol̄. Hanc tr̄a

tenuit Gode de regina Eddid. 7 uend̄e potuit.

137 d

.XIX. **Terra Roberti De Olgi**.

Ⓜ Rotbert de Oilgi. 7 Radulf9 Baſſet de eo ten̄

Theisescote.p̄ iiii.hid ſe deſd.T.R.E. 7 m̄ p̄ duab9.

Tra.ē.iiii.car̄. In dn̄io ſunt.ii̅.7 iii.uilli 7 dim̄ cū

ii.ſochis de una hida 7 v.bord hn̄t.ii.car̄. Ibi

un̄ cot 7 i.ſeruus. 7 i.molin̄ de.x.ſol̄.p̄tū.iii.car̄.

Int totū ual lxx.ſol̄. Qꝺo recep̄:iiii.lib̄.T.R.E.́c.ſol̄.

Hoc Ⓜ tenuer̄.v.ſochi. Hoꝛ duo hōes Briſtrici

unā hid 7 dim̄ habuer̄. 7 alij.ii hōes Oſulfi filij Fran

unā hid 7 dim̄. 7 v.hō Ediner.i.hid tenuit.nullus

eoꝛ ad anteceſſorē Wigot p̄tinuit.ſed unꝗſꝗ tr̄a

ſuā uend̄e potuit. Hoꝛ un̄ tr̄a ſuā emit a.W.rege

nouē unc̄ auri ut hōes de hund teſtant.́ 7 poſtea

ad Wigotū ſe uertit p̄ proteſtione.

137 c, d

In BRAUGHING Hundred

M. The Count holds BRAUGHING himself. It answers for 5 hides.
Land for 11 ploughs. In lordship 3 hides; 3 ploughs there.
   10 villagers with a priest and 9 smallholders have 8 ploughs.
      3 cottagers; 6 slaves.
   1 mill at 12d; meadow for 3 ploughs; pasture for the
      village livestock; woodland, 6 pigs.
The total value is and was £16; before 1066 £20.
   2 thanes held this manor; one of them, King Edward's man,
had 4 hides; the second, Asgar the Constable's man, had 1 hide;
they could not sell because they always lay in the alms (lands) in
the time of King Edward and of all his predecessors, as the Shire
testifies.

8   LAND OF EARL ROGER

In ODSEY Hundred

1   Earl Roger holds ½ hide in BROADFIELD. Land for ½ plough, but it
is not there.
      Woodland, 40 pigs.
The value is and was 5s; before 1066, 10s.
      Gode held this land from Queen Edith; she could sell.

9   LAND OF ROBERT D'OILLY   137d

[In TRING Hundred]

1   M. Robert d'Oilly holds TISCOTT and Ralph Bassett from him.
It answered for 4 hides before 1066; now for 2. Land for 4 ploughs.
In lordship 2.
   *3½ villagers with 2 Freemen, with one hide, and 5 smallholders
      have 2 ploughs. 1 cottager; 1 slave.
   1 mill at 10s; meadow for 3 ploughs.
In total, value 70s; when acquired £4; before 1066, 100s.
   5 Freemen held this manor. 2 of them, Brictric's men, had
1½ hides; 2 others, Oswulf son of Fran's men, 1½ hides;
the fifth, Edmer Ator's man, held 1 hide. None of them
belonged to (Robert's) predecessor, Wigot, but each of them could
sell his land. One of them bought his land from King William
for 9 ounces of gold, as the men of the Hundred testify. Later
he turned to Wigot for protection.

In Polehangre ten̅ Martellus de Roƀto de
de oilgi dim̅ hidā. Tra̅ .e̅. i. car̅. 7 ibi .e̅ cu̅. ii. cot̅.
7 ii. ſeruis . p̅tu̅ . i . car̅ . Silua . ii . porc̅ . Vaɫ 7 ualuit
x . ſoɫ . T.R.E. xx . ſoɫ. Hanc trā tenuit Aluric ho̅
Wallef comitis . 7 uendé potuit.

.XX ## TERRA ROBERTI GERNON.

R OTBERTVS Grenon Aluuard de eo ten̅ in Mer
    delai . i . hiđ . Tra̅ .e̅. iii . car̅. In dn̅io .e̅ una . 7 iiii.
uiɫɫi cu̅ . ii . borđ hn̅t . ii . car̅ . Ibi . iii . cot̅ . Paſtura ad
pecun̅ . Silua . cc . porc̅ . Vaɫ . xxx , ſoɫ. Q̸do recep̅.
xL . ſoɫ . T.R.E. L . ſoɫ. Iſđ qui ten̅ tenuit T.R.E.
7 uendere potuit.

In Aiete ten̅ Wiɫɫs de Roƀto . ii . hiđ 7 dim̅ . Tra̅ .e̅. vL.
car̅ . In dn̅io .e̅ una . 7 alia pot̅ fieri . Ibi vi . uiɫɫi cu̅
iii . borđ hn̅t . iii . car̅ . 7 iiii ta pot̅ fieri . Ibi . i . ſeruus.
P̅tu̅ . i . car̅ . Paſtura ad pec̅ . Silua . c.L . porc̅ . Int totu̅
uaɫ . xL . ſoɫ . Q̸do recep̅. Lx . ſoɫ . T.R.E. vi . liƀ. Hanc
trā tenuer̅ . ii . teigni ho̅es .R.E. 7 uendé potuer̅ . Hanc
.Λ. inuaſit Wiɫɫs ho̅ Roƀti ſup rege̅ . s; reclamat dn̅m ſuu̅
In Gravelai ten̅ Wiɫɫs de Roƀto ⌐ ad ꝓteſtore̅.
dim̅ hiđ . Tra̅ .e̅. i . car̅ . ſed n̅ eſt ibi . Vaɫ . iiii . ſoɫ.
Q̸do recep̅. v . ſoɫ . 7 tn̅tđ T.R.E. Hanc trā tenuer̅
ii . ho̅es Goduini de Benefelle . 7 uendé potuer̅.
In Scelua ten̅ Wiɫɫs de Roƀto dim̅ hiđ . Tra̅ .e̅. i . car̅.
s; ibi n̅ eſt . Vn̅ cot̅ ibi .e̅. Vaɫ 7 ualuit x . ſoɫ . T.R.E.
xx . ſoɫ. Hanc trā tenuit Aluric ho̅ Aluric belinton . 7 uendé pot̅.
In Wluueneuuiche ten̅ Wiɫɫs de Roƀto dim̅ hidā
7 dim̅ uirgā. Tra̅ .e̅. i . car̅ . 7 ibi .e̅ cu̅ . ii . borđ . 7 . ii . cot̅.
P̅tu̅ dim̅ car̅ . Silua . xx . porc̅ Vaɫ . vi . ſoɫ . Q̸do recep̅.
x . ſoɫ . T.R.E. xx . ſoɫ. Hanc trā tenuit Goduin ho̅ Almari
de Benintone . potuit uendere.

*2 In POLEHANGER Martell holds ½ hide from Robert d'Oilly. Land for 1 plough; it is there, with
> 2 cottagers and 2 slaves.
> Meadow for 1 plough; woodland, 2 pigs.

The value is and was 10s; before 1066, 20s.
> Aelfric, Earl Waltheof's man, held this land; he could sell.

20 LAND OF ROBERT GERNON

[In BROADWATER Hundred]

1 Robert Gernon holds 1 hide in MARDLEY and Alfward from him. Land for 3 ploughs. In lordship 1.
> 4 villagers with 2 smallholders have 2 ploughs. 3 cottagers.
> Pasture for the livestock; woodland, 200 pigs.

Value 30s; when acquired 40s; before 1066, 50s.
> The same holder also held it before 1066; he could sell.

*2 In AYOT (ST. PETER) William holds 2½ hides from Robert. Land for 6 ploughs. In lordship 1; another possible.
> 6 villagers with 3 smallholders have 3 ploughs; a fourth possible. 1 slave.
> Meadow for 1 plough; pasture for the livestock; woodland, 150 pigs.

In total, value 40s; when acquired 60s; before 1066 £6.
> 2 thanes, King Edward's men, held this land; they could sell.

*A William, Robert's man, annexed it in the King's despite, but he claims his lord as protector.

3 In GRAVELEY William holds ½ hide from Robert. Land for 1 plough, but it is not there.
Value 4s; when acquired 5s; before 1066 as much.
> Two of Godwin of Benfield's men held this land; they could sell.

*4 In CHELLS William holds ½ hide from Robert. Land for 1 plough, but it is not there.
> 1 cottager.

The value is and was 10s; before 1066, 20s.
> Aelfric, Aelfric (Aelmer?) of Bennington's man, held this land; he could sell.

*5 In WOOLWICKS William holds ½ hide and ½ virgate from Robert. Land for 1 plough; it is there, with
> 2 smallholders and 2 cottagers.
> Meadow for ½ plough; woodland, 20 pigs.

Value 6s; when acquired 10s; before 1066, 20s.
> Godwin, Aelmer of Bennington's man, held this land; he could sell.

In Wimundelai ten Wilłs de Roƀto . 1 . hiđ . Tra . e̅ . 1 . car̅.
sed ibi n̅ eſt . Vn̅ cot ibi . e̅ . p̅t̅u dim car̅ . Val . vi . ſoł . Q̇do
recep̅.́ x . ſoł . T . R . E.́ xv . ſoł . Hanc tr̅a tenuit Alflet ſub
Roƀto . f . Wimarch . die qua rex . E . fuit uiuus 7 mortuus.
n̅ potuit uende̅ p̅ter ej̇ licentiã.

I ſde̅ Wilłs ten de Roƀto LECEWORDE . p̅ x . hiđ ſe
deſđ . Tra . e̅ . vii . car̅ . In dn̅io ſunt . ı̅ı̅ . 7 ıx . uilłi cu̅ p̅bro
hn̅t . v . car̅ . Ibi . 11 . ſochi de una hida 7 dim . 7 iiii . cot.
7 1 . ſeruus . p̅t̅u dim car̅ . paſtura ad pec . Silua . c . porc̅.
In totis ualent ual . vi . liƀ . Q̇do recep̅.́ vii . liƀ . T . R . E.́

Ꝼ viii . liƀ.

Hoc m̅ tenuit G̅oduin̅ de Souƀerie . teign̅ . R . E . 7 uende̅
potuit . 7 ibi . 111 . ſochi ho̅es ej̇ . 11 . hiđ 7 111 . uir̅g habuer̅.
7 uende̅ potuer̅.

In Welga ten Roƀt de pontcardon . 1 . hiđ 7 dim de
Roƀto . 7 xx . ac̅s . Tra . e̅ . 111 . car̅ . In dn̅io . e̅ . una . 7 alia
pot fieri . Ibi . iii . uilłs cu̅ . vi . borđ hn̅t . 1 . car̅ . Ibi . 1 . cot
7 11 . ſerui . p̅t̅u . 11 . boƀʒ . Paſtura ad pec̅ . Val 7 ualuit
xxx . ſoł . T . R . E.́ xl . ſoł . Hanc tr̅a t̅nuit Godric ho̅
Almari de benintone . 7 uende̅ potuit . IN ODESEI HĐ.

In Wallingtone ten Wilłs de Roƀto . 111 . hiđ . xx . ac̅s
min̅ . Tra . e̅ . iiii . c̅ . Ibi ſunt . ı̅ı̅ . 7 aliæ . ı̅ı̅ . poſſ fieri . Ibi
111 . uilłi . 7 vi . cot . Paſtura ad pec̅ . Nem̅ ad ſepes.
Val . xxxv . ſoł . iiii . den min̅ . Q̇do recep̅.́ lx . ſoł . T . R . E.́
c . ſoł . Hanc tr̅a tenuit Aluric ho̅ Goduini . 7 uende̅ pot.
.ſ. Vleſtan

*6 In WYMONDLEY William holds 1 hide from Robert. Land for 1
plough, but it is not there.
 1 cottager.
 Meadow for ½ plough.
Value 6s; when acquired 10s; before 1066, 15s.
 Aelfled held this land under Robert son of Wymarc in
1066; she could not sell without his permission.

*7 William also holds LETCHWORTH from Robert. It answers for 10
hides. Land for 7 ploughs. In lordship 2.
 9 villagers with a priest have 5 ploughs. 2 Freemen with
  1½ hides; 4 cottagers; 1 slave.
 Meadow for ½ plough; pasture for the livestock; woodland, 100 pigs.
Total value £6; when acquired £7; before 1066 £8.
 Godwin of Soulbury, a thane of King Edward's, held this   138a
manor; he could sell. 3 Freemen, his men, had 2 hides and
3 virgates; they could sell.

8 In WELWYN Robert of Pont-Chardon holds 1½ hides and 20 acres from
Robert. Land for 3 ploughs. In lordship 1; another possible.
 3 villagers with 6 smallholders have 1 plough. 1 cottager;
  2 slaves.
 Meadow for 2 oxen; pasture for the livestock.
The value is and was 30s; before 1066, 40s.
 Godric, Aelmer of Bennington's man, held this land; he could sell.

 In ODSEY Hundred
9 In WALLINGTON William holds 3 hides less 20 acres from Robert.
 Land for 4 ploughs; 2 there; another 2 possible.
  3 villagers; 6 cottagers.
 Pasture for the livestock; wood for fences.
Value 35s less 4d; when acquired 60s; before 1066, 100s.
 Aelfric, Godwin son of Wulfstan's man, held this land;
he could sell.

In Sumersele. teñ Witts dim hid de Robto . Tra . e̅   IN EDWI

.i. car̅ 7 ibi . e̅ cū . i. cot . p̃tū dim car̅. Nem ad sepes.   NESTREV.

Vat . vi . sot 7 viii . deñ . Q̨do recep̃:́ x . sot. T.R.E:́   HVND.

xx . sot. Hanc tr̄a tenuit Alured ho̅ Asgari . 7 uende

In Sapehā . teñ Witts de Robto . ii . hid .   ⌐ potuit.

Tra . e̅ . iiii . car̅ . In dñio . e̅ una 7 dim . 7 alia dim

pot fieri. Ibi . iiii . bord hñt . i . car̅ . 7 alia pot fieri.

Ibi . iii . cot. 7 ii . serui. P̃tū dim car̅ . Pastura ad pec̃.

Nem ad sepes. H̄ tra uat . xl . sot . Q̨do recep̃:́ lx . sot.

T.R.E:́ iiii . lib̅. Hoc m̅ tenuer̅ . ii . sochi ho̅es Goduini. benefelle.

In Bordesdene . teñ Witts de Robto   ⌐ 7 uende potuer̅.

dim uirg . Tra . e̅ dim car̅ . 7 ibi . e̅ cū . iiii . bord . p̃tū . ii.

bob . Nem ad sepes . Vat 7 ualuit sep̃ xii . sot . 7 viii . deñ.

Hanc tr̄a tenuit Leuuin ho̅ Goduini de benefelle. Soca

fuit Asgari stalri . uendere potuit. IN BRACHINGES H̄D.

Anschitillus teñ de Robto WESTMELE . p̨ vii . hid

7 una uirg se defd̅ . Tra . e̅ . xiiii . car̅ . In dñio sunt . iiii. or

7 xviii . uitti 7 v . francig cū . xii . bord hñt . x . car̅ . Ibi

xv . cot. 7 ii . serui. 7 iii . moliñ de xxi . sot 7 viii . deñ. p̃tū

iiii . car̅. Pastura ad pec̃. Silua . c . porc̃. In totis ualent

uat . xvii . lib̅. Q̨do recep̃:́ x . lib̅ . T.R.E:́ xx . lib̅. Hoc ti

m̅ tenuit Achi teign̅ Heraldi comit̅. 7 uende potuit.

.XXI.   TERRA ROBERTI DE TODENI. KEVNGE HVND.
Rotbert de Todeni . 7 Radulf de eo teñ MASCEWELLE.

p̨ xiiii . hid se defd̅ . T.R.E. 7 m̅ p̨ . iii . hid 7 ii . uirg 7 dim.

tam sunt sep̃ xiiii . hidæ. Tra . e̅ . vii . car̅ . In dñio sunt

ii. 7 xv , uitti cū . iiii . bord hñt . v . car̅. P̃tū . vii . car̅.

Pastura ad pec̃ . 7 ii . sot. Silua q̨ngent porc̃. In totis ua

In EDWINSTREE Hundred

*10 In HYDE HALL William holds ½ hide from Robert. Land for 1 plough;
it is there, with
1 cottager.
Meadow for ½ plough; wood for fences.
Value 6s 8d; when acquired 10s; before 1066, 20s.
Alfred, Asgar the Constable's man, held this land; he could sell.

*11 In SAPEHAM William holds 2 hides from Robert. Land for 4 ploughs.
In lordship 1½; another ½ possible.
4 smallholders have 1 plough; another possible.
3 cottagers; 2 slaves.
Meadow for ½ plough; pasture for the livestock; wood for fences.
Value of this land 40s; when acquired 60s; before 1066 £4.
2 Freemen, Godwin [of] Benfield's men, held this manor; they
could sell.

12 In BOZEN William holds ½ virgate from Robert. Land for ½ plough;
it is there, with
4 smallholders.
Meadow for 2 oxen; wood for fences.
The value is and always was 12s 8d.
Leofwin, Godwin of Benfield's man, held this land;
the jurisdiction was Asgar the Constable's. He could sell.

In BRAUGHING Hundred

13 Ansketel holds WESTMILL from Robert. It answers for 7 hides
and 1 virgate. Land for 14 ploughs. In lordship 4.
18 villagers and 5 Frenchmen with 12 smallholders have 10 ploughs.
15 cottagers; 2 slaves.
3 mills at 21s 8d; meadow for 4 ploughs; pasture for
the livestock; woodland, 100 pigs.
Total value £17; when acquired £10; before 1066 £20.
Aki, a thane of Earl Harold's, held this manor; he could sell.

21   LAND OF ROBERT OF TOSNY

In TRING Hundred

*1 Robert of Tosny holds MISWELL and Ralph from him. It answered
for 14 hides before 1066; now for 3 hides and 2½ virgates. However
there are 14 hides, always. Land for 7 ploughs. In lordship 2.
15 villagers with 4 smallholders have 5 ploughs.
Meadow for 7 ploughs; pasture for the livestock, and 2s too;
woodland, 500 pigs.

lentijs ual .ç. sol 7 unã unciã Auri. Qdo receƥ. vii. lib.
T.R.E. viii. lib. Hoc M̃ tenuit Osulf fili Frane. teign
R.E. antecessor Roƀti todeniensis. *In Daneis Hvnd.*

In Bereuuorde ten Baldric de Roƀto .v. hið. Tra .ẽ
iii. car. In dñio sunt .ii. 7 tcia pot fieri. Ibi. iii. uilti.
cũ pƀro 7 qdã francig cũ .iiii. bord. Ptũ .i. car. Pasta
ad pec uillæ. Silua .c. porc. Int totũ ual xl. sol. Qdo
receƥ. xxx. sol. T.R.E. lx. sol. Hanc trã tenuit Osulf
fili Frane. 7 uende potuit cui uoluit.

.XXII. **R** TERRA RADVLFI DE TODENI. *In Daneis Hvnd.*

ADVLFVS de Todeni ten *FLAMESTEDE*. ƥ .iiii.
hið se defð .T.R.E. 7 m̃ ƥ duab. Tra .ẽ .xii. car. In
dñio .ii. hidæ. 7 ibi sunt .ii. car. 7 xxii. uilti hñt .viii.
car. 7 adhuc .ii. possunt .ẽe. Ibi .vii. cot 7 iiii. serui.

138 b

Silua mille porc. In totis ualent ual xi. lib. Qdo receƥ.
ix. lib. T.R.E. xii. lib. Hoc M̃ tenuit Achi teign. R.E.

R ogerius ten de Radulfo   *In Brachinges Hd.*

WESMELE . ƥ iiii. hið 7 iii. uirg se defð. Tra .ẽ
x. car. In dñio sunt .ii. 7 tcia pot fieri. Ibi. xiiii.
uilti cũ ix. bord hñt .vii. car. Ibi .iii. cot 7 ii. serui.
7 uñ molin de .x. sol. ptũ .ii. car. Pastura ad pec.
Silua .lx. porc. In totis ualent ual xii. lib. Qdo
receƥ. x. lib. T.R.E. xiiii. lib. Hoc M̃ tenuit Sexi
Huscarle .R.E. 7 ibi socħs un hõ Anschil de Wara
.i. uirg habuit. 7 uende potuit. Et ƥ aduentũ
Regis Willi uendita fuit. 7 apposita huic M̃. ubi
non fuit .T.R.E.

.XXIII. **R** TERRA RADVLFI DE LIMESY. *In Odesei Hvnd.*

ADVLFVS de Limesy ten in Hainstone dim
hið . 7 iiii. part unius uirg. Tra .ẽ dim car.

Total value 100s and 1 ounce of gold; when acquired £7; before 1066 £8.

Robert of Tosny's predecessor, Oswulf son of Fran, a thane of King Edward's, held this manor.

In DACORUM Hundred

*2 In BARWYTHE Baldric holds 5 hides from Robert. Land for 3 ploughs. In lordship 2; a third possible.

3 villagers, with a priest and a Frenchman, with 4 smallholders.

Meadow for 1 plough; pasture for the village livestock; woodland, 100 pigs.

In total, value 40s; when acquired 30s; before 1066, 60s.

Oswulf son of Fran held this land; he could sell to whom he would.

22   LAND OF RALPH OF TOSNY

In DACORUM Hundred

1 Ralph of Tosny holds FLAMSTEAD. It answered for 4 hides before 1066; now for 2. Land for 12 ploughs. In lordship 2 hides; 2 ploughs there.

22 villagers have 8 ploughs; a further 2 possible.

7 cottagers; 4 slaves.

Woodland, 1000 pigs.   138b

Total value £11; when acquired £9; before 1066 £12.

Aki, a thane of King Edward's, held this manor.

In BRAUGHING Hundred

2 Roger holds WESTMILL from Ralph. It answers for 4 hides and 3 virgates. Land for 10 ploughs. In lordship 2; a third possible.

14 villagers with 9 smallholders have 7 ploughs.

3 cottagers; 2 slaves.

1 mill at 10s; meadow for 2 ploughs; pasture for the livestock; woodland, 60 pigs.

Total value £12; when acquired £10; before 1066 £14.

Saxi, one of King Edward's Guards, held this manor. A Freeman, Askell of Ware's man, had 1 virgate; he could sell; after 1066 it was sold and placed in this manor, where it was not before 1066.

23   LAND OF RALPH OF LIMESY

In ODSEY Hundred

*1 In HAINSTONE Ralph of Limesy holds ½ hide and the fourth part of 1 virgate. Land for ½ plough.

Ibi . ē uñ cot . 7 p̄tū . ii . bob₇ . Val 7 ualuit . x . fol.
T . R . E .́ xx . fol. Hanc t̄ra tenuit Lemar hō Stig
archiep̄i . 7 uende potuit.

Ipfe Radulf teñ Caldecota . p una hida 7 i . uirg.
Tra . ē . v . car. In dñio . iii . uirg. 7 iiii . pars uni uirg.
Ibi . ix . uilti cū p̄bro hñt . ii . car 7 dim . 7 i . car
7 dim pot fieri. Ibi . iiii . cot . p̄tū . ii . bob₇ . h̄ tra
ual 7 ualuit . xl . fol . T . R . E .́ c . fol. Hoc M tenuit
Lemar hō Stig Archiep̄i . 7 potuit uende.

Ipfe Radulf teñ PERITONE . p x . hid fe defd.
Tra . ē . xx . car. In dñio . ii . hidæ . 7 ibi funt . vi . car .
Ibi xx . iiii . uilti cū p̄bro 7 xxix . bord hñt . xii . car.
7 adhuc . ii . poff fieri. Ibi uñ miles anglic̄ 7 uñ fochs
cū . iiii . cot. Ibi . iiii . moliñ de . lxxiii . fol. 7 iiii . deñ.
In t̄ra anglici 7 fochi id eft . ii . hidis .́ maneɴ . i . uilts
7 viii . cot . p̄tū . x . car. Ibi . x . ferui. Paftura ad
pec uillæ. Silua q̄ngent porc . De paftura 7 filua .́
x . fol. In totis ualent ual . xx . lib. Q̇do recep̄ .́ xx . ii .
lib . T . R . E .́ xxv . lib. Hoc M tenuit Stig archiep̄s.
7 ibi fuer . ii . fochi. 7 adhuc ibi fuɴ . ñ potuer uende.
H̄ defup . ē dimid HVND DE HIZ . IN HERTFORD HD.
Ipfe Radulf teñ EMMEWELLE . p xiiii . hid 7 dim
fe defd . Tra . ē . xvi . car. In dñio . vii . hidæ . 7 ibi fuɴ
ii . car . 7 aliæ . ii . poff fieri. Ibi . xxiiii . uilti cū p̄bro
7 iiii . franciḡ . 7 vii . bord hñt . viii . car . 7 iiii . poff
fieri. Ibi . xix . cot 7 ii . ferui. 7 i . moliñ de . vi . fol.
p̄tū . xvi . car. Paftura ad pec uillæ. Silua . cc . porc.
7 de paftura 7 feno .́ x . fol. In totis ualent ual xiiii .
lib 7 x . fol. Q̇do recep̄ .́ xii . lib . T . R . E .́ xviii . lib.
Hoc M tenuit Herald comes.

1 cottager.
Meadow for 2 oxen.
The value is and was 10s; before 1066 20s.
Ledmer, Archbishop Stigand's man, held this land; he could sell.

* 2 Ralph holds CALDECOT himself for 1 hide and 1 virgate. Land for 5 ploughs.
In lordship 3 virgates and the fourth part of 1 virgate; [1 plough there].
9 villagers with a priest have 2½ ploughs; 1½ ploughs possible.
4 cottagers.
Meadow for 2 oxen.
The value of this land is and was 40s; before 1066, 100s.
Ledmer, Archbishop Stigand's man, held this manor; he could sell.

[In the Half-Hundred of HITCHIN] *
3 Ralph holds PIRTON himself. It answers for 10 hides. Land
for 20 ploughs. In lordship 2 hides; 6 ploughs there.
24 villagers with a priest and 29 smallholders have 12
ploughs; a further 2 possible. 1 English man-at-arms
and 1 Freeman with 4 cottagers.
4 mills at 73s 4d.
On the land of the Englishman and Freeman, that is on 2 hides, live
1 villager and 8 cottagers.
Meadow for 10 ploughs; 10 slaves; pasture for the village
livestock; woodland, 500 pigs; from pasture and woodland 10s.
Total value £20; when acquired £22; before 1066 £25.
Archbishop Stigand held this manor; 2 Freemen were there and
are still there; they could not sell. The above is in the Half-Hundred
of Hitchin.

In HERTFORD Hundred
* 4 Ralph holds AMWELL himself. It answers for 14½ hides.
Land for 16 ploughs. In lordship 7 hides; 2 ploughs there;
another 2 possible.
24 villagers with a priest, 4 Frenchmen and 7 smallholders
have 8 ploughs; 4 possible. 19 cottagers; 2 slaves.
1 mill at 6s; meadow for 16 ploughs; pasture for the village
livestock; woodland, 200 pigs; from pasture and hay 10s.
Total value £14 10s; when acquired £12; before 1066 £18.
Earl Harold held this manor.

R TERRA RADVLFI BANGIARD.

ADVLFVS Baingiard 7 Wills de eo teñ *ALSIES*
WICHE . p̄ vı. hiđ ſe defđ . Tra̅ . e̅ . vıı . car . In
dñio ſunt . ıı . 7 tcia pot fieri . Ibi . ıııı . uiłłi hn̄t . ııı .
car . 7 ıııı . pot fieri . Ibi . xı . cot 7 vıı . ſerui . P̄tū
. ı . car . Paſtura ad pec uille . Silua . x . porc . In
totis ualent ual . vıı . lib̄ . Q̄do recep̄ . c . ſol . T . R . E .
vııı . lib̄ . Hoc m̅ tenuit Almar h̄o Guert . 7 uende pot .
comitis.

138 c

In Horemede teñ Wills de Radulfo . ı . uirg
Tra̅ . e̅ dim car . sʒ n̄ eſt ibi . Nem tant ad ſepes .
Val 7 ualuit ſep̄ . v . ſol . Hanc trā tenuit Wluuard
H̄o Aſgari ſtalri . Hanc reclamant hōes Euſta
chii comitis . de qua fuer̄ ſaiſiti p̄ . ıı . annos pquā
ipſe comes ad hunc honore uenit . ut hōes de
hundret teſtant . *IN HERTFORD HVND* .

Ipſe Radulf teñ *HEREFORDINGBERIE* . p̄ v .
hiđ ſe defđ . Tra̅ . e̅ . x . car . In dñio . ııı . hidæ 7 una
uirg . 7 ibi ſunt . ıı . car . 7 tcia pot fieri . Ibi . v . uiłłi
cū uno francig 7 vı . borđ hn̄t . v . car . 7 adhuc
ıı . poſſunt fieri . Ibi . xı . cot 7 ıııı . ſerui . 7 ıı . mol
de . vı . ſol . p̄tū . ııı . car . Paſtura ad pec uillæ .
Silua . cc . porc . De ſilua 7 paſtura . vıı . ſol . In
totis ualent ual . vııı . lib̄ . Q̄do recep̄ . vı . lib̄ .
T . R . E . x . lib̄ . Hoc m̅ tenuit Aluuin teign
Heraldi comitis . 7 uende potuit .

24 LAND OF RALPH BAYNARD

[In EDWINSTREE Hundred]
1 Ralph Baynard holds ALSWICK and William from him. It answers for 6
    hides. Land for 7 ploughs. In lordship 2; a third possible.
        4 villagers have 3 ploughs; a fourth possible.
        11 cottagers; 7 slaves.
        Meadow for 1 plough; pasture for the village livestock;
            woodland, 10 pigs.
        Total value £7; when acquired 100s; before 1066 £8.
        Aelmer, Earl Gyrth's man, held this manor; he could sell.

2 In HORMEAD William holds 1 virgate from Ralph. Land for ½   138c
    plough, but it is not there.
        Wood sufficient for fences.
    The value is and always was 5s.
        Wulfward, Asgar the Constable's man, held this land.
    Count Eustace's men claim this land; they had been in possession
    of it for two years after the Count came to this Honour himself,
    as the men of the Hundred testify.

    In HERTFORD Hundred
3 Ralph holds HERTINGFORDBURY himself. It answers for 5 hides.
    Land for 10 ploughs. In lordship 3 hides and 1 virgate. 2
    ploughs there; a third possible.
        5 villagers with 1 Frenchman and 6 smallholders have 5
            ploughs; a further 2 possible. 11 cottagers; 4 slaves.
        2 mills at 6s; meadow for 3 ploughs; pasture for the village
            livestock; woodland, 200 pigs; from woodland and pasture 7s.
        Total value £8; when acquired £6; before 1066 £10.
        Alwin, a thane of Earl Harold's, held this manor; he could sell.

R TERRA RANNVLFI FR̄IS ILGERII.

ANNVLFVS fr̄ Ilgerij. 7 Willms de eo ten̄ in
Stagnehou . I . hid̄ . Tra . ē . III . car̄ . In dn̄io eſt vna.
7 VI . uillti hn̄t alia . 7 tcia pot fieri . Ibi . II . cot.
Silua . xx . porc̄ . H̄ tra ual . L ſol . Q̊do recep̄:
xx . ſol . T . R . E: IIII . lib̄ . Hoc m̄ tenuit Turbern
hō . R . E . 7 uende potuit . *IN BRACHINGES HVND*.

I pſe Rannulf ten̄ in *STANESTEDE* . XVII . hid̄
7 dim̄ uirg . Tra . ē . XVI . car̄ . In dn̄io . XIII . hide.
7 ibi ſunt . II . car̄ . 7 tcia pot fieri . Ibi . IIII . uillti cū
pbro 7 p̄poſito uillæ . 7 IIII . francig hn̄t . VIII . car̄.
7 adhuc . V . poſſuɴ fieri . Ibi . VI . cot 7 II . ſerui . 7 I . mol
de . x . ſol . p̊tū . XVI . car̄ . Paſtura ad pec̄ uille . Silua
c . porc̄ . Ibi etiā . VII . burgenſes . qui redd̄t cū alijs
conſuetudinib p̊ti 7 ſiluæ . xxIII . ſol . In totis ualent.
ual XVII . lib̄ . Q̊do recep̄: x . lib̄ . T . R . E: xx . lib̄.
De hoc m̄ tenuit Aluuin de Godtone . XI . hid̄ 7 dim̄
uirḡ . 7 de his ded̄ Radulf tailgeboſc Rannulfo
cū nepte ſua in maritagio . 7 undecimā hidā
poſuit in · Honeſdone . Alias VII . hid̄ tenuer̄ . IIII.
ſochi . Quattuor ex his hōes Anſchil . IIII . hid̄ habuer̄.
alij ů . x . hōes Aluuini de Godtone . III . hid̄ habuer̄.
7 de c̄ſuetud̄ uicecomiti regis . XII . den̄ p ann̄ reddider̄.
Om̄s aut̄ . XIIII . trā ſua uende potuer̄.

[In the Half-Hundred of HITCHIN]
1 Ranulf brother of Ilger holds 1 hide in STAGENHOE
  and William from him. Land for 3 ploughs.
  In lordship 1; 6 villagers have another; a third possible.
    2 cottagers.
  Woodland, 20 pigs.
  Value of this land, 50s; when acquired 20s; before 1066 £4.
    Thorbern, King Edward's man, held this manor; he could sell.

In BRAUGHING Hundred
2 Ranulf holds 17 hides and ½ virgate in STANSTEAD himself. *
  Land for 16 ploughs. In lordship 13 hides; 2 ploughs there;
  a third possible.
      4 villagers with a priest and the village reeve, and
        4 Frenchmen, have 8 ploughs; a further 5 possible.
        6 cottagers; 2 slaves.
      1 mill at 10s; meadow for 16 ploughs; pasture for the
        village livestock; woodland, 100 pigs.
      Also 7 burgesses who pay 23s, with other customary dues of the
        meadow and woodland.
  Total value £17; when acquired £10; before 1066 £20.
    Alwin of Gotton held 11 hides and ½ virgate of this manor and
  of these Ralph Tallboys gave [10 hides and 1½ virgates] *
  to Ranulf, with his niece,* as a marriage portion; he placed the 11th*
  hide in Hunsdon. [1]4* Freemen held another 7 hides. 4 of them,
  Askell's men, had 4 hides. The other 10, Alwin Gotton's men,
  had 3 hides; they paid the King's Sheriff 12d a year in customary
  dues. All 14 however could sell their land.

.XXVI. **H**TERRA HVGON DE GRENTEM. *IN BRACHINGES HD.*

Vgo de Grentemaifnil ten in *WARAS* .XXIIII.

hid .Tra .e .xxx.viii . car . In dnio xiii .hidæ.

7 ibi funt . iii . car . 7 aliæ . iii . poffuɴ . ee . Ibi . xxxviii .

uilli cu pbro 7 ppofito uillæ 7 cu .iii. francig 7 ii.

anglic hoibʒ hnt . xxvi . car 7 dim . 7 ibi funt

xxvii .bord 7 xii . cot 7 ix . ferui . Sub francig 7 anglic

funt xxxii. hoes int uillos 7 bord . Ibi .ii. molend

de xxiiii. fot 7 cccc. anguill . xxv. min . 7 alij hoes

hnt .iii. molin reddtes p ann . x . fot . ptu . xx . car.

Silua . cccc. porc . Ibi . e parcus beftiaru filuaticar.

7 iiii . Arpendi uineæ nuprime plantatæ . In totis ua

lentijs ual .xlv. lib . Qdo recep: l .lib. 7 tntd T.R.E.

138 d

Hoc M tenuit Anfchil de Waras 7 .i. focchs ho ej . ii.

hid ibi habuit . 7 alt focchs ho Guerd com dimid hid

tenuit .Vtriqʒ uendere potuer . Ipfi . ii . poft aduent

regis. W. huic M appofiti fuer . ubi T.R.E. n ptinuer.

ut fcira teftat.

.XXVII **H**TERRA HVGON DE BELCAMP. *IN HERTFORD HVND.*

Vgo de belcap . 7 ii. milit de eo ten in Belingehou . vi . hid.

p uno M . Tra . e . viii. car . In dnio . ii . car . 7 vii . uitti

cu . vi . bord hnt . ii . car . 7 adhuc . iiii . pofs fieri . Ibi .ii.

ferui . 7 i .molin de .vi. fot 7 viii .den . Ptu . iii . car.

Paftura ad pec uillæ . Silua .xx. porc . In totis ualent

ual 7 ualuit . iii .lib . T.R.E: vi .lib. Hoc M tenuit

Brand hufcarl regis . E.

XXVIII. **W**TERRA WILLELMI DE OW.

ILLELM de Ow. 7 Petr de eo ten in Grauelai

i . uirg 7 dim . Tra . e . dim car . fed n eft . Ibi funt .ii.

uilli . Val h tra . iii . fot . Qdo recep: iiii . fot . 7 .tntd . T.R.E.

26   **LAND OF HUGH OF GRANDMESNIL**

In BRAUGHING Hundred

*1   Hugh of Grandmesnil holds 24 hides in WARE. Land for 38 ploughs.
    In lordship 13 hides; 3 ploughs there; another 3 possible.
      38 villagers with a priest and the village reeve, and with
        3 Frenchmen and 2 Englishmen, have 26½ ploughs;
        [a further 5½ ploughs possible;] *
        27 smallholders; 12 cottagers; 9 slaves. Under the
        Frenchmen and Englishmen are 32 men, of the villagers and
        smallholders.
      2 mills at 24s, and 400 eels less 25; the other men have
        3 mills which pay 10s a year; meadow for 20 ploughs;
        woodland, 400 pigs. A park for woodland beasts; 4 *arpents*
        of vines, just planted.
    Total value £45; when acquired £50; before 1066 as much.
     Askell of Ware held this manor, and 1 Freeman, his man,   138 d
    had 2 hides. Another Freeman, Earl Gyrth's man, held ½ hide;
    both could sell. These two were placed in this manor after 1066;
    they did not belong there before 1066, as the Shire testifies.

27   **LAND OF HUGH OF BEAUCHAMP**

In HERTFORD Hundred

*1   Hugh of Beauchamp holds 6 hides as 1 manor in BENGEO and 2 men-
    at-arms from him. Land for 8 ploughs. In lordship 2 ploughs.
      7 villagers with 6 smallholders have 2 ploughs; a further 4
        possible. 2 slaves.
      1 mill at 6s 8d; meadow for 3 ploughs; pasture for the village
        livestock; woodland, 20 pigs.
    The total value is and was £3; before 1066 £6.
     Brand, one of King Edward's Guards, held this manor.

28   **LAND OF WILLIAM OF EU**

[In BROADWATER Hundred]

1   William of Eu holds 1½ virgates in GRAVELEY and Peter from him.
    Land for ½ plough, but it is not there.
      2 villagers.
    Value of this land 3s; when acquired 4s; before 1066 as much.

De hac ꞇra tenuit Aleſtan de boſcumbe . 1 . uirǵ . 7 jacebat

in Weſtone . 7 Lepſi diḿ uirǵ ſocħs . R . E . uendere poterat.

7 de c̄ſuetuꝺ unū obolū uicecom̄ reddeɓ . 7 de hac diḿ ħ

jacebant . vııı. Acræ 7 una Toft in Stigenace quā . R . E.

deꝺ S̅ Petro de Weſtmon̄ . 7 m̊ teń Roger̊ miniſter petri

I̅n Wilgą teń Wiłłs de Ow diḿ hiꝺ . Tra . ē ⌐ ualonienſis.

diḿ car̄ . ſed n̄ eſt ibi Ħ ꞇra uał 7 ualuit ſ̄ep . ııı . ſoł . Hanc

tenuit Aleſtan de Boſc̄ube . 7 jacebat in Weſtone.

I̅n eaꝺ uilla teń Wiłłs de mara . ıı . hiꝺ de Wiłło de Ow.

Tra . ē . ııı . car̄ . In dn̄io . ē una . 7 v . uiłłi hn̄t aliā . 7 tcia

pot́ fieri . Ibi . ıı . cot́ . Paſtura ad pec̄ . Ħ ꞇra uał 7 ualuit

xxxıı . ſoł . T . R . E꞉́ ıııı . liɓ . Aleſtan̊ de boſc̄ube tenuit . ı . hiꝺ

de hac ꞇra . 7 jaceɓ in Weſtone . 7 Aluiet hō ej̊ . ı . hidā tenuit.

Vtriꝗ uendé potuer̄.

M̅ I̅pſe Wiłłs de ow . teń WESTONE . ꝑ x . hiꝺ ſe defꝺ . Tra . ē

xxııı . car̄ . In dn̄io . v . hidæ . 7 ibi ſunt . v . car̄ . 7 vı̊ᵗᵃ . pot́ fieri.

Ibi . xxxıııᵗᵃ . uiłłi cū p̄ris duoɓ̊ . 7 ı̊ . milite ıı̊ b̄ . franciǵ

hn̄t . xvı . car̄ . 7 adhuc una pot́ fieri . Ibi . xv . borꝺ 7 xıı.

cot́ . 7 x . ſerui . 7 ı . moł de . x . ſoł . p̄tū . ııı . car̄ . Paſtura

ad pec̄ . Silua ꝗngent́ porc̄ . De boſco 7 paſtura xııı.

ſoł 7 ıııı . deń . In totis ualent́ uał . xxᵗⁱ . liɓ . Q̇do recep꞉́

xxv . liɓ . T . R . E꞉́ xxx . liɓ . Hoc M̅ tenuit Aleſtanus

teign̊ . R . E.

I̅n Boxe . teń Petrus de Wiłło de Ow . ıı . hiꝺ . 7 ııı . uirǵ.

Tra . ē . v . car̄ . In dn̄io ſunt . ıı̊ . 7 tcia pot́ fieri꞉ Ibi . ıı̊ . uiłłi

cū . ıııı . borꝺ hn̄t . ıı . car̄ . Ibi . ııı . cot́ . 7 ııı . ſerui . Nemus

ad ſepes . In totis ualent́ Vał . ʟ . ſoł . Q̇do recep꞉́ xxx . ſoł.

*Alstan of Boscombe held 1 virgate of this land; it lay in (the lands of) Weston; Leofsi, a Freeman of King Edward's, ½ virgate; he could sell; he paid ½d to the Sheriff in customary dues.
8 acres and one plot of this ½ hide lay in (the lands of) Stevenage, which King Edward gave to St. Peter's, Westminster; now Roger, Peter of Valognes' officer, holds them.

In WELWYN William of Eu holds ½ hide. Land for ½ plough, but it is not there.
The value of this land is and always was 3s.
    Alstan of Boscombe held it; it lay in (the lands of) Weston.

In the same village William Delamere holds 2 hides from William of Eu. Land for 3 ploughs. In lordship 1;
    5 villagers have another; a third possible.
    2 cottagers.
    Pasture for the livestock.
The value of this land is and was 32s; before 1066 £4.
    Alstan of Boscombe held 1 hide of this land; it lay in (the lands of) Weston. Alfgeat, his man, held 1 hide; either could sell.

M. William of Eu holds WESTON himself. It answers for 10 hides. Land for 23 ploughs. In lordship 5 hides; 5 ploughs there; a sixth possible.
    33 villagers with 2 priests, 1 man-at-arms and 2 Frenchmen have 16 ploughs; a further 1 possible. 15 smallholders;
        12 cottagers; 10 slaves.
    1 mill at 10s; meadow for 3 ploughs; pasture for the livestock; woodland, 500 pigs; from scrub and pasture 13s 4d.
Total value £20; when acquired £25; before 1066 £30.
    Alstan, a thane of King Edward's, held this manor.

In BOX Peter holds 2 hides and 3 virgates from William of Eu. Land for 5 ploughs. In lordship 2; a third possible.
    2 villagers with 4 smallholders have 2 ploughs.
        3 cottagers; 3 slaves.
    Wood for fences.
Total value 50s; when acquired 30s; before 1066, 60s.

T.R.E. lx. fot. Hanc trā tenuit Aluuard hō Aleſtan

de boſcūbe . ñ potuit uende p̄ter . iii . uirg. *IN ODESEI HD.*

In Cladhele ten Wilts dim uirg 7 iii . acs . Tra . ē

dim car 7 ibi . ē . H̄ tra ual 7 ualuit xxix . den . T.R.E.

iii . fot . Hanc trā tenuit Aleſtan 7 jacuit in Weſtone.

In Hamſteuuorde ten . ii . milites·de Wilto . ii . hid

7 dim uirg . Tra . ē . ii . car . 7 ibi ſunt cū . iiii . uillis.

Ibi . iii . cot 7 ii . ſerui . P̄tū . i . car . Paſtura ad pecun.

H̄ tra ual xl.ii . fot 7 vi . den . Q̇do recep̄. xx . fot . T.R.E.

lx . fot . Hanc trā tenuer . iii . fochi . Hoꝛ . ii̯ . hōes R.E.

tenuer . ii . hid 7 dim uirg . 7 tcius hō Aleſtan de boſcūbe

.i . uirg habuit . Om̄s trā ſuā uende potuer . De c̄ſuetud

viii . den 7 dim uicecomiti regis p̱ annū reddider.

139 a

In Offelei ten Wilts de mara . viii . hid ¦ 7·viii·acs.ā de Wilto de Ow.

Tra . ē . xvi . car . In dñio ſunt . iiii . 7 xvi . uilti cū p̄bro

7 iii . milit hn̄t . ix . car . 7 iii . adhuc poſſ fieri . Ibi . viii.

bord 7 iiii . cot . 7 viii . ſerui . Paſtura ad pec uillæ . Silua

xii . porc . In totis ualent ual . xi . lib . Q̇do recep̄.

viii . lib . T.R.E. xv . lib . Hoc M̄ tenuit Aleſtan de

boſcūbe . teign . R.E.

.XXIX.   W̄TERRA WILLI DE ODBVRVILE. *IN EDWINESTREV HD.*
ILLELM de Odburguille . ten in Berlai . iiii . hid

7 dim . 7 x . acs . Tra . ē . v . car . In dñio . ii . hidæ 7 dim 7 x . acræ.

7 ibi ſunt . ii . car . 7 viiii . uilti cū . iii . bord hn̄t . iii . car.

Ibi un cot 7 ii . ſerui . Nem ad ſepes . Int tot ual . iiii . lib.

Q̇do recep̄. l . fot . T.R.E. c . fot . Hoc M̄ tenuit Leuuin

teign . R.E. 7 ibi un hō ej . i . uirg habuit . 7 uende potuer.

Alfward, Alstan of Boscombe's man, held this land;
he could not sell, except for the 3 virgates.

In ODSEY Hundred

6 In CLOTHALL William holds ½ virgate and 3 acres. Land for
½ plough; it is there.
The value of this land is and was 29d; before 1066, 3s.
Alstan held this land; it lay in (the lands of) Weston.

* 7 In HINXWORTH 2 men-at-arms hold 2 hides and ½ virgate from
William. Land for 2 ploughs; they are there, with
4 villagers. 3 cottagers; 2 slaves.
Meadow for 1 plough; pasture for the livestock.
Value of this land, 42s 6d; when acquired 20s; before 1066, 60s.
3 Freemen held this land; two of them, King Edward's men,
held 2 hides and ½ virgate; the third, Alstan of Boscombe's man,
had 1 virgate; they could all sell their land. They paid 8½d a year
to the King's Sheriff in customary dues.*

[In the Half-Hundred of HITCHIN]   139 a

8   In OFFLEY William Delamere holds 8 hides and 8 acres from
William of Eu. Land for 16 ploughs. In lordship 4.
16 villagers with a priest and 3 men-at-arms have 9 ploughs;
a further 3 possible. 8 smallholders; 4 cottagers;
8 slaves.
Pasture for the village livestock; woodland, 12 pigs.
Total value £11; when acquired £8; before 1066 £15.
Alstan of Boscombe, a thane of King Edward's, held this manor.

29   LAND OF WILLIAM OF AUBERVILLE

In EDWINSTREE Hundred

*1 William of Auberville holds 4½ hides and 10 acres in BARLEY.
Land for 5 ploughs. In lordship 2½ hides and 10 acres; 2 ploughs there.
9 villagers with 3 smallholders have 3 ploughs. 1 cottager;
2 slaves.
Wood for fences.
In total, value £4; when acquired 50s; before 1066, 100s.
Leofwin, a thane of King Edward's, held this manor; one
of his men had 1 virgate; they could sell.

TERRA WALTERII FLANDRENS.

Walterivs Flandrenſis teñ *MVNDANE* . p v . hiđ
7 una uirg ſe defđ . Tra . ē . viii . car . In dñio . iii . hidæ
7 dimidia . 7 ibi eſt una car . 7 adhuc . ii . poſſunt fieri.
Ibi xii . uilti cū pbro 7 ii . borđ hñt . v . car . Ibi . ii . ſerui.
Paſtura ad pec uillæ . Silua . cc . porc . In totis ualent
ual . vi . liƀ . Qdo recep: vii . liƀ . T.R.E. viii . liƀ . Hoc ⊙
tenuit Leuuin hō Heraldi . 7 uende potuit.
In Sutrehella teñ Walt . i . hiđ 7 dimiđ uirg . Tra . ē
ii . car . Ibi . ē una . 7 alia pot fieri . In dñio . i . hida.
7 uñ uilts . Silua . xv . porc . Val 7 ualuit . xx . ſol . T.R.E.
xxx . ſol . H tra . ē Bereuuicha de Mundena . Torchil
tenuit de Leuuino . ñ potuit uende pter ej licentiā.
In eađ teñ iſđ Walteri . xi . acs . Val 7 ualueʳ ſep
xii . deñ . Leuuiñ tenuit . 7 uende potuit.

TERRA EVDON FILIJ HVBERTI. *IN BRADEWATRE HĐ.*

Evdo Dapifer . 7 Hunfriđ de eo teñ *CHENEPEWORDE.*
p viii . hiđ 7 una uirg ſe defđ . Tra . ē . xii . car . In dñio
. ii . car . 7 alie . ii . poſs fieri . Ibi . xx . uilti cū . ii militiƀ 7 . ii.
borđ . hñt viii . car . Ibi . iii . cot 7 iiii . ſerui . 7 ii . ruſtici.
7 i . moliñ de . xii . ſol . ptū dim car . paſtura ad pec uillæ.
Silua mille porc . In totis ualent ual . x . liƀ . Qdo recep:
c . ſol . T.R.E. xii . liƀ . Hoc ⊙ tenuit Aſchil teigñ R.E.
7 ibi uñ hō ej habuit . i . hiđ 7 i . uirg . 7 uende potuit.
De cſuetuđ . i . Averā inuenieƀ cū rex in ſcyra ueniebat.
Si non: v . denaʳ reddebat.   *IN ODESEI HVND.*
In Retth . teñ Eudo . i . uirg . Tra . ē . ii . bob; . Val 7 ualuit
ſep . ii . ſol . Hanc trā tenuit Sinod hō S Mariæ de Cetriz.
In Berlai teñ Eudo *IN EDWINESTREV HĐ* . [uende potuit.
ii . hiđ 7 xx . acs . Tra . ē . ii . car . In dñio . i . hiđ 7 dim . 7 xx.

30   LAND OF WALTER THE FLEMING

[In BROADWATER Hundred]

*1 Walter the Fleming holds MUNDEN. It answers for 5 hides and
1 virgate. Land for 8 ploughs. In lordship 3½ hides; 1
plough there; a further 2 possible.

     12 villagers with a priest and 2 smallholders have 5 ploughs.
       2 slaves.

     Pasture for the village livestock; woodland, 200 pigs.

Total value £6; when acquired £7; before 1066 £8.

     Leofwin, Earl Harold's man, held this manor; he could sell.

2 In LIBURY Walter holds 1 hide and ½ virgate. Land for 2 ploughs;
1 there; another possible. In lordship 1 hide;

     1 villager.

     Woodland, 15 pigs.

The value is and was 20s; before 1066, 30s.

     This land is an outlier of Munden. Thorkell held it from
Leofwin; he could not sell without his permission.

3 In the same (village) Walter also holds 11 acres.

The value is and always was 12d. Leofwin held it; he could sell.

31   LAND OF EUDO SON OF HUBERT

In BROADWATER Hundred

1 Eudo the Steward holds KNEBWORTH and Humphrey* from him.
It answers for 8 hides and 1 virgate. Land for 12 ploughs.
In lordship 2 ploughs; another 2 possible.

     20 villagers with 2 men-at-arms and 2 smallholders have
       8 ploughs. 3 cottagers; 4 slaves; 2 countrymen.

     1 mill at 12s; meadow for ½ plough; pasture for the
       village livestock; woodland, 1000 pigs.

Total value £10; when acquired 100s; before 1066 £12.

     Askell, a thane of King Edward's, held this manor; one
of his men had 1 hide and 1 virgate; he could sell.

He found 1 cartage in customary dues, when the King came into
the Shire; if not, he paid 5d.*

In ODSEY Hundred

2 In REED Eudo holds 1 virgate. Land for 2 oxen.

The value is and always was 2s.

     Sinoth, St. Mary's of Chatteris' man, held this land; he could sell.

In EDWINSTREE Hundred

3 In BARLEY Eudo holds 2 hides and 20 acres. Land for 2 ploughs.

acræ . 7 laborat cū ꝓpriis car̃ de Nueſſelle . Ibi . IIII . uitti hn̄t . I . car̃ . Ibi . II . ſerui . H̃ t̃ra uał xxx . ſoł . Q̃do recep̃ x . soł . T.R.E. xL . soł . Hanc t̃rā tenuer̃ . II . f̃rs . Hoꝝ unꝰ ſochs hō R.E . fuit . I . hid 7 x . acs habuit . Alt̃ hō Tochi . I . hidā 7 x . acs habuit . Vtriq; uendere potuer̃.

In Bercheuueig . teñ Eudo *NEVSELA* . ꝓ IIII . hid 7 dim̃ uirg̃ ſe . defđ.

In Ichetone teñ Walterꝰ de Eudone . VI . acs . T̃ra . ē . I . boui. Vał 7 ualuit ſep̃ . XII . deñ . Hanc t̃rā tenuit Aldredꝰ teignꝰ . R.E . 7 uendere potuit.

Ricardꝰ de ſachanuilla teñ de Eudone *ABSESDENE*.

139 b
ꝓ una hida 7 dimid ſe defđ . T̃ra . ē . III . car̃ . In dn̄io ſunt . II . car̃ . Pb̄r cū . VI . bord hĩ . I . car̃ . Ibi . III . ſerui . p̃tū . I . car̃ . Silua . xx . porc̃ . Int̃ tot̃ uał IIII . lib̃ . Q̃do recep̃ xxx . soł . T.R.E. Lx . soł . Hoc ꝍ tenuit Aldred teignus . R.E.

Ipſe Eudo teñ *NEVSELA* . ꝓ . v . hid 7 dim̃ uirg̃ ſe defđ . T̃ra . ē . XIIII . car̃ . In dn̄io . III . hide 7 dim̃ uirg̃ . 7 ibi ſunt . v . car̃ . Ibi . x . uitti cū . VI . bord hn̄t . IX . car̃ . Ibi . VII . cot̃ 7 XXI . ſeruus . p̃tū . I . car̃ . Silua . c . porc̃ . paſtura ad pec̃ uillæ . In totis ualentijs uał . XVIII . lib̃ . Q̃do recep̃ VI . lib̃ . T.R.E. XII . lib̃ . De hoc ꝍ tenuit Aldred teignꝰ . R.E . IIII . hid 7 dim̃ uirg̃ . 7 ibi unꝰ ſochs hō Algari comit̃ tenuit III . uirg̃ . 7 alt̃ ſochs hō Aldredi p̃dicti . I . uirg̃ habuit. Hic . I . denar̃ p annū uicecomiti reddidit . Om̃s ũ terrā ſuā uende potuer̃ . *IN HERTFORD HVND.*

Hunfridꝰ de Eudone teñ dimid hid.

T̃ra . ē . II . car̃ . In dn̄io eſt una . 7 IIII . bord hn̄t unā car̃ . Ibi . VII . cot̃ . 7 I . mol de . VI . soł 7 VIII.

In lordship 1½ hides and 20 acres. He works them with his own ploughs from Newsells.

4 villagers have 1 plough. 2 slaves.

Value of this land, 30s; when acquired 10s; before 1066, 40s.

Two brothers held this land. One of them, a Freeman, was King Edward's man; he had 1 hide and 10 acres. The second, Toki's man, had 1 hide and 10 acres; either could sell.

*4 In BARKWAY Eudo holds NEWSELLS. It answers for 4 hides and ½ virgate.

5 In BUNTINGFORD Walter holds 6 acres from Eudo. Land for 1 ox. The value is and always was 12d.

Aldred, a thane of King Edward's, held this land; he could sell.

*6 Richard of Sackville holds ASPENDEN from Eudo. It answers for 1½ hides. Land for 3 ploughs. In lordship 2 ploughs. 139b

A priest, with 6 smallholders, has 1 plough. 3 slaves.

Meadow for 1 plough; woodland, 20 pigs.

In total, value £4; when acquired 30s; before 1066, 60s.

Aldred, a thane of King Edward's, held this manor.

*7 Eudo holds NEWSELLS himself. It answers for 5 hides and ½ virgate. Land for 14 ploughs. In lordship 3 hides and ½ virgate; 5 ploughs there.

10 villagers with 6 smallholders have 9 ploughs. 7 cottagers;
    21 slaves.

Meadow for 1 plough; woodland, 100 pigs;
    pasture for the village livestock.

Total value £18; when acquired £6; before 1066 £12.

Aldred, a thane of King Edward's, held 4 hides and ½ virgate of this manor. A Freeman, Earl Algar's man, held 3 virgates; a second Freeman, the said Aldred's man, had 1 virgate; the latter paid 1d a year to the Sheriff; all could sell their land.

In HERTFORD Hundred

*8 Humphrey holds ½ hide from Eudo. Land for 2 ploughs. In lordship 1.

4 smallholders have 1 plough. 7 cottagers.

den̅ . Silua . I . porc̅ . Int̅ totū ual 7 ualuit fẽp

LX . fol . Hanc t̅r̅a tenuit Lefsi p̅pofit . R.E.

7 uende potuit . Hanc t̅r̅a abftulit eid Lefsi

eps baiocenfis . 7 dedit Eudoni . 7 occupata eft

fup regẽ . Cū qua fūpfit Hunfrid qdo de Eudone

recep̅. LXVIII . Aalia . 7 ccc̅ . L . oues . 7 cL . porc̅.

7 L . cap̅s . 7 I . equā . 7 XIII . fol 7 IIII . den̅ de cenfu

regis . 7 Int̅ pannos 7 uafa. xx . fol.

.XXXII. **TERRA EDWARDI VICECOM̅ . *IN DANEIS HVND̅.***

Edward de Sarifberie ten̅ *GATESDENE.*

.p . VI . hid̅ fe defd̅ . T.R.E. 7 m̅ .p . III . hid̅ . Sed una

ex iftis fe defd̅ in Treunge hund . 7 hic app̅cianda

eft . Tra . ẽ . XII . car̅ . In dñio . II . hide . 7 ibi funt . IIII.

car̅ . 7 xv . uitti cū p̅bro hn̅t . VI . car̅ . 7 adhuc . II.

poffunt fieri . Ibi . II . bord̅ 7 I . cot̅ . 7 VIII . ferui.

7 I . mot̅ de . V . fol . p̅tū . I . car̅ 7 dim̅ . Paftura ad

pec̅ uillæ . Silua qngent porc̅ . In totis ualent

ual xx.II . lib̅ . Qdo recep̅. xx . lib̅ . T.R.E. xxv.

lib̅ . Hoc M̅ tenuit Wluuen die qua rex . E . fuit

uiuus 7 mortuus . de abbe S̅ Albani . Non poterat

mittere ext̅ æcctam . fed p̅ mortẽ fuā redire

debebat ad æcctam . ut hund̅ teftat̅ . *IN HERTFORD*

In Odefdone . ten̅ Eduuard . IIII . hid̅   *HVND̅.*

xxx . ac̅s min̅ . Tra . ẽ . III . car̅ . In dñio . III . hidæ.

7 ibi . ẽ una car̅ . 7 IIII . uitti cū . II . bord̅ hn̅t

unā car̅ . 7 alia pot̅ fieri . Ibi . V . cot̅ 7 II . ferui.

p̅tū . IIII . car̅ . Silua . xx . porc̅ . De pifcar̅ . cL.

Anguitt . Vat̅ . LX . fol . Qdo recep̅. xxx . fol.

T.R.E. LX . fol . Hoc M̅ tenuit Gode de regina

Eddid . 7 uende potuit.

1 mill at 6s 8d; woodland, 50 pigs.
In total, the value is and always was 60s.

Leofsi, King Edward's reeve, held this land; he could sell.
The Bishop of Bayeux took this land away from Leofsi and
gave it to Eudo; it has been appropriated in the King's despite.
When Humphrey acquired it from Eudo, he took over with it 68 cattle;
350 sheep; 150 pigs; 50 goats; 1 mare; 13s 4d of King's dues;
cloths and vessels, 20s together.

32   LAND OF EDWARD THE SHERIFF

In DACORUM Hundred

*1 Edward of Salisbury holds (GREAT) GADDESDEN. It answered for
6 hides before 1066; now for 3 hides; but one of them
answers in Tring Hundred, and is assessed here. Land
for 12 ploughs. In lordship 2 hides; 4 ploughs there.
    15 villagers with a priest have 6 ploughs; a further 2
        possible. 2 smallholders; 1 cottager; 8 slaves.
    1 mill at 5s; meadow for 1½ ploughs; pasture for the village
        livestock; woodland, 500 pigs.
Total value £22; when acquired £20; before 1066 £25.

Wulfwen held this manor in 1066 from the Abbot of St. Albans;
she could not dispose of it outside the church, but after her
death it was to return to the Church, as the Hundred testifies.

In HERTFORD Hundred

2 Edward holds 4 hides less 30 acres in HODDESDON. Land for
3 ploughs. In lordship 3 hides; 1 plough there.
    4 villagers with 2 smallholders have 1 plough; another
        possible. 5 cottagers; 2 slaves.
Meadow for 4 ploughs; woodland, 20 pigs; from the fishery, 150 eels.
Value 60s; when acquired 30s; before 1066, 60s.

Gode held this manor from Queen Edith; she could sell.

G TERRA GOISFR DE MANNE ᵁᴵᴸᴱ *IN DANEIS HVND.*

OISFRIDVS de Manneuile 7 Radulf⁹
de eo ten in Titeberſt . III . uirg⁷ . Tra . ē diɱ car⁷.

139 c

Ibi . I . uilʌs 7 I . borđ . Silua . XII . porc⁷ . Val 7 ua
luit . v . ſoł . T.R.E. x.ſoł . Hanc trā tenuer⁷
tenuer⁷ . III . ſochi . Duo eoↄ hōes Aſgari ſtalri.
7 tcius hō S̄ Albani . n̄ potuit uende . ſed alij . II.

Ipſe Goisfrid ten̄ *BISSEI* . ᵱ xv.   ᴶ potuer⁷.
hiđ ſe defđ⁷ . Tra . ē . x . car⁷ . In dn̄io . v . hidæ.
7 ibi ſunt . II . car⁷ . 7 tcia poᵗ fieri . ibi . x . uilʌi
cū uno francig⁷ 7 vIII . borđ hn̄t . v . car⁷ . 7 vI.ᵗᵃ
poᵗ fieri . Ibi . II . molin⁷ de . vIII . ſoliđ.
Paſtura ad pecun⁷ . Silua . mille porc⁷ . In totis
ualent⁷ ual 7 ualuit . x . liƀ . T.R.E. xv . liƀ.
Hoc M̄ tenuit Leuuin⁹ teign⁹ R.E . Ibi . ē un⁹
ſochs qui n̄ fuit ibi T.R.E . unā hidā habet.
hō reginæ Eddiđ fuit . T.R.E . 7 uende⁷ poᵗ.

Ipſe Goisfriđ⁹ ten̄⁷ *SENLAI* . ᵱ vIII . hiđ
7 III . uirg⁹ ſe defđ⁷ . Tra . ē . Ix . car⁷ . In dn̄io
III . hidæ . 7 ibi ſunt . II . car⁷ . Ibi . xII . uilʌi
hn̄t . IIII . car⁷ . 7 adhuc . III . poſſunt fieri . P̊tū
un̄ car⁷ . Paſtura ad pec⁷ . Silua ſexcentis
porc⁷ . In totis ualent ual . IIII . liƀ . Qdo recep̷⁷
v . liƀ . T.R.E. vIII . liƀ . Hoc M̄ tenuit Aſgar
7 ibi . II . ſochi hōes ej⁹ habuer⁷ . I . hiđ 7 III . uirg⁷.

In Chaiſſou . *IN ALBANESTOV* H̄ ᴶ 7 uende⁷ poᵗ.
ten̄ Turolđ de Goisfrido . I . hiđ . Tra . ē . I . car⁷.
ſed n̄ eſt ibi . P̊tū . I . car⁷ . Silua . xxx . porc⁷.

In DACORUM Hundred

1 Geoffrey de Mandeville holds 3 virgates in THEOBALD STREET, and
   Ralph from him. Land for ½ plough.
       1 villager; 1 smallholder.   139c
       Woodland, 12 pigs.
   The value is and was 5s; before 1066, 10s.
       3 Freemen held this land. Two of them were Asgar the
   Constable's men; the third, St. Albans' man, could not sell,
   but the other 2 could.

*2 Geoffrey holds BUSHEY himself. It answers for 15 hides. Land for 10
   ploughs. In lordship 5 hides; 2 ploughs there; a third possible.
       10 villagers with 1 Frenchman and 8 smallholders have 5
           ploughs; a sixth possible.
       2 mills at 8s; pasture for the livestock; woodland, 1000 pigs.
   The total value is and was £10; before 1066 £15.
       Leofwin, a thane of King Edward's, held this manor. 1 Freeman
   there, who was not there before 1066; he has 1 hide; before
   1066 he was Queen Edith's man; he could sell.

3 Geoffrey holds SHENLEY himself. It answers for 8 hides and 3
   virgates. Land for 9 ploughs. In lordship 3 hides; 2 ploughs
   there.
       12 villagers have 4 ploughs; a further 3 possible.
       Meadow for 1 plough; pasture for the livestock; woodland, 600 pigs.
   Total value £4; when acquired £5; before 1066 £8.
       Asgar held this manor; 2 Freemen, his men, had 1 hide
   and 3 virgates; they could sell.

In CASHIO Hundred

4 In CASSIO Thorold holds 1 hide from Geoffrey. Land for 1 plough,
   but it is not there.
       Meadow for 1 plough; woodland, 30 pigs.

Val 7 ualuit.v.fot.T.R.E. xx.fot.Hanc tra
tenuit Aiuuin uenator hõ Eddid reginæ.
7 uende potuit.Hanc appofuit Goisfrid in
Biffei.ubi ñ fuit T.R.E. *IN BRADEWATRE HD.*
In Dichelefuuelle.ten Torchil de Goisfrido
II.hid.Tra.ē.vIIII.car 7 dim.In dñio.II.fuŋ car.
7 XII.uilli cũ.III.borð hñt.vI.car 7 dim.Ibi
IIII.cot.7 II.ferui.7 uñ molin 7 dim de.vIII.
fot.7 vIII.deñ.Paftura ad pec.Silua.c.porc.
Int tot ual.IIII.lib.Qdo recep. L.fot.T.R.E.
IIII.lib.Ifd tenuit T.R.E.qui nc ten.hõ Afgari
ftalre fuit.7 uende potuit. *IN ODESEI HD.*
In Wallingtone ten Siuuard de Goisfrido
.I.uirg.Tra.ē dim car.s; ñ ē ibi.nifi.I.cot.
Val.v.fot.Qdo recep. III.fot.T.R.E. x.fot.
Hanc tra tenuit Edred.hõ Afgari.7 uende pot.
In Afceuuelle.ten Germund de Goisfrido
.I.uirg.Tra.ē dim car.7 ibi.ē cũ.II.borð.ptũ
dim car.Val 7 ualuit fep.x.fot.Hanc tra
tenuit Godeue de Afgaro.ñ potuit uende
In Hainftone ten Germund ⌐ pt ej lictia.
de Goisfrido.II.hid.7 IIII.part unius uirg
p uno M.Tra.ē.II.car.Ibi eft una in dñio.
7 alia pot fieri.Ibi.v.uilli cũ.IIII.borð.
Paftura ad pec.ptũ.I.car.H tra ual.III.fot.
Qdo recep. xxx.fot.T.R.E. IIII.lib.Hanc tra
tenuit Wluric hõ Afgari.uende potuit.

The value is and was 5s; before 1066, 20s.

Alwin Hunter, Queen Edith's man, held this land; he could sell. Geoffrey placed this land in Bushey, where it was not before 1066.

In BROADWATER Hundred

5 In DIGSWELL Thorkell holds 2 hides from Geoffrey. Land for 8½ ploughs. In lordship 2 ploughs.

12 villagers with 3 smallholders have 6½ ploughs.

4 cottagers; 2 slaves.

1½ mills at 8s 8d; pasture for the livestock; woodland, 100 pigs. In total, value £4; when acquired 50s; before 1066 £4.

The present holder also held it before 1066; he was Asgar the Constable's man; he could sell.

In ODSEY Hundred

6 In WALLINGTON Siward holds 1 virgate from Geoffrey. Land for ½ plough, but it is not there; only

1 cottager.

Value 5s; when acquired 3s; before 1066, 10s.

Edred, Asgar's man, held this land; he could sell.

*7 In ASHWELL Germund holds 1 virgate from Geoffrey. Land for ½ plough; it is there, with

2 smallholders.

Meadow for ½ plough.

The value is and always was 10s.

Godiva held this land from Asgar; she could not sell without his permission.

*8 In HAINSTONE Germund holds from Geoffrey 2 hides and the fourth part of 1 virgate as one manor. Land for 2 ploughs. 1 is there, in lordship; another possible.

5 villagers with 4 smallholders.

Pasture for the livestock; meadow for 1 plough.

Value of this land, 3s; when acquired 30s; before 1066 £4.

Wulfric, Asgar the Constable's man, held this land; he could sell.

In Bercheuuei . tenͧ Hugo   *IN EDWINESTREV HD.*

de Goisfrido . iii . hidͤ ꝑ uno M̄ . Tͧra .ē . vii . carͧ . In

dñio funt . iii . 7 xii . uilti cū pͣbro 7 xv . bordͤ hn̄t

iiii . carͧ . ibi . iiii . cotͧ 7 vi . ſerui . p̄tū dim carͧ . Paſtura

ad pecͧ . Silua . l . porcͧ . De paſtura 7 ſilua . ii . ſolidͤ

7 iii . ſocos . In totis ualent ualͧ . vi . libͤ . Qͤdo recep̄.

iii . libͤ . T.R.E. vi . libͤ . Hoc M̄ tenuerͧ . ii . hͦes Aſgari ᶠᵗᵃˡʳᵉ

Iṇ Langeport tenͧ Sauuardͧ de Goisfrͧ 𝄐 7 uendeͧ potuerͧ .

. i . uirgͧ . Tͧra .ē dim carͧ . 7 ibi eſt cū . i . cotͧ 7 ii . ſeruis .

Valͧ 7 ualuit ſͤep . v . ſolͧ . Alured tenuit hͦ Aſgari . uendeͧ

Iṇ Bordeſdene tenͧ Turaldͧ de Goisfrido 𝄐 potuit .

dim hidͤ 7 . ix . acͧs . Tͧra .ē . ii . carͧ 7 dim . In dñio .ē una .

7 ii . uilti cū . ii . bordͤ hn̄t . i . carͧ 7 dimͧ . Paſtura ad pecͧ .

p̄tū . i . carͧ . Nemͧ ad ſepes . H̄ tͧra ualͧ . xx . ſolͧ Qͤdo recep̄.

x . ſolͧ . T.R.E. xl . ſochͧ . Hanc tͧra tenuerͧ . iiii . ſochi

de ſoca Aſgari ſtalri . 7 uendeͧ potuerͧ . *IN HERTFORD HD.*

Iṇ Stiuiceſuuorde tenͧ Germundͧ de Goisfrͧ . i . hidͤ

Tͧra .ē . i . carͧ 7 dim . Ibi .ē una . 7 dim pot fieri . Ibi . iii . cotͧ

7 ii . ſerui . P̄tū . i carͧ 7 dimͧ . 7 ad dñicū opͧ . Silua . c . porcͧ .

Paſtura ad pecunͧ . Valͧ 7 ualuit . xx . ſolͧ . T.R.E. xl . ſolͧ .

Hoc M̄ tenuit Burgiͧ hͦ Aſgari . 7 uendeͧ potuit .

Iṇ hodeſdone tenͧ Radulfͧ de Goisfrͧ . i . hidͤ . Tͧra .ē . i . carͧ .

7 ibi .ē cū . iii . bordͤ 7 ii . cotͧ . Ibi . i . ſeruͧ . p̄tū . i . carͧ . Paſtaͧ

ad pecͧ . Silua . l . porcͧ . De gugite . xxii . anguilt . H̄ tͧra

ualͧ . xx . ſolͧ . Qͤdo recep̄. v . ſolͧ . T.R.E. xl . ſolͧ . Hanc

tͧra tenuit Godid hͦ Aſgari ſtalri . 7 uendeͧ potuit .

In EDWINSTREE Hundred

9 In BARKWAY Hugh holds 3 hides from Geoffrey as 1 manor.
Land for 7 ploughs. In lordship 3.
    12 villagers with a priest and 15 smallholders have 4 ploughs.
       4 cottagers; 6 slaves.
    Meadow for ½ plough; pasture for the livestock; woodland,
       50 pigs; from pasture and woodland, 2s, and [he has] 3
       ploughshares.*
Total value £6; when acquired £3; before 1066 £6.
    Two of Asgar the Constable's men held this manor; they could sell.

10 In HARE STREET Saeward holds 1 virgate from Geoffrey. Land
for ½ plough; it is there, with
    1 cottager; 2 slaves.
The value is and always was 5s.
    Alfred, Asgar's man, held it; he could sell.

11 In BOZEN Thorold holds ½ hide and 9 acres from Geoffrey.
Land for 2½ ploughs. In lordship 1.
    2 villagers with 2 smallholders have 1½ ploughs.
    Pasture for the livestock; meadow for 1 plough; wood for fences.
Value of this land, 20s; when acquired 10s; before 1066, 40[s].*
    4 Freemen, of Asgar the Constable's jurisdiction, held this land;
they could sell.

In HERTFORD Hundred
*12 In 'STETCHWORTH' Germund holds 1 hide from Geoffrey.
Land for 1½ ploughs; 1 there; ½ possible.
    3 cottagers; 2 slaves.
    Meadow for 1½ ploughs, and for the lord's work;
       woodland, 100 pigs; pasture for the livestock.
The value is and was 20s; before 1066, 40s.
    Burgi, Asgar's man, held this manor; he could sell.

* 13 In HODDESDON Ralph holds 1 hide from Geoffrey. Land for 1 plough;
it is there, with
    3 smallholders; 2 cottagers. 1 slave.
    Meadow for 1 plough; pasture for the livestock;
       woodland, 50 pigs; from weirs, 22 eels.
Value of this land, 20s; when acquired 5s; before 1066, 40s.
    Godith, Asgar the Constable's man, held this land; she could sell.

In Brichendone ten̄ Walteri⁹ de Goisfr̄.ɪ.uirg trǽ.
Tra.ē dim̄ car̄.7 ibi.ē cū.ɪ.cot.Silua.xʟ.porc.Val
7 ualuit.v.ſoł.T.R.E.́x.ſoł.Hanc tr̄a tenuit Oſuui
hō Aſgari ſtalri.7 uendē potuit.
In Belingehou.ten̄ Huard⁹ de Goisfr̄.ɪɪɪ.hiđ 7 ɪ.uirḡ.
Tra.ē.ɪɪɪɪ.car̄.In dn̄io.ē una.7 alia car̄ pot fieri.Ibi
ɪɪɪ.uiłłi cū.ɪɪ.borđ hn̄t.ɪɪ.car̄.Ibi.vɪ.cot.7 ɪ.molin̄
de.x.ſoł.P̃tū.ɪ.car̄.Paſt̄a ad pecuñ.Silua.ɪɪɪɪ.porc.
Int tot̄ ual̄.xʟv.ſoł.Q̇do recep.́xʟ.ſoł.T.R.E.́ɪɪɪɪ.liƀ.
Hoc m̄ tenuit Turchil hō Aſgari ſtalri.7 uendē potuit.
In Staneſtede ten̄ q̇d̄a ſochs de Goisfr̄ IN BRACHINGS HD̆.
dim̄ uirḡ.Tra.ē.ɪɪ.bob.7 ibi ſunt.p̃tū.vɪ.bob.Silua.ɪ.porc.
Val 7 ualuit ſēp.ɪɪ.ſoł.Iſtemet tenuit T.R.E.hō Aſgari
fuit.7 uendē potuit.
Ipſe Goisfrid⁹ ten̄ SABRIXTEWORDE.p̣.xxɪɪɪɪ.hiđ
7 dim̄.Tra.ē.xʟ.car̄.In dn̄io.xv.hidǽ.7 ibi ſunt.x.
car̄.7 adhuc.ɪɪ.poſ̄ fieri.Ibi.ʟ.uiłłi.7 ɪɪɪɪ.ſochi cū pƀro
hn̄t.xxvɪɪɪ.car̄.P̃poſit ħt dim̄ hiđ.Pƀr.ɪ.hiđ.Ex
uiłłis.xɪɪɪɪ.́q̇ſq̢ una uirḡ.7 xxxv.́uiłłi.́q̇ſq̢ dim̄ uirḡ.
7 p̃dicti uiłłi ten.ɪ.uirḡ 7 dim̄ 7 ɪx.ac̄s unde reddunt
xvɪɪ.ſoł 7.ɪɪɪɪ.deñ.p̣ annū.Ibi.xʟvɪ.borđ q̇ſq̢ ħt.vɪɪɪ.
ac̄s.7 ɪɪ.borđ de.x.ac̄s.7 xx.cot de.xxvɪ.ac̄s.7 ibi
xxx.cot.7 xxx.ſerui.Sub ſochis.ſunt.vɪɪ.cot.Aſgar⁹
ħt.ɪɪ.hiđ.Sub eo ſuɴ.ɪɪ.uiłłi.7 vɪɪ.borđ.7 ɪɪɪ.cot.7 ɪɪɪɪ.
ſerui.Kip.ħt dim̄ hiđ.7 ɪ.molin̄ de.xx.ſoł.7 alter
ſochs de.v.ſoł 7 ɪɪɪɪ.deñ.p̃tū.xx.car̄.Paſt̄a ad pec.́
Silua.ccc.porc.7 de reddita earū.́ɪɪɪɪ.ſoł.In totis
ualent.́ual̄.ʟ.liƀ.Q̇do recep.́ʟx.liƀ.7 tn̄tđ.T.R.E.

14 In BRICKENDON Walter holds 1 virgate of land from Geoffrey.
Land for ½ plough; it is there, with
1 cottager.
Woodland, 40 pigs.
The value is and was 5s; before 1066, 10s.
Oswy, Asgar the Constable's man, held this land; he could sell.

*15 In BENGEO Howard holds 3 hides and 1 virgate from Geoffrey.
Land for 4 ploughs. In lordship 1; another plough possible.
3 villagers with 2 smallholders have 2 ploughs. 6 cottagers.
1 mill at 10s; meadow for 1 plough; pasture for the livestock;
woodland, 4 pigs.
In total, value 45s; when acquired 40s; before 1066 £4.
Thorkell, Asgar the Constable's man, held this manor; he could sell.

In BRAUGHING Hundred
16 In STANSTEAD a Freeman holds ½ virgate from Geoffrey.
Land for 2 oxen; they are there.
Meadow for 6 oxen; woodland, 1 pig.
The value is and always was 2s.
He held it himself before 1066; he was Asgar's man; he could sell.

*17 Geoffrey holds SAWBRIDGEWORTH himself for 24½ hides. Land for 40
ploughs. In lordship 15 hides; 10 ploughs there; a further 2 possible.
50 villagers and 4 Freemen with a priest have 28 ploughs.
A reeve has ½ hide; a priest 1 hide. 14 of the villagers, 1 virgate
each; 35 villagers, ½ virgate each; and the said villagers
hold 1½ virgates and 9 acres, from which they pay 17s 4d a year.
46 smallholders have 8 acres each; 2 smallholders with 10 acres;
20 cottagers with 26 acres. 30 cottagers; 30 slaves.
Under the Freemen are 7 cottagers.
Asgar has 2 hides; under him are
2 villagers, 7 smallholders, 3 cottagers and 4 slaves.
Kip has ½ hide and
1 mill at 20s.
Another Freeman at 5s 4d.
Meadow for 20 ploughs; pasture for the livestock;
woodland, 300 pigs; and from their payments 4s.
Total value £50; when acquired £60; before 1066 as much.

Hoc m̄ tenuit Afgar ftalr. 7 ibi fuer̄. II. fochi. Duo eoꝛ

hoēs ejđ Afgari. dim̄ hiđ habuer̄. 7 uende pot

p̄ter foca. Terci hō Heraldi. I. uirg habuit.

7 quart hō Aluuini de Godtone. I. uirg habuit.

hi uende 7 dare potuer̄. Soca fuit Afgari ftalri.

7 adhuc. I. focħs hō Afgari. II. hiđ habuit. fed

uende n̄ potuit.

Ipfe Goisfr̄ ten̄ *TORLEI*. p IIII. hiđ fe defđ. Tra

ē. VIII. car̄. In dn̄io. II. hidæ. 7 ibi funt. IIII. car̄.

Ibi. V. uiłłi 7 q̄đa milite. 7 cū p̄bro 7 IX. borđ.

hnt. III. car̄ 7 dim̄. 7 adhuc dim̄ pot fieri. Ibi. XI.

ferui. 7 I. moliñ de. X. fol. p̄tū. II. car̄. Silua

XL. porc̄. Pafta ad pecuñ. In totis ualent uał. VIII.

lib. Q̄do recep̄. c. fol. T.R.E. x. liƀ. Hoc m̄ te

nuit Godid hō Afgari ftalre. 7 uende potuit.

Hoc m̄ emit Wiłłs ep̄s Lundon a rege Wiłło.

p cceffionē ejđ Godid. 7 m̄ reclamat ep̄s Lundon.

In Wicheħa ten̄. I. focħs de Goisfr̄. VIII. acs.

Tra. ē. II. boƀ. Silua. II. porc̄. Vał 7 ualuit fēp. XVI.

den̄. Iftemet tenuit. T.R.E. hō Godid fuit. 7 uende

potuit. De foca regis fuit. In Wicheħa jacuit T.R.E.

Hunc focħum appofuit Goisfr̄ in Torlei. ubi n̄ fuit

In Wicheħa ten̄. II. milites de Goisfr̄   ⌐ T.R.E.

. I. hiđ 7 III. acs. Tra. ē. II. car̄. In dn̄io. ē una. 7 alia

pot fieri. p̄tū. I. car̄. Silua. XIIII. porc̄. Int tot uał

x. fol. Q̄do recep̄. XX. fol. T.R.E. XL. fol. Hanc tra

tenuer̄. II. fochi hoēs Afgari. 7 uende potuer̄.

Asgar the Constable held this manor. There were 4 Freemen 140 a
there; two of them, Asgar's men, had ½ hide; they could sell,
except for the jurisdiction; the third, Earl Harold's man, had 1
virgate; the fourth, Alwin of Gotton's man, had 1 virgate; these
could sell and grant. The jurisdiction was Asgar the Constable's. 1
further Freeman, Asgar's man, had 2 hides; but he could not sell.

*18 Geoffrey holds THORLEY himself. It answers for 4 hides.
Land for 8 ploughs. In lordship 2 hides; 4 ploughs there.
    5 villagers, [with] a man-at-arms and with a priest and 9
       smallholders, have 3½ ploughs; a further ½ possible. 11 slaves.
    1 mill at 10s; meadow for 2 ploughs; woodland, 40 pigs;
       pasture for the livestock.
Total value £8; when acquired 100s; before 1066 £10.
    Godith, Asgar the Constable's man, held this manor;
she could sell. William, Bishop of London, bought this manor
from King William with Godith's consent; the Bishop of
London now claims it.

19 In WICKHAM 1 Freeman holds 8 acres from Geoffrey. Land for 2 oxen.
    Woodland, 2 pigs.
The value is and always was 16d.
    He held it himself before 1066; he was Godith's man;
he could sell; he was of the King's jurisdiction. Before 1066
it lay in (the lands of) Wickham. Geoffrey placed this Freeman
in Thorley; he was not there before 1066.

20 In WICKHAM 2 men-at-arms hold 1 hide and 3 acres from Geoffrey.
Land for 2 ploughs. In lordship 1; another possible.
    Meadow for 1 plough; woodland, 14 pigs.
In total, value 10s; when acquired 20s; before 1066, 40s.
    2 Freemen, Asgar's men, held this land; they could sell.

TERRA GOISFRIDI DE BECH . *IN DANEIS HVND.*

GOISFRID de Bech In Wenriga 7 Radulf de eo ten
.i.hid 7 dim.Tra.ē.ii.car.Ibi.ē una.7 alta pot fieri.
Ibi.iii.bord.Silua.ccc.porc.Paftura ad pec. Ħ tra
ual 7 ualuit.xx.fot.T.R.E.'l.fot.Hanc trā tenuit Æilmar
hō Leuuini.7 uende potuit.

In Titeberft ten Louet de Goisfr dim hid .Tra.ē.vi.bob.
7 ibi.ē un uilts.Silua.xxiiii.porc.Val 7 ualuit fēp.
v.fot.Hanc trā tenuit qdā fochs hō abbis S Albani.
7 uende potuit.   *IN BRADEWATRE HVND.*

In Daceuuorde ten.ii.milit.ii.uirg 7 dim.de Goisfrido.
Tra.ē.i.car.7 ibi.ē cū.iii.uiltis.Val 7 ualuit.xii.fot
7 viii.den .T.R.E.'xx.fot.Hanc trā tenuer.iii.fochi
hōes.R.E.7 uende potuer.

In Welge ten Rogeri de Goisfr.ii.hid.Tra.ē.vii.
car.In dñio eft una.7 alia pot fieri.Ibi.vi.uilti cū
iiii.bord hñt.iiii.car.7 v.pot fieri.Ibi.iiii.cot
7 i.feruus.7 i.molin de.viii.fot.ptū.ii.car.Paftura
ad pecun.Silua.xx.porc.Int tot ual.l.fot.Qdo
recep.'xx.fot.T.R.E.'vi.lib.Hanc trā tenuer Gode
7 filius ej de Eddid regina.7 uende potuer.

In Langelei.ten Otbtus de Goisfr.i.hid 7 dim.Tra.ē
iii.car.Ibi.ē una.7 ii.pofs fieri.Ibi.ii.uilti.7.iiii.
cot.Ibi.i.feruus.ptū.i.boui.Silua.ci.porc.Val
xxx.fot.Qdo recep.'xxv.fot.T.R.E.'xxx.fot.Hoc ⊕
tenuit Suuen hō Heraldi.7 uende potuit.

LAND OF GEOFFREY OF BEC

In DACORUM Hundred

1 Geoffrey of Bec holds 1½ hides in WINDRIDGE and Ralph from him.
Land for 2 ploughs; 1 there; a second possible.
3 smallholders.
Woodland, 300 pigs; pasture for the livestock.
The value of this land is and was 20s; before 1066, 50s.
Aelmer, Earl Leofwin's man, held this land; he could sell.

2 In THEOBALD STREET Lovett holds ½ hide from Geoffrey. Land
for 6 oxen.
1 villager.
Woodland, 24 pigs.
The value is and always was 5s.
A Freeman, the Abbot of St. Albans' man, held this land; he could sell.

In BROADWATER Hundred

3 In DATCHWORTH 2 men-at-arms hold 2½ virgates from Geoffrey.
Land for 1 plough; it is there, with
3 villagers.
The value is and was 12s 8d; before 1066, 20s.
3 Freemen, King Edward's men, held this land; they could sell.

*4 In WELWYN Roger holds 2 hides from Geoffrey. Land for 7 ploughs.
In lordship 1; another possible.
6 villagers with 4 smallholders have 4 ploughs; a fifth
possible. 4 cottagers; 1 slave.
1 mill at 8s; meadow for 2 ploughs; pasture for the
livestock; woodland, 20 pigs.
In total, value 50s; when acquired 20s; before 1066 £6.
Gode and her son held this land from Queen Edith; they could sell.

*5 In LANGLEY Osbert holds 1½ hides from Geoffrey.
Land for 3 ploughs; 1 there; 2 possible.
2 villagers; 4 cottagers. 1 slave.
Meadow for 1 ox; woodland, 150 pigs.
Value 30s; when acquired 25s; before 1066, 30s.
Swein, Earl Harold's man, held this manor; he could sell.

Ìn Scelue . teñ Aluric de Goisfr̃ dim̃ uirg̃ . Tra . ẽ

II . boḃ . 7 ibi ſunt . H̃ tra ual 7 ualuit ſẽp . v . ſol . Iſtemet

tenuit T.R.E. hõ Suuen fuit de ſoca regis . E . de c̃ſue

tudine . I . obolũ reddeḃ uicecomiti p̃ annũ .

Ìn Wilie . teñ ipſe Goisfrid de bec̃h . v . hid 7 I . uirg̃ .

Tra . ẽ . IX . car̃ . In dñio . II . hidæ . 7 ibi ſunt . II . car̃ . 7 aliæ

II . poſſ fieri . Ibi . x . uilti cũ . I . milite 7 IIII bord̃ hñt

. v . car̃ . p̃tũ dim̃ car̃ . Paſtura ad pecuñ . Nem̃ ad ſepes .

Int̃ tot̃ ual . x . liḃ 7 XIIII . ſol . Q̃do recep̃ . IIII . liḃ .

T.R.E. XII . liḃ . Hoc m̃ tenuit Leuric Huſcarl Leuuini com̃ .

7 uende̅ potuit . 7 ibi . I . ſoc̃hſ hõ Elmari de Benintone

dim̃ hid̃ habuit . 7 uende̅ potuit . 7 una uidua dim̃ hid̃

habuit . x . ac̃s miñ . ñ potuit uende̅ p̃t licentiã Goduini

Ìn Rodehangre teñ Louet de Goisf̃ ſ de Laceuuorde .

. I . uirg̃ . Tra . ẽ . II . bobʒ . Val 7 ualuit ſẽp . XLIIII . deñ .

Hanc tr̃a tenuit Aluuin ſoc̃hs . R.E. 7 uende̅ potuit .

7 uñ denariũ reddeḃ uicecomiti de c̃ſuetudine .

Ìn Berlai teñ Ansfrid Goisf̃r . *IN EDWINESTREV HD.*

xx . ac̃s . Tra . ẽ . II . bobʒ . Val 7 ualuit ſẽp . III . ſol . Hanc

tram tenuit Algar hõ Wigar . 7 uende̅ potuit .

Ìn Cochenac teñ Ansfrid de Goisf̃r . I . hid̃ 7 XII . ac̃s .

Tra . ẽ . IIII . car̃ . In dñio ſunt . II . 7 ibi . I . uiltſ cũ . VIII .

bord̃ hñt . II . car̃ . Ibi . VI . cot 7 I . ſeruus . P̃tũ . I . car̃ .

6 In CHELLS Aelfric Bush holds ½ virgate from Geoffrey.
Land for 2 oxen; they are there.
The value of this land is and always was 5s.
   He held it himself before 1066; he was Swein's man, of
King Edward's jurisdiction; he paid ½d a year to the
Sheriff in customary dues.

*7 In WILLIAN Geoffrey of Bec holds 5 hides and 1 virgate himself.
Land for 9 ploughs. In lordship 2 hides; 2 ploughs there;
another 2 possible.
   10 villagers with 1 man-at-arms and 4 smallholders have 5 ploughs.
   Meadow for ½ plough; pasture for the livestock; wood for fences.
In total, value £10 14s; when acquired £4; before 1066 £12.
   Leofric, one of Earl Leofwin's Guards, held this manor; he could sell.
A Freeman, Aelmer of Bennington's man, had ½ hide;
he could sell. A widow had ½ hide less 10 acres; she could not
sell without Godwin of Letchworth's permission.

*8 In 'RODHANGER' Lovett holds 1 virgate from Geoffrey.
Land for 2 oxen.
The value is and always was 44d.
   Alwin, a Freeman of King Edward's, held this land; he could sell.
He paid 1 penny to the Sheriff in customary dues.

   In EDWINSTREE Hundred
*9 In BARLEY Ansfrid holds 20 acres from Geoffrey. Land for 2 oxen.
The value is and always was 3s.
   Algar, Withgar's man, held this land; he could sell.

10 In COKENACH Ansfrid holds 1 hide and 12 acres from Geoffrey.
Land for 4 ploughs. In lordship 2.
   1 villager with 8 smallholders have 2 ploughs. 6 cottagers; 1 slave.
   Meadow for 1 plough; woodland, 50 pigs.

Silua . L . porc . Hoc ⓜ ual . LX . fol . Q̃do recep̃ẽ xL .
fol . T.R.E.ẽ c . fol . Hoc ⓜ tenuit Algar hõ Wigar
7 uendẽ potuit . *In Dimidio Hvnd de Hiz.*

Ĩn Hegeſtaneſtone teñ Radulf de Goisfr . I . hid .
Trã . ẽ . I . car̃ 7 dim̃ . Ibi . ẽ dim̃ car̃ . 7 alia car̃ pot
fieri . Ibi . II . borđ . p̃tū dim̃ car̃ . Paſtã ad pecuñ .
Ibi . II . cot̃ . 7 I . molin de . xL . deñ . Ħ trã ual . xxx .
fol . Q̃do recep̃ẽ x . fol . T.R.E.ẽ xL . fol . Hanc
terrã tenuit Alric hõ Aſgari ſtalri . uendẽ potuit .
Soca remanſit in Hiz . 7 ibi . I . Auerã inuenit .

Ĩpſe Goisfr̃ teñ *Linlei* . p̃ . v . hiđ ſe defđ . Trã . ẽ
. IX . car̃ . In dñio . II . hidæ . 7 ibi ſunt . III . car̃ . Ibi . XIX .
uilłi cū p̃bro hñt . v . car̃ . 7 vi . pot fieri . Ibi . vi . borđ
7 IIII . cot̃ . 7 vi . ſerui . Paſtura ad pecuñ . Silua . vi .
porc̃ . In totis ualent̃ ual 7 ualuit . c . fol . T.R.E.ẽ
vii . lib̃ . Hoc ⓜ tenuit Leueua de Heraldo comite .
7 ibi . I . focħs hõ Heraldi de eađ trã . III . uirg̃ 7 dim̃
habuit . 7 uendẽ potuit . 7 unã Auerã in hiz reddidit .
uel . III . deñ 7 I . obolū . *In Herfort Hvnd.*

Ĩpſe Goisfr̃ teñ *Hailet* . p̃ . II . hiđ ſe defđ . Trã . ẽ
. II . car̃ . In dñio . I . hida 7 III . uirg̃ . 7 ibi . ẽ una car̃ .
7 adhuc dim̃ pot fieri . Ibi . II . uilłi cū . II . borđ
hñt dim̃ car̃ . Ibi . III . cot̃ . 7 un ſeruus . p̃tū . I . car̃ .
Paſtura ađ pecuñ . Silua . L . porc̃ . De gurgite ẽ
. L . Anguilł . Val . xxx . fol . Q̃do recep̃ẽ x . fol . T.R.E.ẽ

140 b

Value of this manor, 60s; when acquired 40s; before 1066, 100s.
Algar, Withgar's man, held this manor; he could sell.

In the Half-Hundred of HITCHIN
11 In HEXTON Ralph holds 1 hide from Geoffrey.
Land for 1½ ploughs; ½ plough there; another plough possible.
2 smallholders.
Meadow for ½ plough; pasture for the livestock.
2 cottagers.
1 mill at 40d.
Value of this land, 30s; when acquired 10s; before 1066, 40s.
Alric, Asgar the Constable's man, held this land; he could sell.
The jurisdiction remained in Hitchin; he found 1 cartage there.

12 Geoffrey holds LILLEY himself. It answers for 5 hides.
Land for 9 ploughs. In lordship 2 hides; 3 ploughs there.
19 villagers with a priest have 5 ploughs; a sixth possible.
6 smallholders; 4 cottagers; 6 slaves.
Pasture for the livestock; woodland, 6 pigs.
The total value is and was 100s; before 1066 £7.
Leofeva held this manor from Earl Harold. 1 Freeman,
Harold's man, had 3½ virgates of this land; he could sell; he
paid 1 cartage in Hitchin, or 3½d.

In HERTFORD Hundred
13 Geoffrey holds HAILEY himself. It answers for 2 hides. Land
for 2 ploughs. In lordship 1 hide and 3 virgates; 1 plough
there; a further ½ possible.
2 villagers with 2 smallholders have ½ plough. 3 cottagers; 1 slave.
Meadow for 1 plough; pasture for the livestock;
woodland, 50 pigs; from a weir, 50 eels.
Value 30s; when acquired 10s; before 1066 £4.

IIII.lib. Hanc trã tenuit Wluuini hõ Heraldi. ^{comitis.}

De quadã filua reclam Radulf de Limefi tant

qtũ ptin ad . III . hid de Emmeuuelle . 7 II . uiltos

140 c

de . I . uirg . 7 I . bord de . x . acs . 7 adhuc . xxIIII . acs træ.

quas fupfit Ilbt de Hertfort . 7 appofuit huic ᴄᴑ

ut hões de Scirã teftant. 7 Canonici de Walthã

reclam tant filuæ qtũ ptin ad unã hidã.

In Brichendone ten Ifenbard de Goisfr . v . uirg

p uno ᴄᴑ . Tra . ẽ . I . car . 7 ibi . ẽ . ptũ . I . car . Silua

xL . porc . Val 7 ualuit . x . fol . T.R.E: xL . fol.

Hanc trã tenuit Leueron hõ Stig Arch . 7 uende

In Belingehou . ten ifd Goisfridus ⌐potuit.

.v.hid 7 I.uirg p uno ᴄᴑ . Tra . ẽ . v . caruc . In

dñio . III . hidæ 7 dim . 7 ibi . ẽ una car . 7 alia pot

fieri . Ibi . II . francig 7 II . uilti cũ . vI . bord . hñt

III . car . Ibi . xxx.IIII . cot . Ptũ . II . car . Paftura

ad pecun . 7 vIII . den . Nem ad fepes . In totis ua

lentijs ual 7 ualuit . c . fol . T.R.E: vIII . lib . Hoc

ᴄᴑ tenuit Anand hufcarl . R.E . 7 ibid . I . fochs

dim uirg habuit . 7 uende potuit.

In ead uilla ten ifd Goisfr . vI . hid 7 dim p uno . ᴄᴑ .

Tra . ẽ . vIII . car . In dñio . II . hidæ 7 dim . Ibi . IIII .

milit hñtes . IIII . hid cũ . II . uiltis. hñt . III . car

7 dim . 7 IIII . car 7 dim adhuc pofs fieri . Ibi . x . bord

7 v . ferui . Ptũ . III . car . Paftura ad pecun . Silua:

140 b, c

Wulfwin, Earl Harold's man, held this land. Ralph of Limesy
claims as much of a woodland as belongs to 3 hides
of Amwell, and 2 villagers with 1 virgate, 1 smallholder   140c
with 10 acres, and a further 24 acres of land, which Ilbert
took from Hertford* and placed in this manor, as the
men of the Shire testify. The Canons of Waltham claim
as much woodland as belongs to 1 hide.

14 In **BRICKENDON** Isambard holds 5 virgates from Geoffrey as one
manor. Land for 1 plough; it is there.
　Meadow for 1 plough; woodland, 40 pigs.
The value is and was 10s; before 1066, 40s.
　Leofrun, Archbishop Stigand's man, held this land; she could sell.

15 In **BENGEO** Geoffrey also holds 5 hides and 1 virgate as one manor.
Land for 5 ploughs. In lordship 3½ hides; 1 plough there;
another possible.
　2 Frenchmen and 2 villagers with 6 smallholders have 3 ploughs.
　　34 cottagers.
　Meadow for 2 ploughs; pasture for the livestock, and 8d too;
　　wood for fences.
The total value is and was 100s; before 1066 £8.
　Anand, one of King Edward's Guards, held this manor;
there 1 Freeman also had ½ virgate; he could sell.

16 In the same village Geoffrey also holds 6½ hides as one manor.
Land for 8 ploughs. In lordship 2½ hides.
　4 men-at-arms who have 4 hides with 2 villagers have 3½ ploughs;
　　a further 4½ ploughs possible. 10 smallholders; 5 slaves.
　Meadow for 3 ploughs; pasture for the livestock; woodland, 30 pigs.

xxx . porc . In totis ualent . ual . c . fol . Qdo recep.
lx . fol . T.R.E. viii . lib . Hoc ω tenuit Elaf . teign

In ead uilla ten . iii . milit de Goisfr   R.E.
. i . hid . 7 i . uirg 7 dim . Tra . e . iii . car . Ibi non fuɴ
car nifi dñic car . Ibi . iiii . bord . Ptu . iiii . bob.
Nem ad fepes . Val 7 ualuit . xx . fol . T.R.E. xl . fol.
Hanc tra tenuer . iii . fochi . Duo ex his Walcra 7 Lepfi
habuer . i . hid de foca regis . 7 iiii . den reddeb de cfue
tudine . 7 tcius Aleftan . i . uirg 7 dim tenuit . de foca
regis . 7 iii . obolos reddidit . Oms u tras fuas uende

In ead uilla ten Roger de Goisfrido   potuer.
v . uirg 7 dim . Tra . e . ii . car . Ibi . e una . 7 altera pot
fieri . Ibi . iiii . uilti . Val 7 ualuit . xx . fol . T.R.E. xl.
fol . Hanc tra tenuer . iiii . fochi . R.E. 7 uende potuer.
7 vi . den uicecom reddider p annum.

In ead uilla ten qda pbr 7 qda francig de Goisfr
iii . uirg 7 dim . Tra . e . i . car . Ibi . e dimid . 7 dimid
pot fieri . Val 7 ualuit . v . fol . T.R.E. x . fol . Hanc
tra tenuer . ii . fochi . R.E. 7 uende potuer . 7 ii . den
p annu uicecom reddider.

In SELA . ten Goduin de Goisfr dim hid . Tra . e
i . car . 7 ibi eft cu . ii . feru . 7 i . molin de . ii . folid.
ptu . i . car . Nem ad fepes . Paftura ad pec . Valet
7 ualuit fep . x . fol . Iftemet tenuit T.R.E. 7 uende
In Rochesforde ten Wido pbr   potuit.
de Goisfrido dim hid . Tra . e . i . car 7 dim . In dñio
e una . 7 dimid pot fieri . Ibi . iit . bord . 7 i . molin

Total value 100s; when acquired, 60s; before 1066 £8.

Elaf, a thane of King Edward's, held this manor.

17 In the same village 3 men-at-arms hold 1 hide and 1½ virgates
from Geoffrey. Land for 3 ploughs; no ploughs there except
for the lordship ploughs.

4 smallholders.

Meadow for 4 oxen; wood for fences.

The value is and was 20s; before 1066, 40s.

3 Freemen held this land; two of them, Walcra and Leofsi,
had 1 hide, of the King's jurisdiction; they paid 4d in
customary dues; the third, Alstan, held 1½ virgates, of the
King's jurisdiction; he paid 3 halfpence; all could sell their lands.

18 In the same village Roger holds 5½ virgates from Geoffrey.
Land for 2 ploughs; 1 there; a second possible.

4 villagers.

The value is and was 20s; before 1066, 40s.

4 Freemen of King Edward's held this land; they could sell;
they paid 6d a year to the Sheriff.

19 In the same village a priest and a Frenchman hold 3½ virgates
from Geoffrey. Land for 1 plough; ½ there; ½ possible.

The value is and was 5s; before 1066, 10s.

2 Freemen of King Edward's held this land; they could sell;
they paid 2d a year to the Sheriff.

20 In SELE Godwin holds ½ hide from Geoffrey. Land for 1 plough;
it is there, with

2 slaves.

1 mill at 2s; meadow for 1 plough; wood for fences;
pasture for the livestock.

The value is and always was 10s.

He held it himself before 1066; he could sell.

21 In ROXFORD the priest Guy holds ½ hide from Geoffrey. Land for
1½ ploughs. In lordship 1; ½ possible.

3 smallholders.

de . v . fol . p̃tu . 1 . car̃ . Paſta ad pecuñ . Silua . L .
porc . Int totũ ual 7 ualuit . xv . fol . T . R . E : xx . fol .
Hanc trã tenuit Goduin teigñ . R . E . 7 uende potuit .

140 d

In Blachemene . teñ Goisfr̃ Runeuile de Goisfr̃
. 1 . hiđ . Tra . ẽ . 11 . car̃ . In dñio . ẽ una . 7 alia pot fieri .
Ibi . 1 . uilłs 7 11 . borđ . p̃tu . 11 . car̃ . Paſtura ad pecuñ .
Silua . xL . porc . H̃ tra ual 7 ualuit xv . fol . T . R . E :
xL . fol . Hanc trã tenuer̃ . 11 . teigni . R . E . 7 uende pot .
In Staneſtede . teñ Goisfr̃   IN BRACHINGES HVND .
de Goisfr̃ de bech dim hiđ . Tra . ẽ dim car̃ . 7 ibi eſt
cũ . 1 . cot . P̃tu dim car̃ . H̃ tra ual . x . fol . Qđo recep :
v . fol . T . R . E : x . fol . Hanc trã tenuit Bettice hõ
Wluuini de Eſteuuiche . 7 uende potuit . 7 11 . deñ
In Eſteuuiche teñ Rainalđ de Goisfrido   £ reddiđ .
11 . hiđ . Tra . ẽ . 1111 . car̃ . In dñio funt . 111 . 7 1111 . uilłi
cũ pƀro 7 11 . borđ hñt . 11 . car̃ . Ibi . v . ferui . 7 1 . moliñ
de . v . fol . p̃tu . v . car̃ . Silua . xx . porc . In totis ua
lentijs ual . Lx . fol . Qđo recep : xL . fol . T . R . E : 1111 . liƀ .
Hoc M̃ tenuit Wluuin teigñ Heraldi . 7 uende pot .
In Wichehã . teñ Rog̃ 7 Oſƀtus de Goisfrido
111 . uirg̃ 7 v . acs . Tra . ẽ . 1 . car̃ 7 dim . 7 ibi funt cũ
. v111 . borđ . P̃tu dim car̃ . Silua . v111 . porc . Val 7 ua
luit . xxx . fol . T . R . E : xL . fol . Hanc trã tenuer̃
111 . focħi . R . E . 7 uende potuer̃ . 7 111 . deñ uicecomiti
p annũ reddider̃ .

1 mill at 5s; meadow for 1 plough; pasture for the livestock;
    woodland, 50 pigs.
In total, the value is and was 15s; before 1066, 20s.
    Godwin, a thane of King Edward's, held this land; he could sell.

140 d

22 In PANSHANGER Geoffrey of 'Runeville' holds 1 hide from Geoffrey.
Land for 2 ploughs. In lordship 1; another possible.
    1 villager; 2 smallholders.
    Meadow for 2 ploughs; pasture for the livestock; woodland, 40 pigs.
The value of this land is and was 15s; before 1066, 40s.
    Two thanes of King Edward's held this land; they could sell.

In BRAUGHING Hundred

23 In STANSTEAD (ABBOTS) Geoffrey holds ½ hide from Geoffrey of Bec.
Land for ½ plough; it is there, with
    1 cottager.
Meadow for ½ plough.
Value of this land 10s; when acquired 5s; before 1066, 10s.
    Bettica, Wulfwin of Eastwick's man, held this land; he could
sell; he paid 2d.

24 In EASTWICK Reginald holds 2 hides from Geoffrey.
Land for 4 ploughs. In lordship 3.
    4 villagers with a priest and 2 smallholders have 2 ploughs. 5 slaves.
    1 mill at 5s; meadow for 5 ploughs; woodland, 20 pigs.
Total value 60s; when acquired 40s; before 1066 £4.
    Wulfwin, a thane of Earl Harold's, held this manor; he could sell.

25 In WICKHAM Roger and Osbert hold 3 virgates and 5 acres from
Geoffrey. Land for 1½ ploughs; they are there, with
    8 smallholders.
Meadow for ½ plough; woodland, 8 pigs.
The value is and was 30s; before 1066, 40s.
    3 Freemen of King Edward's held this land; they could sell;
they paid 3d a year to the Sheriff.

TERRA GOISBERT DE BELVACO.

Goisbertvs De beluaco ten *Wimvndeslai*.
p̄.iii.hid̄ 7 i.uirg̃ se defd̄.Tra̅.e̅.iiii.car̃.In
dn̄io.ii.hide.7 ii.uirg̃ 7 dim.7 ibi sunt.ii.car̃.
7 tcia pot̃ fieri.Ibi.iiii.uilli cū.iii.bord̄ hn̄t.i.car̃.
Ibi.iiii.cot̃ 7 ii.serui.p̄tū.i.car̃.Pastura ad pec̃.
Silua.x.porc̃.In totis ualent̃ ual.lx.sol̃.Q̊do
recep̄:xx.sol̃.T.R.E:lx.sol̃.hoc m̅ tenuit Suuen
hō Heraldi.7 uendẽ potuit.

In Grauelai.ten isd̄ Goisb̄t̃.ii.hid̄.Tra̅.e̅.iii.car̃.
In dn̄io.v.uirg̃ 7 dim.7 ibi.e̅ una car̃.7 alia pot̃
fieri.Ibi.iii.uilli hn̄t.i.car̃.Ibi.i.cot̃.7 i.seruus.
Past̃a ad pecuñ.Rispalia ad sepes.Ual.xl.sol̃.
Q̊do recep̄:xx.sol̃.T.R.E:xl.sol̃.Hoc m̅ tenuit
Suuen hō Heraldi.7 uendẽ potuit. *In Odesei hvnd̄.*

In Wallingtone ten Fulco de Goisb̄to.iii.hid̄ 7 xl
ac̃s træ.Tra̅.e̅.v.car̃.In dn̄io sunt.ii.7 iiii.uilli cū.iii.
bord̄ hn̄t.ii.car̃.7 iii.cia pot̃ fieri.Ibi.i.cot̃.7 ii.serui.
Past̃a ad pec̃.Nem̃ ad sepes.Int̃ tot̃ ual.l.sol̃.Q̊do
recep̄:xxx.sol̃.T.R.E:c,sol̃.Hoc m̅ tenuit Ederic̃
hō Algari.7 uendẽ potuit.7 de ead̄ tra tenuit q̊dā
sochs.xxiiii.ac̃s.hō Eddeuæ pulchre.7 uendẽ potuit.
De q̊b̊z Radulf̃ com fuit saisit.s; die qua forisfecit
non erat saisit testante Hundret.

TERRA PETRI DE VALONGIES. *In Bradewatre Hd̄.*

Petrvs de Valongies.7 Rob̄t̃ de eo ten|uirg̃ dimid'
in Daceuuorde.Tra̅.e̅.ii.bob̃.sed ibi n̄ suŋ.H̄ tra
ual 7 ualuit sep̃.vi.sol̃.Hanc tra̅ tenuit Alstan hō
Alm de belintone.7 uendẽ potuit.

35   LAND OF GOSBERT OF BEAUVAIS

[In BROADWATER Hundred]

1 Gosbert of Beauvais holds WYMONDLEY. It answers for 3 hides and
  1 virgate. Land for 4 ploughs. In lordship 2 hides and 2½ virgates;
  2 ploughs there; a third possible.
    4 villagers with 3 smallholders have 1 plough. 4 cottagers; 2 slaves.
    Meadow for 1 plough; pasture for the livestock; woodland, 10 pigs.
  Total value 60s; when acquired 20s; before 1066, 60s.
    Swein, Earl Harold's man, held this manor; he could sell.

2 In GRAVELEY Gosbert also holds 2 hides. Land for 3 ploughs.
  In lordship 5½ virgates; 1 plough there; another possible.
    3 villagers have 1 plough. 1 cottager; 1 slave.
  Pasture for the livestock; brushwood for fences.
  Value 40s; when acquired 20s; before 1066, 40s.
    Swein, Earl Harold's man, held this manor; he could sell.

In ODSEY Hundred

*3 In WALLINGTON Fulk holds 3 hides and 40 acres of land from
  Gosbert. Land for 5 ploughs. In lordship 2.
    4 villagers with 3 smallholders have 2 ploughs; a third possible.
    1 cottager; 2 slaves.
  Pasture for the livestock; wood for fences.
  In total, value 50s; when acquired 30s; before 1066, 100s.
    Edric, Earl Algar's man, held this manor; he could sell.
  A Freeman, Edeva the Fair's man, held 24 acres of this land;
  he could sell. Earl Ralph was in possession of them, but on
  the day of his forfeiture he was not in possession, as the
  Hundred testifies.

36   LAND OF PETER OF VALOGNES *

In BROADWATER Hundred

1 Peter of Valognes holds ½ virgate in DATCHWORTH and Robert
  from him. Land for 2 oxen, but they are not there.
  The value of this land is and always was 6s.
    Alstan, Aelmer of Bennington's man, held this land; he
  could sell.

In Dichelefuuelle . teñ Roger de Petro . ɪ . ħid . Tra . ē . ɪɪɪ . car.

In dñio . ē una . 7 v . uilti cū . ɪɪɪ . borđ ħnt . ɪɪ . car . Ibi . vɪɪɪ . cot.

7 dim molenđ de . xʟ . deñ . Ptū . ɪɪ . bob . Paftura ad pecuñ .

Silua . ʟ . porc . Int totū ual . xxxv . fol . Q̆do recep̃ . xx . fol.

T . R . E . ʟ . fol . Hanc trā tenuit Topi ħo Almari . 7 uende pot.

In Grauelai teñ Godefriđ de Petro . ɪɪ . hiđ . 7 ɪ . uirg 7 dim.

Tra . ē . ɪɪɪ . car . In dñio funt . ɪɪ . 7 ɪɪɪ . uilti cū . ɪɪɪɪ . borđ ħñt

. ɪ . car . Ibi . ɪɪ . cot . 7 ɪɪ . ferui . Paftura ad pecuñ . Nem̄ āđ fepes

7 domos . Val . xʟ . fol . Q̆do recep̃ . x . fol . T . R . E . ɪɪɪɪ . liƀ.

Hoc M̄ tenuit Lemar de Ælmaro de belint . 7 uende pot.

In Efcelucia . teñ Godefriđ de petro . ɪ . hiđ 7 dim . Tra . ē

. ɪ . car . 7 ibi . ē cū . ɪɪ . borđ 7 ɪ . feruo . Val . xxx . fol . Q̆do recep̃

xx . fol . T.R.E . xʟ . fol . De hac tra tenuit Aluuiñ hiđ 7 dim.

exceptis . x . acris 7 ɪ . toft . q̃s teñ Aluuiñ ħo Alurici . 7 jace

bant in Wilga . ñ pot uende extra.

In Wluueneuuiche teñ Roger de petro . ɪ . uirg 7 dim . Tra . ē

dim car . s; ibi non . ē . Ibi . v . cot . Ptū . ɪɪ . bob; . Silua . x̃ . porc.

Val 7 ualuit . ɪɪɪ . fol . T.R.E . x . fol . Hanc trā tenuit Aluuin

ħo Ælmari de Belintone . 7 uende potuit.

In Boxe . teñ Petrus . ɪ . hiđ 7 ɪɪɪ . uirg . Tra . ē . ɪɪ . car . Ibi . ē

un borđ . H̄ tra jacet 7 app̃ciat in Belintone . 7 colit p̃pis car.

Ipfe Petrus teñ *BELINTONE* . p̃ . x . hiđ fe defđ . Tra . ē . xɪ.

car . In dñio . vɪ . hidæ 7 dim . 7 ibi funt . ɪɪɪ . car . 7 duæ adhuc

pofs fieri . Ibi . xvɪ . uilti cū pƀro . 7 xvɪɪ . borđ ħñt . vɪɪɪ . car.

Ibi . ɪ . cot 7 . v . ferui . Silua . c . porc . Parc filuatic beftiaƀ.

In totis ualent ual . xɪɪ . liƀ . Q̆do recep̃ . vɪ . liƀ . T.R.E . xɪɪɪɪ . liƀ.

Hoc M̄ tenuit Ælmer de Belintone.

2 In DIGSWELL Roger holds 1 hide from Peter. Land for 3 ploughs.
In lordship 1.
　　5 villagers with 3 smallholders have 2 ploughs. 8 cottagers.
　　½ mill at 40d; meadow for 2 oxen; pasture for the livestock;
　　　woodland, 50 pigs.
In total, value 35s; when acquired 20s; before 1066, 50s.
　　Topi, Aelmer's man, held this land; he could sell.

3 In GRAVELEY Godfrey holds 2 hides and 1½ virgates from Peter.
Land for 3 ploughs. In lordship 2.
　　3 villagers with 4 smallholders have 1 plough. 2 cottagers; 2 slaves.
　　Pasture for the livestock; wood for fences and houses.
Value 40s; when acquired 10s; before 1066 £4.
　　Ledmer held this manor from Aelmer of Bennington; he could sell.

*.4 In CHELLS Godfrey holds 1½ hides from Peter. Land for 1 plough;
it is there, with
　　2 smallholders and 1 slave.
Value 30s; when acquired 20s; before 1066, 40s.
　　Alwin held 1½ hides of this land, apart from 10 acres and
1 plot, which Alwin Dod [son], Aelfric Little's man, holds; they lay
in (the lands of) Welwyn; he could not sell outside.

5 In WOOLWICKS Roger holds 1½ virgates from Peter.
Land for ½ plough, but it is not there.
　　5 cottagers.
　　Meadow for 2 oxen; woodland, 10 pigs.
The value is and was 3s; before 1066, 10s.
　　Alwin, Aelmer of Bennington's man, held this land; he could sell.

*6 In BOX Peter holds 1 hide and 3 virgates. Land for 2 ploughs.
　　1 smallholder.
　　This land lies and is assessed in Bennington; it is cultivated
with his own ploughs.

7 Peter holds BENNINGTON himself. It answers for 10 hides.
Land for 11 ploughs. In lordship 6½ hides; 3 ploughs there;
a further 2 possible.
　　16 villagers with a priest and 17 smallholders have 8
　　　ploughs. 1 cottager; 5 slaves.
　　Woodland, 100 pigs; a park for woodland beasts.
Total value £12; when acquired £6; before 1066 £14.
　　Aelmer of Bennington held this manor.

In Stuterehele ten. ii ſochi de Petro. i. hiđ 7 iii.uirg. Tra. ē
ii. car 7 ibi ſunt cū. i. borđ. Ptū dim car. Paſta ad pec. Int
totū ual 7 ualuit. xx. ſol. T.R.E. xl. ſol. De hac tra tenuit Le
ueron. i. hiđ hō Elmer de belintone. ñ potuit uende pt ej lictiā.
7 Aluuin habuit. iii. uirg hō | Ælmæri. de ſoca R.E. 7 uen
dere potuit. 7 inuenieb. iii. partes Aueræ ł iii. den uicecomiti.
In Stuterehele ten Petr dim uirg 7 x. acſ. Tra. ē. iii. bob.
Ibi. i. borđ. Silua. iiii. porc. H tra ual. ii. ſol. T.R.E. Hanc
tenuit qđā ſochs. R.E. 7 uende potuit. 7 de cſuetuđ. iiii.
parté uni Aueræ ł unū den inuenieb uicecom regis p annū.
Hanc trā ſupſit Petr uicecom de iſto ſocho. R.W. in manu
ejđ regis. p forisfactura de gildo regis ſe ñ reddidiſſe ut hōes
ſui đnt. Sed hōes de Scira ñ portant uicecomiti teſtimon.
qa ſep quieta fuit de gildo 7 de alijs erga regē. quādiu te
nuit. teſtante hundret.
In eađ uilla ten Aluuard de Petro dim uirg. Tra. ē. i. boui.
Val 7 ualuit ſep. xvi. den. Hanc trā tenuit qđā femina
In Seuechāpe ten Petrus. ix. hiđ. i. uirg min. de Almaro.
Tra. ē. vii. car. In dnio. vi. hidæ. 7 ibi ſunt. iii. car. 7 iiii. pot
fieri. Ibi. v. uilti cū. vi. borđ 7 i. clerico hnt. iii. car. Ibi
vi. cot 7 iiii. ſerui. 7 i. molenđ de xx. ſol. Silua. lx. porc.
In totis ualent ual 7 ualuit. vi. lib. T.R.E. viii. lib.
De hoc M tenuit Elmær. iiii. hiđ p uno M. teſtante hund.
7 Leuuin tenuit. ii. hiđ. i. uirg min p uno M. hō Heraldi fuit.
7 uende potuit.
In M qđ Elmer tenuit fuer. iiii. ſochi. Vn eoq dimiđ
hiđ tenuit 7 uende potuit. 7 alt. i uirg tenuit ſed
uende ñ potuit. pt ej lictiā đni ſui Almæri. Terci 7 qrt
dim hiđ habuer. vi. acſ min. 7 uende potuer. Sup hos

141 b

141 a, b

*8 In LIBURY 2 Freemen hold 1 hide and 3 virgates from Peter.
Land for 2 ploughs; they are there, with
   1 smallholder.
Meadow for ½ plough; pasture for the livestock.
In total, the value is and was 20s; before 1066, 40s.
   Leofrun, Aelmer of Bennington's man, held 1 hide of this
land; she could not sell without his permission. Alwin, also
Aelmer's man, of King Edward's jurisdiction, had 3 virgates;
he could sell; he found 3 parts of a cartage, or 3d for the Sheriff.

9 In LIBURY Peter holds ½ virgate and 10 acres. Land for 3 oxen.
   1 smallholder.
   Woodland, 4 pigs.
Value of this land 2s before 1066. *
   A Freeman of King Edward's held it; he could sell; in customary
dues, he found the fourth part of one cartage, or 1 penny a year,
for the King's Sheriff. Peter the Sheriff took this land from this
Freeman of King William's; it is in the King's hands, in forfeiture,
for his not paying the King's tax, as (the Sheriff's) men say.
But the men of the Shire do not bear witness to the Sheriff,
because it was always exempt from tax and from other things
concerning the King for as long as he held it, as the Hundred
testifies.

10 In the same village Alfward holds ½ virgate from Peter.
Land for 1 ox.
The value is and always was 16d. A woman held this land from Aelmer.

11 In SACOMBE Peter holds 9 hides less 1 virgate. Land for 7 ploughs.
In lordship 6 hides; 3 ploughs there; a fourth possible.
   5 villagers with 6 smallholders and 1 cleric have 3 ploughs.
     6 cottagers; 4 slaves.
   1 mill at 20s; woodland, 60 pigs.
The total value is and was £6; before 1066 £8.
   Aelmer held 4 hides of this manor as one manor, as the Hundred
testifies; Leofwin held 2 hides less 1 virgate as one manor;
he was Earl Harold's man; he could sell.
   In the manor which Aelmer held were 4 Freemen.   141 b
One of them held ½ hide; he could sell. The second held 1
virgate, but he could not sell, except with the permission of
his lord, Aelmer. The third and fourth had ½ hide less 6 acres;
they could sell.

ıı .habuit rex .E .Sacā 7 Socā . 7 q́ſq̇ uicecomiti q́rtā
parte̅ Aeræ inuenieƀ p annū .ł unū denariū . Ipſe ıııı .
hōes Ælmeri de Belintone fuer̄ . In hoc eod ꝋ quædā
femina tenuit . v . uirg̊ ſub Anſchil de Waras . 7 uende̊
potuit p̄t̊ . ı . uirg̊ q̇ poſuit in uadim̊ Almero de Belint̊
p . x . ſoł . 7 inuenieƀ . ı . auerā . 7 ıııı . parte̅ alteri
aeræ . aut quinq̇ denarios . *IN EDWINESTREV HD̊.*
In Ichetone ten̊ Hunfrid de petro dim̊ hid̊ . Tra . e̅
un̊ car̊ . 7 ibi . e̅ cū . ıı . borđ . P̊tū . ıı . boƀ . H̅ tra
uał . xv . ſoł . Q̇do recep̊ x . ſoł . T.R.E.́ xx . ſoł . Harc
trā tenuit Elmer de belint̊ . 7 uende̊ potuit .
Ipſe Petr̄ ten̊ *STANES* . p una hida 7 dim̊ ſe
defđ . Tra . e̅ . ı . car̊ 7 dim̊ . Ibi . e̅ una . 7 dim̊ pot̊ fieri .
Ibi . e̅ . ı . uilłs cū . ıııı . borđ . Vał . xv . ſoł . Q̇do recep̊
x . ſoł . T.R.E.́ xL . ſoł . Hanc trā tenuer̄ . ıııı . ſochi
Vn̊ eoᵹ p̄poſit̊ regis dim̊ hid̊ habuit . 7 tras alioᵹ
triū ſochoᵹ occupauit ſup rege̅ Willelm̅ . ut
tota ſcira teſtat.́ De cſuetuđ reddeƀ p annū
ıııı . deñ 7 dim̊ . Modo ten̊ Petr̄ uicecom̊ .
In Eſceuuelle . ten̊ Petrus . ıı . hiđ *IN ODESEI HD̊.*
p uno ꝋ . Tra . e̅ . vı . car̊ . In dn̅io . ııı . uirg̊ . 7 ibi
ſuᵹ . ıı . car̊ . 7 vııı . uilłi cū . vııı . borđ hn̅t . ıııı . car̊ .
Ibi . ıı . cot̊ . 7 ıııı . ſerui , 7 ı . molin̊ de . x . ſoł . P̊tū
. ı . car̊ . Paſtura ad pecun̊ . Int̊ tot̊ uał . c . ſoł .
Q̇do recep̊ Lx . ſoł . T.R.E.́ vıı . liƀ . Hoc ꝋ tenuit
Elmer de belintone . teign̊ . R.E. 7 unā uirg̊
In Hainſteuuorde ten̊ iſđ Petr̄ . ı . hiđ | Tra . e̅ . ıı . car̊ .
7 ibi ſunt . In dn̅io dim̊ hida . 7 ibi . e̅ una car̊ . 7 ı . uilłs

King Edward had full jurisdiction over these two; each found a fourth part of a cartage a year for the Sheriff, or 1 penny. These four were Aelmer of Bennington's men.*

In the same manor a woman held 5 virgates under Askell of Ware; she could sell, except for the 1 virgate, which she placed in pledge with Aelmer of Bennington for 10s; she found 1 cartage and a fourth part of another cartage, or 5d.

In EDWINSTREE Hundred

12 In BUNTINGFORD Humphrey holds ½ hide from Peter.
Land for 1 plough; it is there, with
   2 smallholders.
   Meadow for 2 oxen.
Value of this land, 15s; when acquired 10s; before 1066, 20s.
   Aelmer of Bennington held this land; he could sell.

13 Peter holds STONE himself. It answers for 1½ hides.
Land for 1½ ploughs; 1 there; ½ possible.
   1 villager with 4 smallholders.
Value 15s; when acquired 10s; before 1066, 40s.
   4 Freemen held this land. One of them, a reeve of the King's, had ½ hide; he appropriated the lands of the other three Freemen in King William's despite, as the whole Shire testifies. He paid 4½d a year in customary dues. Now Peter the Sheriff holds it.

In ODSEY Hundred

14 In ASHWELL Peter holds 2 hides as one manor. Land for 6 ploughs.
In lordship 3 virgates; 2 ploughs there.
   8 villagers with 8 smallholders have 4 ploughs. 2 cottagers; 4 slaves.
   1 mill at 10s; meadow for 1 plough; pasture for the livestock.
In total, value 100s; when acquired 60s; before 1066 £7.
   Aelmer of Bennington, a thane of King Edward's, held this manor.

15 In HINXWORTH Peter also holds 1 hide and 1 virgate. Land for 2 ploughs; they are there. In lordship ½ hide; 1 plough there.
   1 villager with 4 smallholders have 1 plough. 2 cottagers.

cū . iiii . borđ hn̄t . i . car̄ . Ibi . ii . cot . P̄tū dim car̄.

Val . xx . ſol . Q̄do recep̄ . x . ſol . T.R.E. xxx . ſol . Ħ tra
fuit Bereuuiche de Eſceuuelle Almer tenuit.

In Radeuuelle . ten̄ Roger de Petro . ii . hiđ p̄ uno
Ѡ . Tra . ē . iii . car̄ . In dn̄io ſunt . ii . 7 v . borđ hn̄t
dim car̄ . 7 dim adhuc pot fieri . Ibi . ii . ſerui . 7 uñ
molin de vi . ſol 7 viii . den . P̄tū dim car̄ . Paſtura
ad pecun̄ . Hoc Ѡ tenuit Elmer de Belinton . 7 de
eađ tra tenuit fr̄ ej dim hiđ . hō ej fuit 7 uendē pot.

In Flexmere ten̄ Petr̄ *IN DIMID̄ HVND DE HIZ.*
dim uirḡ . Tra . ē dim car̄ . Ibi . ē . i . borđ . Silua . v.
porc̄ . Val 7 ualuit . iii . ſol . T.R.E. xl . den . Hanc tra
tenuit Aluric hō Ælmari . 7 uendē pot . In hiz unā
Auerā reddidit.   *IN HERTFORT HVND.*

In Belingehou . ten̄ Petr̄ dim uirḡ . Tra . ē . dim car̄
7 ibi . ē cū . i . uillo . Val 7 ualuit . v . ſol ſēp . Hanc tra
tenuit Elmer de belintone teign̄ . R . E.

In Teuuinge ten̄ Aldene de Petro . v . hiđ 7 dim .
Tra . ē . v . car̄ . 7 dim . In dn̄io . ē una . 7 alia pot fieri.

141 c
7 iiii . uilli cū . v . borđ hn̄t . iii . car̄ 7 dim . Ibi . v . cot 7 i.
ſeruus . 7 i . molin de . viii . ſol . P̄tū . ii . car̄ . Paſtura ad
pecun̄ . Silua . l . porc̄ . 7 de reddita ſiluæ . ii . ſol . In totis
ualent ual . lx . ſol . Q̄do recep̄ . xxx . ſol . T.R.E. iiii . liƀ.
Hoc Ѡ tenuit iſđ Aldene teign̄ . R . E . 7 uendē potuit.
Sed . W . rex deđ hoc Ѡ huic Aldene 7 matri ej pro
anima Ricardi filij ſui . ut ipſemet dicit 7 p̄ breue
ſuū oſtenđ . Modo dicit Petrus qđ habet hoc Ѡ ex
dono regis.

Meadow for ½ plough.
Value 20s; when acquired 10s; before 1066, 30s.
This land was an outlier of Ashwell; Aelmer held it.

16   In RADWELL Roger holds 2 hides from Peter as one manor.
Land for 3 ploughs. In lordship 2.
   5 smallholders have ½ plough; a further ½ possible. 2 slaves.
   1 mill at 6s 8d; meadow for ½ plough; pasture for the livestock.
   Aelmer of Bennington held this manor. His brother held ½ hide
of this land; he was his man; he could sell.

   In the Half-Hundred of HITCHIN
*17   In FLEXMORE Peter holds ½ virgate. Land for ½ plough.
   1 smallholder.
   Woodland, 5 pigs.
The value is and was 3s; before 1066, 40d.
   Aelfric, Aelmer of Bennington's man, held this land; he could
sell; he paid one cartage in Hitchin.

   In HERTFORD Hundred
18   In BENGEO Peter holds ½ virgate. Land for ½ plough; it is there, with
   1 villager.
The value is and always was 5s.
   Aelmer of Bennington, a thane of King Edward's, held this land.

*19   In TEWIN Haldane holds 5½ hides from Peter. Land for 5½ ploughs.
In lordship 1; another possible.
   4 villagers with 5 smallholders have 3½ ploughs.   141 c
      5 cottagers; 1 slave.
   1 mill at 8s; meadow for 2 ploughs; pasture for the livestock;
      woodland, 50 pigs, and from the payments of the woodland 2s.
Total value 60s; when acquired 30s: before 1066 £4.
   Haldane also held this manor; he was King Edward's thane; he could
sell. But King William granted this manor to this Haldane and
his mother for the soul of his son Richard, as he says himself
and shows through his writ. Peter now says that he has this
manor by the King's gift.

H TERRA HARDVINI DE SCALERS *IN BRADEWATRE HD.*

ARDVINVS De Scalers ten̄ in Sueuecāpe

.ı.hıđ.Terra.ē.ı.car̄.7 ibi.ē cū.ıııı.uiłłis.

Vał 7 ualuit.vııı.soł.T.R.E.́xx.soł.Hanc trā te

nuer̄.ııı.socħi.Hoꝗ.ıı.hōēs Anschil de Wares

.ııı.uirḡ tenuer̄.7 uendē potuer̄.7 tcius hō Aluric.^{blac}

unā uirḡ habuit 7 uendē pot̄.Ipsi.ııı.unā Auerā

ł.ıııı.den̄ reddeꝑ uicecomiti p annū.^{or} *IN ODESEI HD.*

In Lufenel ten̄ Tetbałd de Harduino dim̄ hıđ.Tra.ē

.ı.car̄.Ibi n̄ est.nisi.ıı.borđ.Vał 7 ualuit.v.soł.T.R.E.́

x.soł.Hanc trā tenuit Aluuard hō Algari.^{com} 7 uendē

In Cladhele.ten̄ Tetbałd de Harđ.ı.uirḡ. ⌐potuit.

ııı.acs mim̄.Vał 7 ualuit.v.soł.T.R.E.́x.soł.Hanc

trā tenuit Turꝑt pꝓr Stiḡ arcħ.7 uendē pot̄.Inuen̄.ı.

In Wallingtone ten̄ Siuuard de Harđ ⌐denar̄.

.ı.hıđ 7 dim̄.7 xxvı.acs.Tra.ē ıı.car̄.Ibi.ē una.7 alia

pot̄ fieri.Ibi.ııı.borđ.Vał xxv.soł.Ꝗdo recēꝑ.́xx.

soł.T.R.E.́xxx.soł.Hanc trā tenuit Wluuar hō

Anschil de Wares.7 uendē potuit.

In Bradefelle.ten̄ Tetbałd de Harđ.ı.hıđ 7 ıııı.^{tam}

part̄.ı.uirḡ.Tra.ē.ı.car̄.7 ibi.ē cū.ııı.borđ 7 ıı.seru̅.

7 ı.cot̄.Ptū dim̄ car̄.Pastura ad pecun̄.Vał.xx.soł.

Ꝗdo recēꝑ.́x.soł.T.R.E.́xL.soł.Hanc trā tenuer̄

.ıı.frs hōēs Stiḡ archiepi.7 uendē potuer̄.

In **BROADWATER** Hundred

1 Hardwin of Scales holds 1 hide in SACOMB. Land for 1 plough;
it is there, with
    4 villagers.
The value is and was 8s; before 1066, 20s.
    3 Freemen held this land. Two of them, Askell of Ware's men,
held 3 virgates; they could sell. The third, Aelfric Black's man, had 1
virgate; he could sell. These three paid one cartage, or 4d a year,
to the Sheriff.

In **ODSEY** Hundred

2 In **LUFFENHALL** Theobald holds ½ hide from Hardwin.
Land for 1 plough; it is not there, only
    2 smallholders.
The value is and was 5s; before 1066, 10s.
    Alfward, Earl Algar's man, held this land; he could sell.

3 In **CLOTHALL** Theobald holds 1 virgate less 3 acres from Hardwin.
The value is and was 5s; before 1066, 10s.
    Thorbert, a priest of Archbishop Stigand's, held this land;
he could sell; he found 1d.

4 In **WALLINGTON** Siward holds 1½ hides and 26 acres from Hardwin.
Land for 2 ploughs; 1 there; another possible.
    3 smallholders.
Value 25s; when acquired 20s; before 1066, 30s.
    Wulfmer, Askell of Ware's man, held this land; he could sell.

5 In **BROADFIELD** Theobald holds 1 hide and the fourth part of 1 virgate
from Hardwin. Land for 1 plough; it is there, with
    3 smallholders, 2 slaves; and 1 cottager.
    Meadow for ½ plough; pasture for the livestock.
Value 20s; when acquired 10s; before 1066, 40s.
    Two brothers, Archbishop Stigand's men, held this land; they
could sell.

In Orduuelle ten̅ Wiſgar de Hard̄ . I . hid̄ 7 dim̅ . v . aĉs
min̅ . Tra . e̅ . I . car̅ 7 dim̅ . 7 ibi ſunt cu̅ . I . uiɫɫo 7 III . cot.
Ibi . II . ſerui . Ptu̅ nil . Paſtura ad pecun̅ . H̅ tra uaɫ
xxvIII . ſoɫ . Qdo recep̅ : xv . ſoɫ . T . R . E . xx . v . ſoɫ . Hanc
tra̅ tenuer̅ . II . ſochi ho̅es Stig Archiep̅i . 7 uende̅ potuer̅.
In Dereuelde . ten̅ Wigar de Harduino . III . uirg̅.
Tra . e̅ . I . car̅ . Ibi . II . uiɫɫi 7 II . cot cu̅ . I . ſeruo . Paſtura ad
pecun̅ . Vaɫ 7 ualuit . x . ſoɫ . T . R . E . xx . ſoɫ . Hanc tra̅
tenuit Alric p̅br ſub ab̅be de Rameſy̅ . n̅ potuit uende̅
p̅ter licentia̅ ab̅bis.
In Retth . ten̅ Harduin̅ . v . hid̄ . 7 I . uirg 7 dim̅ . Tra . e̅ . vI.
car̅ . In d̅nio . III . hidæ 7 dim̅ 7 vIII . aĉ . 7 ibi ſunt . II . car̅ . Ibi
x . uiɫɫi cu̅ p̅bro 7 v . bord̄ h̅nt . IIII . car̅ . Ibi . II . cot 7 vI.
ſerui . Ptu̅ dim̅ car̅ . Paſta̅ ad pecun̅ . Silua . x . porc̅ . In
totis ualent uaɫ . c . ſoɫ . Qdo recep̅ : IIII . lib̅ . T . R . E . vI . lib̅.
De hoc M̅ tenuit Siret ho̅ Heraldi . IIII . hid̄ 7 I . uirg̅
7 dim̅ . 7 Sinod ho̅ S̅ Mariæ de Cetriz . I . hid̄ tenuit.
Ambo uende̅ potuer̅.
In Eſceuuelle . ten̅ Tetbald̄ de Hard̄ dimid̄ hid̄ . Tra . e̅
. I . car̅ . ſed n̅ eſt ibi . Ibi . vI . cot . Ptu̅ dim̅ car̅ . H̅ tra uaɫ
xx . ſoɫ . Qdo recep̅ : x . ſoɫ . T . R . E . xxx . ſoɫ . Hanc tra̅
tenuit Vĉtred ſub Rob̅to filio Wimarch . n̅ potuit
uende̅ p̅ter ej lictia̅ . ut ho̅es de hund̄ teſtant̅.

6   In ORWELL Withgar holds 1½ hides less 5 acres from Hardwin.
Land for 1½ ploughs; they are there, with
    1 villager and 3 cottagers. 2 slaves.
    No meadow; pasture for the livestock.
Value of this land, 28s; when acquired 15s; before 1066, 25s.
    2 Freemen, Archbishop Stigand's men, held this land; they
could sell.

7   In THERFIELD Withgar holds 3 virgates from Hardwin. Land for 1 plough.
    2 villagers and 2 cottagers with 1 slave.
    Pasture for the livestock.
The value is and was 10s; before 1066, 20s.
    Aelfric, a priest, held this land under the Abbot of Ramsey; he
could not sell without the Abbot's permission.

8   In REED Hardwin holds 5 hides and 1½ virgates. Land for 6 ploughs.
In lordship 3½ hides and 8 acres; 2 ploughs there.
    10 villagers with a priest and 5 smallholders have 4 ploughs.
      2 cottagers; 6 slaves.
    Meadow for ½ plough; pasture for the livestock;woodland, 10 pigs.
Total value 100s; when acquired £4; before 1066 £6.
    Sired, Earl Harold's man, held 4 hides and 1½ virgates of this
manor, and Sinoth, St. Mary of Chatteris' man, held 1 hide;
both could sell.

9   In ASHWELL Theobald holds ½ hide from Hardwin. Land for 1 plough,
but it is not there.
    6 cottagers.
    Meadow for ½ plough.
Value of this land 20s; when acquired 10s; before 1066, 30s.
    Uhtred held this land under Robert son of Wymarc; he could
not sell without his permission, as the men of the Hundred testify.

In Haingeſteuuorde ten̅ Tetbalđ de Harđ . II . hiđ . Tra . e̅ . II .
car̅ . 7 ibi ſunt cu̅ . v . uiłłis 7 q̊đa̅ francig̅ . 7 III . cot̅ . P̊tu̅ . I . car̅ .
Paſta ad pecun̅ . H̅ tra uał . xl . ſoł . Qdo recep̅⳹ xx . ſoł . T . R . E ⳹
lx . ſoł . Hanc tra̅ tenue꞊r̅ . vi . ſochi . Ho꞊ꝥ . IIII . ho̅es Almer de
belinton . I . hiđ 7 I . uir̅g habue꞊r̅ . 7 v . denar̅ p ann̅ redde᷑ 7 q̊nt
h̅o Stig arch̅ dimiđ habuit . 7 vͣi . h̅o R . E . una̅ uir̅g habuit .
7 unu̅ denar̅ redditđ . Om̅s ů uende꞊ potue꞊r̅ .   *IN EDWINESꞰEV HD.*

In Berlai . ten̅ Tetbalđ de Harđ . IIII . hiđ 7 x . acs̅ . Tra . e̅
III . car̅ 7 dim̅ . In dn̅io ſunt . II . 7 III . uiłłi cu̅ p᷑ro 7 vIII . borđ
hn̅t . I . car̅ 7 dim̅ . Ibi . IIII . cot̅ 7 II . ſerui . Int tot̅ uał . xl . v . ſoł .
Qdo recep̅⳹ xv . ſoł . T . R . E ⳹ lx . ſoł . Hoc M͡ tenue꞊r̅ . v . ſochi .
Ho꞊ꝥ . III . ho̅es Algari . I . hiđ 7 x . acs̅ habue꞊r̅ . 7 quart h̅o
Guert co᷑m . II . hiđ habuit . 7 q̊nt h̅o Heraldi co᷑m . I . hiđ habuit . Hi
om̅s . uende꞊ potue꞊r̅ .

In Bercheuuei . ten̅ . II . ho̅es de Harđ . I . uir̅g 7 dim̅ . Tra . e̅
una car̅ . ſed n̅ eſt ibi . niſi . I . cot̅ . H̅ tra uał 7 ualuit . vII . ſoł .
T . R . E ⳹ x . ſoł . Hanc tra̅ tenue꞊r̅ . II . ſochi . Ho꞊ꝥ un̅ h̅o Algari co᷑m
. I . uir̅g habuit . 7 alt h̅o Eldret dim̅ uirg tenuit . dim̅ denar̅
reddebat p annu̅ . uende꞊ potuit .

In Helſangre ten̅ . III . ho̅es de Harđ . IIͣs . part uni̅ hidæ . Tra . e̅
. I . car̅ . 7 ibi . e̅ . H̅ tra uał . x . ſoł . Qdo recep̅⳹ v . ſoł . T . R . E ⳹ xx . ſoł .
Hanc tra̅ tenuit Ordmer h̅o ab᷑bis de Rameſẏ . 7 uende꞊ pot̅ .

Ipſe Harduin ten̅ *WIDIHALE* . ꝑ . v . hiđ 7 đim̅ ſe defđ . Tra
e̅ . vIII . car̅ . In dn̅io . II . hide . xx . acs̅ min̅ . 7 ibi ſunt . III . car̅ .
Ibi . xI . uiłłi cu̅ p᷑ro cu̅ . v . borđ hn̅t . v . car̅ . Ibi . IIII . cot̅
7 vI . ſerui . P̊tu̅ dim̅ car̅ . Paſtura ad pecun̅ . Nem̅ ad ſepes .
In totis ualent uał . Ix . lib᷑ . Qdo recep̅⳹ vI . lib᷑ . T . R . E ⳹ x . lib᷑ .

10 In HINXWORTH Theobald holds 2 hides from Hardwin.   141 d
    Land for 2 ploughs; they are there, with
        5 villagers, a Frenchman and 3 cottagers.
    Meadow for 1 plough; pasture for the livestock.
Value of this land, 40s; when acquired 20s; before 1066, 60s.
    6 Freemen held this land. Four of them, Aelmer of Bennington's
men, had 1 hide and 1 virgate, and paid 5d a year; the fifth,
Archbishop Stigand's man, had ½ (hide); the sixth, King Edward's
man, had 1 virgate; he paid 1 penny. All could sell.

    In EDWINSTREE Hundred
11 In BARLEY Theobald holds 4 hides and 10 acres from Hardwin.
    Land for 3½ ploughs. In lordship 2.
        3 villagers with a priest and 8 smallholders have 1½ ploughs.
            4 cottagers; 2 slaves.
    In total, value 45s; when acquired 15s; before 1066, 60s.
        5 Freemen held this manor. Three of them, Earl Algar's men, had
1 hide and 10 acres; the fourth, Earl Gyrth's man, had 2 hides;
the fifth, Earl Harold's man, had 1 hide. All of them could sell.

12 In BARKWAY 2 men hold 1½ virgates from Hardwin. Land for 1 plough,
    but it is not there, only
        1 cottager.
    The value of this land is and was 7s; before 1066, 10s.
        2 Freemen held this land. One of them, Earl Algar's man, had 1
virgate; the second, Aldred's man, held ½ virgate; he paid ½d a year;
he could sell.

13 In 'HAZELHANGER' 3 men hold 2 parts of 1 hide from Hardwin.
    Land for 1 plough; it is there.
    Value of this land, 10s; when acquired 5s; before 1066, 20s.
        Ordmer, the Abbot of Ramsey's man, held this land; he could sell.

14 Hardwin holds WYDDIAL himself. It answers for 5½ hides.
    Land for 8 ploughs. In lordship 2 hides less 20 acres; 3 ploughs there.
        11 villagers with a priest, with 5 smallholders, have 5 ploughs.
            4 cottagers; 6 slaves.
    Meadow for ½ plough; pasture for the livestock; wood for fences.
Total value £9; when acquired £6; before 1066 £10.

Hoc M̄ tenuer̃ . ix . ſocħi . Hoᷔ un̄ Sired hō Heraldi . i . hiđ 7 iii . uirg̃
habuit ꝑ uno M̄ . 7 Aluuarđ hō Algari . i . hiđ 7 dim̄ ꝑ . uno M̄ .

7 alij . vii . ſocħi . R . E . ii . hiđ 7 un̄a uirg̃ habuer̃ . hi ꝑ annū uice
comiti inuenieƀ . ix . deñ . uel . ii . aueras . 7 iiii . parte uni̅ aueræ .

In Odenhou . ten̄ Tetbalđ de harđ . i . hiđ 7 i . uirg̃ . Tra . ē . i . car̃
7 ibi . ē cū . i . borđ . Nem ad ſepes . H̄ tra ual xx . ſol . Qᷔdo recep̃ .
x . ſol . T . R . E . xxv . ſol . Hanc trā tenuer̃ . ii . ſocħi hōēs Algari .

In Trochinge . ten̄ Tetbalđ de Harđ . i . hidā   ſ uendē potuer̃ .
7 un̄a uirg̃ . Tra . ē . i . car̃ 7 dim̄ . 7 ibi ſuᷔ cū . ii . borđ . 7 i . ſocħo
de . iii . uirg̃ . Ibi . vi . cot . 7 ii . ſerui . P̃tū . vi . boƀ . Paſtura ađ
pecuñ . Nem ad ſepes . Int totū ual . xxv . ſol . Qᷔdo recep̃ . x . ſol .
T . R . E . xxv . ſol . Hanc trā tenu   ii . ſocħi . hōēs Stig
Archiepi . 7 uendē potuer̃ .

In Ichetone ten̄ Tetbalđ de Harđ . iii . uirg̃ 7 vi . acs . Tra . ē
. i . car̃ . 7 ibi . ē cū uno uilło 7 vi . borđ . 7 i . cot . P̃tū . v . boƀ .
Paſtura ad pecuñ . Val . xv . ſol . Qᷔdo recep̃ . x . ſol . T . R . E .
. xx . ſol . Hanc trā tenuer̃ . ii . ſocħi . R . E . uendē potuer̃ .

7 uicecomiti . iii . deñ ꝑ annū reddider̃ .

In Wachelei . ten̄ Tetbalđ de Harđ . xl . acs . Tra . ē . i . car̃ .
7 ibi . ē cū . vii . cot . P̃tū . ii . boƀᷔ . Nem ad ſepes . H̄ tra ual
xv . ſol . Qᷔdo recep̃ . vii . ſol . T . R . E . xv . ſol . Hanc trā tenuit
Edric hō Algari comit . uendē potuit .

In Berchedene ten̄ Petr̃ 7 Tetbalđ de Harđ . i . uirg̃ . Tra . ē
. i . car̃ . 7 ibi . ē cū . ii . borđ . p̃tū . ii . boƀ . Valuit ſēp 7 ual . x . ſol .
Hanc trā tenuer̃ . iii . ſocħi . Hoᷔ un̄ hō Eddeuæ pulchræ . iiii .
part̃ . i . uirg̃ habuit . 7 alt̃ hō Algari . iiii . part̃ ſimił habuit .

9 Freemen held this manor. One of them, Sired, Earl Harold's man, had 1 hide and 3 virgates as one manor, and Alfward, Earl Algar's man, 1½ hides as one manor. The other seven, King Edward's Freemen, had 2 hides and 1 virgate; they found 9d a year for the Sheriff, or 2 cartages and a fourth part of one cartage.

15 In HODENHOE Theobald holds 1 hide and 1 virgate from Hardwin. Land for 1 plough; it is there, with
    1 smallholder.
    Wood for fences.
Value of this land, 20s; when acquired 10s; before 1066, 25s.
    2 Freemen, Earl Algar's men, held this land; they could sell.

16 In THROCKING Theobald holds 1 hide and 1 virgate from Hardwin. Land for 1½ ploughs; they are there, with
    2 smallholders, and 1 Freeman with 3 virgates. 6 cottagers; 2 slaves.
    Meadow for 6 oxen; pasture for the livestock; wood for fences.
In total, value 25s; when acquired 10s; before 1066, 25s.
    2 Freemen, Archbishop Stigand's men, held this land; they could sell.

17 In BUNTINGFORD Theobald holds 3 virgates and 6 acres from Hardwin. Land for 1 plough; it is there, with
    1 villager, 6 smallholders and 1 cottager.
    Meadow for 5 oxen; pasture for the livestock.
Value 15s; when acquired 10s; before 1066, 20s.
    2 Freemen of King Edward's held this land; they could sell.
They paid 3d a year to the Sheriff.

18 In WAKELY Theobald holds 40 acres from Hardwin. Land for 1 plough; it is there, with
    7 cottagers.
    Meadow for 2 oxen; wood for fences.
Value of this land, 15s; when acquired 7s; before 1066, 15s.
    Edric, Earl Algar's man, held this land; he could sell.

*19 In BERKESDEN Peter and Theobald hold 1 virgate from Hardwin. Land for 1 plough; it is there, with
    2 smallholders.
    Meadow for 2 oxen.
The value is 10s and always was.
    3 Freemen held this land. One of them, Edeva the Fair's man, had a fourth part of 1 virgate; the second, Algar's man, likewise had a fourth part; the third, Gyrth's man, had ½ virgate; they could sell.

7 tcius hō Guerd dim̄ uirḡ habuit . 7 uende potuer̄ . De hac

uirga reclamat Alanus . iii . partes ſe habe juſte|.Nā inde

erat ſaiſit q̄do mare nuprime tranſiuit . ut hōes de hund

ſibi portaɴ teſtimon̄ . Sed Harduin reclamat Petrū uicecom̄

142 a

ad ᵱteċtorē 7 lib̄atorē juſſu ep̄i baioc̄ . qđ ei lib̄auit ᵱ excābio

In Aneſtei ten̄ Pagan de Harđ dim̄ hiđ. ᛒ de Suterehele.

Tra . ē . i . car̄ 7 dim̄ . 7 ibi ſunt cū . iiii . borđ . 7 iiii . cot̄ . 7 uno

ſeruo . p̄tū dim̄ car̄ . Paſta ađ pecun̄ . Silua . xii . porc̄.

Ħ tra ual̄ . xx . ſol̄ . Q̄do recep̄. x . ſol̄ . T . R . E. xx . ſol̄.

Hanc tenuit Aluuard hō Algari . 7 uende potuit.

Ipſe Harđ ten̄ BERCHEHÁSTEDE . IN HERFORD HVND́.

ᵱ . v . hiđ ſe defđ . Tra . ē . viii . car̄ . In dn̄io . iii . hidæ . 7 ibi

ſunt . ii . car̄ . 7 tcia pot̄ fieri . Ibi . vi . uiłłi cū . v . borđ . hn̄t

iiii . car̄ . 7 v . pot̄ fieri . Ibi . vi . cot̄ . 7 i . ſeruus . p̄tū . iii . car̄.

Silua . l . porc̄ . In totis ualent̄ ual̄ . c . ſol̄ . Q̄do recep̄.

l . ſol̄ . T . R . E. c . ſol̄ . De hoc ᛗ tenuit Semar . ii . hiđ . 7 q̄dā

uidua Leueſa . ii . hiđ . 7 Wluric . i . hiđ . Hæ træ fuer̄ de ele

moſina . R . E . 7 om̄iū regū Anteceſſoꝛ ſuoꝗ . ut ſcira teſtat̄.

ᛗ Ipſe Harduin ten̄ BRANDEFELLE . ᵱ . v . hiđ ſe defđ . Tra . ē

vi . car̄ . In dn̄io . iii . hidæ . 7 ibi . ē . i . car̄ 7 dim̄ . 7 dim̄ pot̄ fieri.

Ibi . x . uiłłi hn̄t . ii . car̄ 7 dim̄ . 7 adhuc . i . car̄ 7 dim̄ pot̄ fieri.

Ibi . i . ſeruus . P̄tū . i . car̄ . Paſtura ađ pec̄ . Silua . c . porc̄.

7 xii . den̄ de ea . In totis ualent̄ ual̄ . iiii . lib̄ . Q̄do recep̄.

xl . ſol̄ . T . R . E. c . ſol̄ . Hoc ᛗ tenuit Achi teign̄ Heraldi.

In Briceuuold ten̄ Balduin de Harđ ᛒ 7 uende pot̄.

iii . uirḡ . Tra . ē . ii . car̄ . Ibi . ē una . 7 alia poteſt fieri . Ibi . ii.

uiłłi . 7 iii . borđ . P̄tū . iiii . bob̄ . Silua . xv . porc̄ . Ħ tra ual̄

v . ſol̄ . Q̄do recep̄. x . ſol̄ . 7 tntđ T . R . E.

Count Alan claims that he should rightly have three parts of this virgate;* for he was in possession thereof when he recently crossed the sea, as the men of the Hundred bear witness for him. But Hardwin claims Peter the Sheriff as protector and deliverer, by order of the Bishop of Bayeux, because he delivered it to him in exchange for Libury.

142 a

0 In ANSTEY Payne holds ½ hide from Hardwin. Land for 1½ ploughs; they are there, with
    4 smallholders, 4 cottagers and 1 slave.
    Meadow for ½ plough; pasture for the livestock; woodland, 12 pigs.
Value of this land, 20s; when acquired 10s; before 1066, 20s.
    Alfward, Earl Algar's man, held it; he could sell.

In HERTFORD Hundred
21 Hardwin holds (LITTLE) BERKHAMSTED himself. It answers for 5 hides.
    Land for 8 ploughs. In lordship 3 hides; 2 ploughs there; a third possible.
    6 villagers with 5 smallholders have 4 ploughs; a fifth possible.
      6 cottagers; 1 slave.
    Meadow for 3 ploughs; woodland, 50 pigs.
Total value 100s; when acquired 50s; before 1066, 100s.
    Saemer the priest held 2 hides of this manor; a widow, Leofeva, 2 hides; and Wulfric Warden 1 hide. These lands were of the alms(lands) of King Edward, and of all the Kings his predecessors, as the Shire testifies.

22 M.Hardwin holds BRAMFIELD himself. It answers for 5 hides.
    Land for 6 ploughs. In lordship 4* hides; 1½ ploughs there; ½ possible.
    10 villagers have 2½ ploughs; a further 1½ ploughs possible. 1 slave.
    Meadow for 1 plough; pasture for the livestock; woodland, 100 pigs, and 12d from it.
Total value £4; when acquired 40s; before 1066, 100s.
    Aki, a thane of Earl Harold's, held this manor; he could sell.

23 In BRICEWOLD Baldwin holds 3 virgates from Hardwin. Land for 2 ploughs; 1 there; another possible.
    2 villagers; 3 smallholders.
    Meadow for 4 oxen; woodland, 15 pigs.
Value of this land, 5s; when acquired 10s; before 1066 as much.

TERRA EDGARI ADELING. *IN EDWINESKEV HD*

Edgarvs Adeling 7 Goduin dé eo ten in Bercheuuei
.I. hid 7 dim. Tra . e . II . car. In dnio . e una . 7 IIII . bord
cu . IIII . cot hnt . I . car. Ibi . I . seruus. Pasta ad pecun . Silua
xv . porc . H tra ual xl . sol . Qdo recep. x . sol . T.R.E. xl . sol.
Hanc tenuer . II . sochi hoes Asgari . 7 uende potuer.

Isde Goduin ten de Edgaro *HOREMEDE* . p . vi . hid 7 iii.
uirg se defd . Tra . e . x . car . In dnio sunt . iiii . 7 v . pot fieri.
Ibi . vi . uitti cu . xv . bord hnt . v . car . Ibi . ii . cot 7 vi . serui.
Ptu . i . car . Pasta ad pecun . Silua . xxiiii . porc . In totis ua
lent ual . viii . lib . Qdo recep. vi . lib . T.R.E. xii . lib.
De hoc M tenuit Alnod teign Stig arch . i . hid 7 dim p . i . M.
7 Vluuin ho Asgari . i . hida . 7 Aluuard ho Ælmær de belint
. i . hida . 7 vii . sochi . R.E . tenuer . iii . hid 7 i . uirg . uicecomiti
xiii . denar p annu reddider . Oms hi tra sua uende potuer.
Hos . vii . sochos 7 Vluuin 7 Aluuard apposuit Ilbt uicec
huic M tepore . R.W . qui n fuer ibi T.R.E. ut hund testat.

TERRA MANNON BRITONIS. *IN KEDVNGE HVND.*

Maino Brito ten in Deneslai tcia part de dim hida.
Tra . e uno boui . Val 7 ualuit sep . xii . den . Hanc tra te
nuit Engelri T.R.E. 7 jacuit in Tredunge 7 est de . vii . hid
quas com morit assupsit.

XL. TERRA GISLEBERTI FILIJ SALOMON.

Gislebertvs fili Salom ten *MAPTESHALE* . p . iii.
hid 7 una uirg se defd . Ibi sunt . iii . uitti 7 iiii . cot.
H tra . e appciata in Bedefordscyre cu alia tra.
Hanc tra tenuit Leuuin teign . R.E.

38   LAND OF PRINCE EDGAR*

In EDWINSTREE Hundred

1   Prince Edgar holds 1½ hides in BARKWAY and Godwin from him.
Land for 2 ploughs. In lordship 1.
     4 smallholders with 4 cottagers have 1 plough. 1 slave.
     Pasture for the livestock; woodland, 15 pigs.
     ·Value of this land, 40s; when acquired 10s; before 1066, 40s.
     2 Freemen, Asgar the Constable's men, held it; they could sell.

2 M.Godwin also holds HORMEAD from Edgar. It answers for 6 hides
and 3 virgates. Land for 10 ploughs. In lordship 4; a fifth possible.
     6 villagers with 15 smallholders have 5 ploughs.
       2 cottagers; 6 slaves.
     Meadow for 1 plough; pasture for the livestock; woodland, 24 pigs.
     Total value £8; when acquired £6; before 1066 £12.
     Of this manor Alnoth, a thane of Archbishop Stigand's, held 1½
hides as one manor; Wulfwin, Asgar the Constable's man, 1 hide;
Alfward, Aelmer of Bennington's man, 1 hide; 7 Freemen of King
Edward's held 3 hides and 1 virgate; they paid 13d a year to the
Sheriff; all these could sell their land. Ilbert the Sheriff placed
these 7 Freemen and Wulfwin and Alfward in this manor after
1066; they were not there before 1066, as the Hundred testifies.

39   LAND OF MAINOU THE BRETON

In TRING Hundred

1   Mainou the Breton holds the third part of ½ hide in DUNSLEY.
Land for 1 ox.
The value is and always was 12d.
     Engelric held this land before 1066; it lay in Tring and is
of the 7 hides which the Count of Mortain took.

40   LAND OF GILBERT SON OF SOLOMON

1   Gilbert son of Solomon holds MEPPERSHALL. It answers for 3 hides
and 1 virgate.
     3 villagers; 4 cottagers.
This land is assessed in Bedfordshire with (his) other land*.
     Leofwin, a thane of King Edward's, held this land.

Sᴵɢᴀʀ Dᴇ Cɪᴏᴄʜᴇꜱ . *Iɴ Oᴅᴇꜱᴇɪ ʜᴠɴᴅʀᴇᴛ.*

Sɪɢᴀʀ de Cioches ten᷑ *Rɪꜱᴇɴᴅᴇɴᴇ* . ᵽ . v . hiđ ſe defđ.

Tra᷑ . e̅ . vɪɪɪ . car᷑ . In dn̅io . ɪɪɪ . hidæ . 7 ibi ſunt . ɪɪ . car᷑ . 7 tcia᷑

pot fieri . Ibi . vɪɪɪ . uilti cu̅ . ɪɪɪ . borđ . hn̅t . v . car . Ibi un⁹

ſocħs . 7 ɪɪɪ . cot᷑ 7 ɪɪɪɪ . ſerui . p̊tu̅ dim᷑ car᷑ . Paſta᷑ ad pecun᷑.

142 b

Silua . ʟ . porc᷑ . In totis ualent᷑ ual᷑ 7 ualuit . c . x . ſol . T . R . E꞊᷑

x . ſol . Hoc m̅ tenuer᷑ . ɪɪ . ſocħi hões Stig᷑ archieᵽi . 7 uendᵉ᷑

Iɴ Bradefelle ten᷑ Sigar . ɪ . hiđ . 7 ɪɪɪ . partes   ⌐ potuer᷑.

uni uirg⁹᷑ . Tra᷑ . e̅ . ɪɪ . car᷑ . Ibi . e̅ una . 7 alia pot fieri . Ibi . ɪɪɪɪ,

uilti cu̅ . ɪɪ . borđ . P̊tu̅ dim᷑ car᷑ . Paſtura ad pecun᷑ . Silua . ʟ.

porc᷑ . Int totu̅ ual᷑ 7 ualuit . xxx . ſol . T . R . E꞊᷑ ʟx . ſol . Hanc

tra᷑᷑ tenuit Anſgot hõ Stig᷑ Archieᵽi . 7 uendᵉ᷑ potuit.

Dᴇʀᴍᴀɴ 7 Aʟᴡᴀʀᴅ⁹᷑ ten᷑ de rege *Wᴏᴅᴛᴏɴᴇ* . ᵽ . v.

hiđ ſe defđ . Tra᷑ . e̅ . vɪɪ . car᷑ . In dn̅io . ɪɪɪ . hidæ 7 dim᷑.

7 ibi ſunt . ɪɪ . car᷑᷑ . 7 adhuc dim᷑ pot fieri . Ibi . x . uilti cu̅ . ɪɪɪɪ.

borđ hn̅t . ɪɪɪɪ . car᷑ 7 dim᷑ . Ibi . ɪɪɪɪ . ſerui . 7 ɪ . molin᷑ de xɪɪɪ.

ſolid᷑ . 7 ɪɪɪɪ . den᷑ . P̊tu̅ . ɪ . car᷑ . Paſtura ad pecun᷑ . Silua

c . porc᷑ . Int totu̅ ual᷑ 7 ualuit . c . ſol . T . R . E꞊᷑ vɪɪ . liƀ.

Hanc tra᷑᷑ tenuit Aluuin⁹ Horne teign⁹ . R . E . 7 uendᵉ᷑ pot᷑.

m̅ Iᴘꜱᴇ Dᴇʀᴍᴀɴ ten᷑ *Wᴀʟᴄʜʀᴀ* . ᵽ . x . hiđ ſe defđ . Tra᷑ . e̅

xɪɪ . car᷑ . In dn̅io . v . hidæ . 7 ibi ſunt . ɪɪ . car᷑ 7 aliæ dụæ

poſſunt fieri . Ibi . xɪɪɪɪ . uilti cu̅ pƀro 7 vɪ . borđ hn̅t

vɪɪɪ . car᷑ . Ibi . vɪɪɪ . cot᷑ 7 ɪɪɪɪ . ſerui . Paſtura ad pecun᷑.

Silua . cc . porc᷑ . In totis ualent᷑ ual᷑ . x . liƀ . Q̷do receᵽ꞊᷑

vɪɪɪ . liƀ . T . R . E꞊᷑ xvɪ . liƀ . Hoc m̅ tenuit Aluuin⁹ horne

teign⁹ . R . E . 7 uendᵉ᷑ potuit.

Iɴ Stuterehele . ten᷑ Derman . ɪɪɪ . uirg᷑ . Tra᷑ . e̅ . ɪ . car᷑.

ſ꞊ n̅ eſt ibi car᷑ . H̅ tra᷑ . e̅ apᵽciata in Watone m̅ derman.

LAND OF SIGAR OF CHOCQUES

In ODSEY Hundred

1 Sigar of Chocques holds RUSHDEN.* It answers for 5 hides.
Land for 8 ploughs. In lordship 3 hides; 2 ploughs there;
a third possible.
    8 villagers with 3 smallholders have 5 ploughs.
      1 Freeman; 3 cottagers; 4 slaves.
    Meadow for ½ plough; pasture for the livestock;   142 b
      woodland, 50 pigs.
The total value is and was 110s; before 1066, 10s*.
    2 Freemen, Archbishop Stigand's men, held this manor; they
could sell.

2 In BROADFIELD Sigar holds 1 hide and 3 parts of 1 virgate.
Land for 2 ploughs; 1 there; another possible.
    4 villagers with 2 smallholders.
    Meadow for ½ plough; pasture for the livestock; woodland, 50 pigs.
In total, the value is and was 30s; before 1066, 60s.
    Asgot, Archbishop Stigand's man, held this land; he could sell.

42   LAND OF THE KING'S THANES

In BROADWATER Hundred

1 Derman and Alfward hold WATTON from the King. It answers for 5
hides. Land for 7 ploughs. In lordship 3½ hides; 2 ploughs there;
a further ½ possible.
    10 villagers with 4 smallholders have 4½ ploughs. 4 slaves.
    1 mill at 13s 4d; meadow for 1 plough; pasture for the livestock;
      woodland, 100 pigs.
In total, the value is and was 100s; before 1066 £7.
    Alwin Horne, a thane of King Edward's, held this land; he could sell.

2 M.Derman holds WALKERN himself. It answers for 10 hides.
Land for 12 ploughs. In lordship 5 hides; 2 ploughs there;
another 2 possible.
    14 villagers with a priest and 6 smallholders have 8 ploughs.
      8 cottagers; 4 slaves.
    Pasture for the livestock; woodland, 200 pigs.
Total value £10; when acquired £8; before 1066 £16.
    Alwin Horne, a thane of King Edward's, held this manor; he
could sell.

3 In LIBURY Derman holds 3 virgates. Land for 1 plough,
but there is no plough there.
    This land is assessed in Watton, Derman's manor.

In ead uilla ten̅ Derman . iii . ac̅s . Val̅ 7 ualuer̅ ſep̅ . iii . den̅.

In Sueuecha̅p ten̅ Derman dim̅ uirg̅ . Tra . e̅ . ii . bob₇.

Val̅ 7 ualuit ſep̅ . xii . den̅ . Hanc tra̅ 7 alias ſupiores
tenuit Aluuin̊ horne teign̊ . R.E . 7 uende̅ potuit.

In Wermelai . ten̅ Aluuin̊ dodeſone . ii . hid̅ 7 dim̅ de
rege . Tra . e̅ . ii . car̅ . 7 ibi ſunt cu̅ . vi . uilliṣ 7 uno ſeruo.
P̊tu̅ . ii . car̅ . Paſtura ad pecun̅ . Silua . cl . porc̅ . Int̅ totu̅
ual̅ . xl . ſol̅ . Q̊do recep̅꞉ l . ſol̅ . T.R.E꞉ lx . ſol̅ . Hoc m̅
tenuit Wluuard hō Aſgari ſtalri . 7 uende̅ potuit.

Hoc m̅ fuit uenditu̅ . iii . mark̅ auri . p̊ aduen̅t regis Willi̅.

Petrus q̊da̅ burgenſis ten̅ . ii . hid̅ de rege in Dodeſdone.

Tra . e̅ . i . car̅ 7 dim̅ . 7 ibi ſunt cu̅ . i . uilto . 7 iii . cot
7 ii . ſeruis . P̊tu̅ . ii . car̅ . Paſta̅ ad pecun̅ . Silua . x . porc̅.
Int̅ totu̅ ual̅ . xx . ſol̅ . Q̊do recep̅꞉ x . ſol̅ . T.R.E꞉ xxx . ſol̅.
Hoc m̅ tenuit Goda hō Eddid reginæ . 7 uende̅ potuit.

Balduin̊ q̊da̅ ſeruiens regis ten̅ . iii . uirg̅ in Brichedone.
Tra . e̅ . i . car̅ . 7 ibi . e̅ . Silua . xl . porc̅ . H̅ tra ual̅ 7 ualuit
x . ſol̅ . T.R.E꞉ xv . ſol̅ . Hanc tra̅ tenuer̅ . iii . frs̅ . 7 uende̅

In Briceuuolde ten̅ q̊da̅ pbr̅ 7 ſoror ej̊   ⌐ potuer̅.
de rege . iii . uirg̅ . Tra . e̅ . ii . car̅ . Ibi . e̅ una . 7 alia pot̅
fieri . Ibi . i . uilts 7 i . cot̅ . p̊tu̅ . iiii . bob̅ . Silua . xv . porc̅ . H̅ tra
ual̅ . v . ſol̅ . Q̊do recep̅꞉ x . ſol̅ . 7 t̅nt̅d T.R.E꞉ Iſtimet tenuer̅
T.R.E . de ſoca ej̊ . 7 uende̅ potuer̅.

In Thepeca̅pe ten̅ q̊da̅ pbr̅ de elemoſina regis dim̅ hida̅.
Tra . e̅ . i . car̅ . 7 ibi . e̅ cu̅ . ii . ſeruis . P̊tu̅ . i . car̅ . 7 i . molin̅ de . xii.
den̅ . H̅ tra ual̅ 7 ualuit . xv . ſol̅ . T.R.E꞉ xx . ſol̅ . Iſtemet
tenuit . T.R.E . 7 adhuc ten̅ in elemoſina . IN BRADEWATRE HD̅.

In WELGE ten̅ q̊da̅ pbr̅ . i . hid̅ in elemoſina de rege . Tra . e̅

4· In the same village Derman holds 3 acres.
The value is and always was 3d.

5 In SACOMBE Derman holds ½ virgate. Land for 2 oxen.
The value is and always was 12d.
Alwin Horne, a thane of King Edward's, held this land and
the others above; he could sell.

In HERTFORD Hundred
6 In WORMLEY Alwin Dodson holds 2½ hides from the King.
Land for 2 ploughs; they are there, with
6 villagers; 1 slave.
Meadow for 2 ploughs; pasture for the livestock; woodland, 150 pigs.
In total, value 40s; when acquired 50s; before 1066, 60s.
Wulfward, Asgar the Constable's man, held this manor; he
could sell. This manor was sold for 3 marks of gold after 1066.

*7 Peter, a burgess, holds 2 hides from the King in HODDESDON.
Land for 1½ ploughs; they are there, with
1 villager, 3 cottagers and 2 slaves.
Meadow for 2 ploughs; pasture for the livestock; woodland, 10 pigs.
In total, value 20s; when acquired 10s; before 1066, 30s.
Gode, Queen Edith's man, held this manor; she could sell.

8 Baldwin, a Servant of the King's, holds 3 virgates in BRICKENDON.
Land for 1 plough; it is there.
Woodland, 40 pigs.
The value of this land is and was 10s; before 1066, 15s.
·Three brothers held this land; they could sell.

9 In BRICEWOLDE a priest and his sister hold 3 virgates from the
King. Land for 2 ploughs; 1 there; another possible.
1 villager; 1 cottager.
Meadow for 4 oxen; woodland, 15 pigs.
Value of this land, 5s; when acquired 10s; before 1066 as much.
They held it themselves before 1066, of King Edward's jurisdiction;
they could sell.

10 In EPCOMBS a priest holds ½ hide, of the King's alms.
Land for 1 plough; it is there, with
2 slaves.
Meadow for 1 plough; 1 mill at 12d.
The value of this land is and was 15s; before 1066, 20s.
He held it himself before 1066 and still holds it, in alms.

In BROADWATER Hundred
11 In WELWYN a priest holds 1 hide, in alms from the King.

.iii.car̄. In dn̄io.ē una. 7 alia pot fieri.Ibi.vi.bord̄ hn̄t
.i.car̄.Ibi.ii.cot.P̄tu.i.car̄.Paſtura ad pecun̄.Silua.L.porc̄.
Int totū ual 7 ualuit ſēp.xxv.ſol.Iſtemet tenuit de rege.E.

In elemoſina.7 jacet in̄ æccła ejd̄ uillæ.De hac elemoſina
inuaſit Witts blach hō ep̄i baioc̄ ſup regē.xii.ac̄s.

In Aiete ten̄ p̄poſit de iſto hundret ƒ ut hund̄ teſtat.̄
ix.ac̄s.de rege.Tra.ē uno boui.Val 7 ualuit ſēp.ix.
denar̄.Hanc tr̄a tenuit Siuuard hō Aluuini de Godtone.

In Rodenehangre ten̄ Aluuard̄ de Merde ƒ 7 uend̄e pot.
łai.iii.uirḡ de rege.Tra.ē.i.car̄.s; n̄ eſt ibi.niſi.i.cot.
Silua.xxiiii.porc̄.H̄ tra ual 7 ualuit ſēp.v.ſolid̄.
Iſtemet tenuit.T.R.E.7 dare potuit cui uoluit.7 iii.den̄
p̄ ann̄u redded̄ uicecomiti.

In Sueuech̄ap.ten̄.i.ſochs regis dim uirḡ.Tra.ē.ii..
boḃȝ.Val 7 ualuit ſēp xv.den̄.Iſtemet tenuit.T.R.E.
hō Leuuini.7 redded̄.i.obolū p̄ ann̄u de c̄ſuetudine.

In Staneſtede ten̄ Godmund̄ IN BRACHINGES HVND.
iii.uirḡ de rege.Tra.ē.vi.boḃȝ.7 ibi ſunt cū.iiii.bord̄.
p̄tu.i.car̄.Silua.viii.porc̄.H̄ tra ual 7 ualuit ſēp
.x.ſol.Iſtemet tenuit de rege.E.7 uend̄e potuit.

.XLII. TERRA VXORIS RICARDI. IN BRACHINGES HD.
Rothais uxor Ricardi.f Gislebti ten̄ STANDONE.
p̄ xi.hid̄ ſe defd̄.Tra.ē.xxiiii.car̄.In dn̄io.vi.hide.
7 ibi ſunt.v.car̄.Ibi xxix.uitti cū p̄bro 7 xv.bord̄
7 ii.ſochis 7 q̄d̄a franciḡ hn̄t.xii.car̄.7 adhuc.vii.
poſſunt fieri.Ibi.ix.cot.7 viii.ſerui.7 v.molend̄

Land for 3 ploughs. In lordship 1; another possible.
   6 smallholders have 1 plough. 2 cottagers.
   Meadow for 1 plough; pasture for the livestock; woodland, 50 pigs.
In total, the value is and always was 25s.
   He held it himself from King Edward in alms. It lies in the   142 c
(lands of the) church of this village.
   William Black, the Bishop of Bayeux's man, annexed 12 acres of
this alms land in the King's despite, as the Hundred testifies.

12   In AYOT (ST. LAWRENCE) the reeve of this Hundred holds 9 acres
from the King. Land for 1 ox.
The value is and always was 9d.
   Siward, Alwin Gotton's man, held this land; he could sell.

13   In 'RODHANGER' Alfward of Mardley holds 3 virgates from the King.
Land for 1 plough, but it is not there, only
   1 cottager.
   Woodland, 24 pigs.
The value of this land is and always was 5s.
   He held it himself before 1066 and could grant to whom he
would; he paid 3d a year to the Sheriff.

14   In SACOMBE 1 Freeman of the King's holds ½ virgate.
Land for 2 oxen.
The value is and always was 15d.
   He held it himself before 1066; [he was] Earl Leofwin's man;
he paid ½d a year in customary dues.

In BRAUGHING Hundred
15   In STANSTEAD (ABBOTS) Godmund holds 3 virgates from the King.
Land for 6 oxen; they are there, with
   4 smallholders.
   Meadow for 1 plough; woodland, 8 pigs.
The value of this land is and always was 10s.
   He held it himself from King Edward; he could sell.

42 [a]   LAND OF RICHARD SON OF GILBERT'S WIFE   142 d

In BRAUGHING Hundred
1   Rothais, wife of Richard son of Count Gilbert, holds STANDON.
It answers for 11 hides. Land for 24 ploughs. In lordship 6 hides;
   5 ploughs there.
      29 villagers with a priest, 15 smallholders, 2 Freemen
         and a Frenchman have 12 ploughs; a further 7 possible.
      9 cottagers; 8 slaves.

de . xlv . fot . P̊tū . xxiiii . car̄ . Paſtura ad pecuń .

Silua fexcent porc̄ . Ibi . ii . aripend uineæ . In totis ua

lentijs ual . xxxiii . liƀ . Q̊do recep̄ xvi . liƀ . T . R . E .⁊

xxxiiii . liƀ . Hoc M̃ tenuit Stigand Archieṗs .

In hoc M̃ fuer̄ . vi . focħi hões ejdem archi . 7 q́fq̷ unā

hidā habuit . 7 uende̅ potuer̄ præt foca . Vnus aut̄

eoꝗ etiā focā fua cū tra uende̅ poterat .

.XLIII **A**TERRA VXORIS HVG⁊ DE GRENTE ᵐᵃⁱᶠⁿⁱˡ IN HERTFORD HVND̊ .

DELIZ uxor Hugon̄ de Grentmaifnil ten̄ BROCHES

BORNE . ꝑ . v . hid̄ 7 dim̄ fe defd̄ . Tra . e̅ . vi . car̄ . In dnĩo

iii . hidæ 7 iii . uirg̅ . 7 ibi . e̅ una car̄ . Ibi . iiii . uiłłi cū

pƀro 7 uno focħo 7 ii . bord̄ . ħnt . v . car̄ . Ibi . ii . ſerui .

7 . i . molend̄ . de . viii . fot . P̊tū . vi . fot . 7 iiii . fot de fæno .

Paſtura ad pecuń . Silua . cc . porc̄ . In totis ualent̄

iiii . liƀ . Q̊do recep̄⁊ lx . fot . T.R.E.⁊ vii . liƀ . Hoc M̃

tenuit Stig archieṗs . 7 ibi fuit . i . focħs hō 7 ꝑpofit̄⁹

ejd̄ archiepĩ . dim̄ hid̄ habuit . 7 uende̅ potuit .

.XLII. II **F**TERRA filie RADVLFI Tailgebos IN BRÆCHINGES HVND⁊ .

ilia Radulfi tailgebofch ten̄ in Hodefdone . iiii . hid̄ .

de feudo Hugon̄ de belcāp . Tra . e̅ . v . car̄ . In dnĩo . ii . hidæ .

7 ibi . e̅ una car̄ . 7 alia pot̄ fieri . Ibi . iiii . uiłłi cū pƀro

7 q̊dā francig̅ . 7 viii . bord̄ . ħnt . ii . car̄ . 7 tcia pot̄

fieri . Ibi . ii . cot 7 iii . ſerui . 7 i . moliñ de . x . fot . P̊tū

v . car̄ . Paſtura ad pecuń . Silua . xl . porc̄ . 7 de paſta

x . deń . In totis ualent̄ ual 7 ualuit . lxx . fot . T.R.E.⁊

vi . liƀ . Hoc M̃ tenuit Leuuin hō Heraldi comitis .

7 uende̅ potuit . 7 de hac tra tenuit ᴳᵒᵈᵗᵒⁿ Aluuin⁹ hō R . E .

. i . hidā . 7 uende̅ potuit . Radulf⁹ tailgebofc accep̄

eā de Staneſtede . 7 |ᵃᵖ pofuit huic Manerio .

5 mills at 45s; meadow for 24 ploughs; pasture for the livestock;
woodland, 600 pigs; 2 *arpents* of vines.
Total value £33*; when acquired £16; before 1066 £34.

Archbishop Stigand held this manor. In this manor were 6 Freemen,
the Archbishop's men; each had 1 hide; they could sell, except
the jurisdiction. One of them however could also sell his
jurisdiction with the land.

43 ' LAND OF HUGH OF GRANDMESNIL'S WIFE

In HERTFORD Hundred

* 1 Adelaide, wife of Hugh of Grandmesnil, holds BROXBOURNE. It
answers for 5½ hides. Land for 6 ploughs. In lordship 3 hides
and 3 virgates; 1 plough there.
4 villagers with a priest, a Freeman and 2 smallholders have
5 ploughs. 2 slaves.
1 mill at 8s; meadow, 6s, and 4s from hay; pasture for the
livestock; woodland, 200 pigs.
Total value £4; when acquired 60s; before 1066 £7.

Archbishop Stigand held this manor. There was a Freeman there,
the Archbishop's man and reeve; he had ½ hide; he could sell.

44 LAND OF RALPH TALLBOYS' DAUGHTER

In BRAUGHING Hundred

1 Ralph Tallboys' daughter holds 4 hides in HUNSDON* from the
Holding of Hugh of Beauchamp. Land for 5 ploughs.
In lordship 2 hides; 1 plough there; another possible.
4 villagers with a priest, a Frenchman and 8 smallholders
have 2 ploughs; a third possible. 2 cottagers; 3 slaves.
1 mill at 10s; meadow for 5 ploughs; pasture for the
livestock; woodland, 40 pigs, and from pasture 10d.
The total value is and was 70s; before 1066 £6.

Leofwin, Earl Harold's man, held this manor; he could sell.
Alwin Gotton, King Edward's man, held 1 hide of this land;
he could sell. Ralph Tallboys received it from Stanstead and
attached it to this manor.

BEDFORDSHIRE
8   LAND OF ST. BENEDICT'S OF RAMSEY   210 d

In CLIFTON Hundred

* EB
1
  8 M. The Abbot holds HOLWELL himself for 3½ hides.
Land for 4 ploughs. In lordship 1 hide; 1 plough there.
8 villagers have 3 ploughs; 1 smallholder and 2 slaves.
Meadow for 1 plough.
Value £4; the value always was as much.
This manor lay and lies in the lordship of St. Benedict's Church.

9   LAND OF ST.PETER'S OF WESTMINSTER   211 a

In CLIFTON Hundred

EB
2
  1 M. The Abbot of Westminster holds 6½ hides in HOLWELL.
Land for 6 ploughs. In lordship 3 hides and ½ virgate; 2
ploughs there.
11 villagers have 4 ploughs. 4 smallholders and 2 slaves.
2 mills, 20s; meadow for 1 plough.
The value is and was 100s.
This manor lay and lies in the lordship of St. Peter's Church.

23   LAND OF HUGH OF BEAUCHAMP

* EB
3

7; 41-43	GOLDINGTON...		212 d; 213 d
16	SALPH...		213 a
(49) 56	COPLE...		214 a

Ralph Tallboys had this land in exchange for WARE.

CAMBRIDGESHIRE
32 (30)   LAND OF PICOT OF CAMBRIDGE

* EC
1
  10 In HATLEY Picot holds 2 hides ...   200 c
Picot states that he has one hide of this land in exchange for
EYNESBURY and the other in exchange for RUSHDEN, which
Ilbert of Hertford delivered to him.

EC
2
  25 In the same village (HATLEY) Picot holds 1 hide ...   201 a
Picot states that he has it in exchange for RUSHDEN, which
Sigar (of Chocques) holds.

ESSEX   AMWELL, HERTFORD, HODDESDON see 23,4 note.

NOTES

ABBREVIATIONS used in the notes.

DB..Domesday Book. MS..Manuscript. EPNS..English Place-Name Society Survey.[*]
VCH..Victoria County History.[*] OEB..G. Tengvik *Old English Bynames*, Uppsala 1938
(*Nomina Germanica* volume 4). KCD..Kemble *Codex Diplomaticus*. BCS.. Birch
Cartularium Saxonicum. IE and ICC..see Appendix (App.) ff.. and following pages.
    [*]refers to the County volume, unless otherwise stated.

The manuscript is written on leaves, or folios, of parchment (sheep-skin), measuring about 15
inches by 11 (38 by 28 cm), on both sides. On each side, or page, are two columns, making
four to each folio. The folios were numbered in the 17th century, and the four columns of
each are here lettered a,b,c,d. The manuscript emphasises words and usually distinguishes
chapters and sections by the use of red ink. Underlining indicates deletion.

HERTFORDSHIRE. In red, across the top of the page, spread above both columns:
Herfordscire folios 132-136, *Hertfordscire* folios 137-142.

B		HERTFORD. See also 23,4 note.
B	2	DUES. *Consuetudo,* normally translated 'customary dues'; in the Borough chapter 'customary' is here omitted, to avoid excessive repetition; so B 2-4 and 6-10.
B	11	BOROUGH TOWN. The *burgus* (borough) was in origin a garrisoned fortress. Hertford was fortified by Edward the Elder in 912, as a base of operations against the Danes of Bedford, Huntingdon and Cambridge , and its first *burgenses* (burgesses) were its garrison. The *suburbium* (here translated 'borough town'), is a word rare enough to be misconceived in the ·Berkhamsted entry (15,1), and was probably intended to comprise the whole population, including those who lived without the walls, and those who did not have burgess rights and status. Elsewhere in Hertfordshire, DB burgesses were resident at Berkhamsted, which may or may not have been fortified before 1066, and also at Ashwell (9,10), which was still described as a *burgus*, and at Stanstead (25,2) where they paid local dues. Both places were strategically sited for the initiation of Edward's campaign and may have originated as subsidiary fortresses of the army of Hertford. It is theoretically possible that the 46 burgesses of St. Albans (10,5) were not residents, but Londoners, like those of Staines (Middlesex 4,5), who lived at *Staeningehaga withinne Lundne* (possibly around Staining Lane), whom Edward the Confessor granted to Westminster's manor of Staines (KCD 855). But the St. Albans burgesses, who held half a hide there,were probably resident; and the town is located in the middle of 'Danish' Hundred (see 5,2 note). At·Berkhamsted the burgesses had the right to levy tolls, and tolls are otherwise named in Hertfordshire only at the Borough of Ashwell and at St. Albans. In Hertfordshire, as in other counties, markets were located in the Boroughs, their profits and tolls assigned to the burgesses. St. Alban's Abbey acquired Kingsbury about 1000, EPNS 90.
		£7 10s. DB uses the old English currency system, which endured for a thousand years until 1971. The pound contained 20 shillings, each of 12 pence, and the abbreviations £.s.d. preserved the DB terms librae, solidi and denarii.
L	11	ABBOT OF RAMSEY. Omitted from the List of Landholders. Chapters 12-42 are
L	12	misnumbered 11-41 in the List of Landholders, but chapters 42-44 are numbered in the text as the List, so that two chapters are numbered 42 in the text. The second of these is therefore here given as 42[a].
1,4		WAIN. See EPNS 14; the name survives in Wain Wood. See also 7,4, note.
1,5		WESTONING. In Bedfordshire; *-ing* is a later suffix, EPNS Beds 141.
1,6		CARTAGE, ESCORT. *Avera,* provision of a cart with a mule or other animal, *inward,* of a horse and rider, originally 'when the King came into the Shire'. These obligations are virtually confined to Cambridgeshire, and Hertfordshire, there chiefly to Hitchin and the King's Freemen. They were commonly commuted, for 4d in Hertfordshire, 8d in Cambridgeshire. In Hertfordshire 1 *avera* was normally paid on 1 hide.
1,11		OF HERTFORD. See 34,13 note.
1,12		LILLEY. Previously also held by Leofeva, later by Geoffrey of Bec (34,12).
1,19		£86. *quater xx. lib et vi.* It is possible that *sol* has been omitted after *vi,* which would give an alternative reading of £80 6s.

4,1	WILLIAM. Bishop of London 1051-1075.
4,2	HADHAM. Probably Much Hadham, where the *dominium* of the Bishopric's manor was perhaps centred on the large moated site still termed 'The Lordship', at TL 429 199, immediately north of the Palace and the church.
4,5	RODHERE. *Roderius* is probably distinct from *Rodericus* (Suffolk 26,1; 398a).
4,8	LEVERAGE. Its Common is now divided by the Widford/Much Hadham parish boundary. The smaller portion is named Leverage (centered on TL 436 156), in Much Hadham (Parish Map of 1833, Hertfordshire Record Office), but Great Levenage in Widford, to which it is joined by Levenage Lane, with Levenage Spring nearby (Tithe Map of 1839; Mingers Farm map of 1759). Interchange of 'n' and 'r' is normal (EPNS 1 i (Introduction) 106). Since the place had little meadow, its lands probably lay either in or about the modern Common, or else in the cultivated area around the moated site of Mingers Farm (TL 43 16). Since Leofwara could sell the ½ hide, but not the whole hide, the distinction between 'Great' and ('Little') may date back to the 11th century. The modern spelling is a normal derivation from the DB form, the *wick*, specialised farmstead, of *Leware;* though she evidently named the place, she was not necessarily its first founder. Lever Mead (with Lever Wood) in the north of the parish is a strip of land by a brook, probably *laefer maed,* 'rush-grown' meadow; not connected with Leverage. The editor is indebted to Mr. Peter Walne, Hertfordshire County Archivist, to Mr. James Fox of the Ordnance Survey, and to Mr. John Dodgson of the English Place-Name Society for help in locating this place.
4,9	KING'S JURISDICTION. It is sometimes unclear whether *de soca regis* refers to people (see 4,16 note) or to land; here probably to land. 2d TO THE SHERIFF. Evidently for half an *avera* (1,6 note) on ½ hide.
4,11	SIWARD. Farley misprints *Siuurad* for MS *Siuuard.*
4,14	GODWIN BENFIELD. Of Benfield (Bentfield) in Stansted Mountfitchet in Essex, TL 50 25, one mile north of the county boundary, 2½ miles east of Stocking Pelham parish.
4,16	KING EDWARD'S JURISDICTION. *de soca regis* here probably refers to people, rather than to land, as in 4,9 note; see also 5,9; 5,11 etc.
4,21	HADHAM. See 8,3.
4,23	RODHERE. See 4,5 note.
5,1	TRING HUNDRED. The DB forms *Tredunga, Treunga* suggest that the origin might be a 'third', a Scandinavian 'thriding', as in the three Ridings of Yorkshire (EPNS 25); if so, the place took its name from the Hundred, the reverse of normal practice. The Hundred is in fact one of three which are probably divisions of an earlier whole, see 5,2; 5,3 notes. But the dominant 12th century spellings are variants of *Trehangra;* which seems the more probable origin, meaning 'tree-slope'.
5,2	DACORUM HUNDRED. *Daneis,* 'Danish' in DB; 'Dacorum' (of the Danes) is the product of 12th century literary affectation, which allotted classical names to later barbarians, *Getae* to the Goths, *Daci* to the Danes, etc. There is no record of Danish rule in the area, and Scandinavian settlement names are rare. The name, however, implies Danish control at some period, perhaps about the years 890/910, which may have occasioned the possible fortification of St. Albans (B 11 note). Dacorum later absorbed Tring, but was already split into separated portions by Cashio Hundred (5,3 note), probably a recent formation. 12th century tradition (Roger of Wendover and related Chronicles, A.D. 1178) remembered that in 'ancient times' the folk used to meet at the 'Standard Hills' in Redbourn, by description Roman barrows with early 7th century secondary pagan English burials. Redbourn may have been the original meeting place, and the name, of the Hundred, before the intervention of the Danes and the creation of Cashio. ADAM. Probably the magnate Adam son of Hubert, brother of Eudo, the King's Steward.
5,3	CASHIO HUNDRED. Called 'Albanstow', St. Albans Hundred, in the 11th and 12th centuries; elsewhere almost entirely confined to St. Albans' holdings. These however are given in separate northern and southern lists, with holdings in the other Hundreds listed between them. This order suggests that the southern holdings (10,15-17) were newly added to an ecclesiastical Hundred, separating portions of Dacorum, which was itself recently formed and still expanding. Expansion continued, and St. Albans' holdings all over Hertfordshire were later detached from their geographical Hundreds and annexed to Cashio.

5,9	JURISDICTION. Or *terram...de soca regis;* see 4,16 note.
5,11	VALUE IS AND WAS. For *et* (and) Farley prints '7'; MS '&'. JURISDICTION. See 5,9 note.
5,13	2½ HIDES. The MS leaves space for about 5 letters after *dim.*
5,15	ORWELL. Orwell Bury in Kelshall, EPNS 159.
5,16	MAN. *Homo,* as commonly, includes 'woman'. See also 5,20.
5,18	..HELD. Adam (5,2 note) was almost certainly a Norman magnate, who did not hold before 1066; the name of the then holder has evidently been omitted.
5,23	BUNTINGFORD. *Ichetone* was a manor in Layston (J.H. Round, VCH 310); Layston has now been absorbed in Buntingford.
7,4	WELWYN. 'The Willows', EPNS 144, identified in DB by spellings *Wil-* or *Wel-* followed by *-ge* or *-ga, -we* or *-wes.*
8	ELY ABBEY. These holdings are also described in the Ely Inquiry (IE...see Appendix), where details of the livestock, and also of the Hundred Representatives, are reproduced. Most of IE's account is identical with that of DB. Differences and additional information are given below (IE 49 b 1-2 (b 2 misprinted as a 2), pp. 124-5).
8,1	HATFIELD. The 18 villagers, 1 virgate each; the priest, ½ hide. Also, omitted in DB, 4 men *(homines)* with 4 hides, and the entry 'Adam son of Robert son of William (holds) under the Abbot 2 hides'. The 18 smallholders, 12 with ½ hide, 6 others with ½ hide. The value of the mill is given as 46s 4d, but 47s 4d in DB. The hides listed (20 in lordship, 12 between the priest, villagers, smallholders and Adam) total 32, in contrast with the 40 answerable.
8,2	KELSHALL. The 12 villagers, 2 with ½ hide, 10 with 5 virgates; the 9 smallholders with 1 virgate. These holdings total 2 hides; with the 2 lordship hides they give a total of 4, in contrast with the 5 answerable.
8,3	HADHAM. The 15 villagers, 1 with 1 virgate, 14 with ½ virgate each. But, in place of DB's 15 smallholders, IE has 7 cottagers with ½ virgate. With the lordship hides. these figures give a total of 4 hides and ½ virgate, as against the 4 hides answerable. In IE the word *cot(arii)* is an interlinear insertion, possibly in error for *b(ordarii);* but, since the IE figures correspond with the hidage, and are also repeated in its summary A (see below), DB's '15' may be an error, repeating the figure given for villagers in the line above. IE gives the value when acquired as £10, DB as £15. IE (the main, Cottonian MS and MS B, but not C) here reads *silva ad c.p.* (woodland (sufficient) for 100 pigs). The main MS gives 8 slaves, as against 7 in DB and MSS B,C.

The IE text entry concludes with the statement *De toto quod habemus in tota scira Hertford l lib* (From all that we have in the whole of Hertfordshire, £50), which agrees with its own summary and with DB.

IE gives two summaries, A (68 a 2, p. 173) giving figures for each holding and a total of the whole, and B (48 a 2, p. 122) giving the total only. The figures are given below; a star (*) marks discrepancies.

Summary	A				B	Totals of DB figures
	Hatfield	Kelshall	Hadham	Total	Total	
Lordship ploughs	3	3*	3	9*	8	8
Men's ploughs	20	6	8	34	34	34
Villagers	18	12	15	45	50*	45
Smallholders	30	9	7	46	55*	54*
Slaves	6	7	6	20	20	20

*The 3 Kelshall lordship ploughs are evidently an error for 2, given in the text and DB, and implied in Summary B. Summary B's villagers total clearly includes the priest and 4 men of Hatfield. Its total for smallholders evidently follows the draft which gave 15 for Hadham, as against 7 cottagers in IE text (in Summary A, 7 smallholders) and found its way into DB. '55' is probably an error for '54'. Summary B also totals 49 hides, a value of £50, and land for 53 ploughs, all of which figures agree with the texts of IE and DB. IE also summarises Hardwin's Hertfordshire lands, see chapter 37 note.

8,3	HADHAM. The Abbot's holding was probably in Little Hadham, where, with 4,6, it would make 6 hides, as against 9 hides for the other Hadham holdings, 4,2 (see note), 4,7 and 4,9. The present parish of Much Hadham is about one and a half times the size of Little Hadham. The figures suggest an assessment fixed at 15 hides before Hadham was divided.
9,4	ALDENHAM. The boundaries of the Westminster holding are detailed in BCS 245 (discussed in EPNS 59); they exclude a small portion of the north of the parish (see 10,17 note). 3 PLOUGHS. In the MS *vi* seems to have been corrected to *iii*, with *(tr)es* inserted above the line.
9,6	RANCH. *Hardwich*, a *wick*, or specialised farmstead, for herds.
9,9	GEOFFREY. De Mandeville, whose heirs held Ayot St. Lawrence, VCH 313. ALWIN. Alwin Gotton (10,6 note), who granted Ayot to Westminster, with King Edward's consent, F.E. Harmer *Anglo-Saxon Writs* no. 91 = KCD 864. ABBOT OF WESTMINSTER. *Abb(as) W(illelmum) regem* is a possible but less likely alternative expansion of the Latin.
9,10	ASHWELL. See B 11 note.
10,1	HANSTEAD. EPNS 97.
10,4	ST. PAUL'S WALDEN. The only DB Hertfordshire holding detached from its geographical Hundred. Its annexation to Cashio may have been the first step in the process which later attached most St. Albans manors to the Abbey's Hundred. But it is a mile from the old border of Sandridge in Cashio; in 1086 it may have been joined to Sandridge by a narrow corridor, now in Kimpton in Hitchin, flanking the probable course of the Baldock-Wheathamstead Roman road, which spans the gap. The place was named 'St. Paul's' when it was granted to the see of London in 1544, after the dissolution of St. Albans Abbey.
10,5	ST. ALBANS..BURGESSES. See B 11 note.
10,6	EIGHTH. Read *viii [ma]*. ALWIN [of] GOTTON. Possibly but not probably Gotton in Somerset, as OEB 43; or Gotten in the Isle of Wight (early forms *Godetone, Godyngtone etc.*) (H. Koekeritz, *Place Names of the Isle of Wight* (Nomina Germanica 6, Uppsala 1940,p.115)), in which case he might have been a near neighbour of Alstan of Boscombe (28,1 note), if Alstan came from Hampshire. But Alstan was more probably from Wiltshire, and held land in several western counties, as well as in Hertfordshire and Bedfordshire, whereas Alwin was local, recorded only in Hertfordshire (with one holding at Quickbury (Essex 22,4; f.36a), half a mile from the Hertfordshire border at Sawbridgeworth). His principal holdings were in Stanstead and Hoddesdon, and Gotton is therefore more probably a lost place-name in that region. Goods Green in Hoddesdon (now Goose Green) (TL 35 09); *Gode* in the 14th century (EPNS 229), may preserve the name. Geddings (TL 38 08), also in Hoddesdon (whose variant spelling *Geddyngesholme* suggests that it was named in or before the period of Scandinavian settlement) may also be relevant, as is Goldings in Bengeo (EPNS 217), since Golde and Gode occur as variant spellings of the same name (e.g. Hunts DB 19,21 and 29,5).
10,17	ALDENHAM. Perhaps the northern portion of the parish, excluded from the boundaries of the Westminster holding (see 9,4 note), centred on the lands about the Roman villa of Netherwild (TL 143 012) and perhaps including the site of Radlett (first named in the 15th century, EPNS 61).
12,1	[1 PLOUGH THERE]. In line 3 read 7 *dimid [7 ibi est i car] et adhuc*.. 8 FREE MEN. The only *liberi homines* entered in Hertfordshire DB. At the end of the line 3, the MS reads *Ibi viii v;* Farley omits the 'v', and the MS suggests a half-hearted attempt to delete the letter. Evidently the compiler began to write *villani,* from force of habit, and noticed his mistake after the first letter.
13,1	KENSWORTH. In Bedfordshire since 1897.
13,2	CADDINGTON. In Bedfordshire since 1897.
13,5	13 PLOUGHS' Farley and MS *xiii;* a fault in the facsimile shows *xii*, and misled VCH 317, causing J.H. Round's mistaken note to the translation.
14,1	MEADOW FOR 4 PLOUGHS. Accidentally duplicated in the MS.
15,1	BOROUGH OF THIS TOWN. The word *burbium* is otherwise unknown, and is probably a botched version of *suburbium,* used of Hertford (B11 note). The form might be influenced by late 11th century continental *burban* (Ducange *Glossarium*), for *burgi bannum (bannum leugae,* French *banlieu,* 'suburb').

15,2	SHENLEY. In the southern portion of Dacorum Hundred, not in Tring Hundred. In the Count of Mortain's chapter the Hundred headings are omitted, but the wording indicates their position. Throughout Hertfordshire, the normal arrangement is to list first within each Hundred the places held by the landholder himself, those held by his men thereafter. The words *Ipse comes,* at the beginning (15,3) of Aldbury, in Tring Hundred, suggest that it was in a different Hundred from Shenley, and that a Hundred heading has therefore also been omitted before Shenley. Berkhamsted is entered first, since it was the Count's principal Hertfordshire manor, and the site of his castle. Shenley follows, as the only detached portion of his otherwise contiguous holding. After Aldbury come the manors of his men in Tring, to 15,9; Hemel Hempstead (15,10, see note), with *Ipse comes,* begins the manors in the northern part of Dacorum. It is therefore probable that Dacorum (south) Hundred should also have been entered before Shenley. It is however possible that the entry refers to Shenley in Buckinghamshire (13,2-3), mistakenly included in the Hertfordshire list, since it adjoins the Count's holding of Loughton (Bucks 12,32), and, like the Shenley here entered, was held by one of King Edward's Guards before 1066. Such misplacements, remote from the county boundary, occasionally occur elsewhere, and are especially frequent in Northamptonshire.

100s. An omission, *silva c[porc et ii] sol,* is more probable than *sol* written in error for *porc,* as VCH 299.

15,3	MEADOW ½ HIDE. *hid* is possibly an error for *car,* (as suggested by Round, VCH 299), with perhaps a figure missing, the normal Hertfordshire measurement; but hidage of meadows sometimes occurs, e.g. Cambs 5,2, where the wording *dim hid prati* is confirmed both by ICC and IE.
15,4	ENGELRIC. A notable priest, founder of St. Martin's-le-Grand in London, see J.H. Round *Commune of London* 28 ff. He was the former holder of Tring (17,1). 7 HIDES. Those of 15, 4-6; 15,9; and 39,1, bordering on Tring, held by Count Eustace, (17,1), taken from it by the Count of Mortain.
15,10	DACORUM HUNDRED ? Tring Hundred (5,1 note) is not mentioned after DB, and was absorbed by Dacorum (5,2 note). It was not a private jurisdiction of the Count's, comparable with the ecclesiastical Hundreds of some major monasteries, since it is specifically named under the other Landholders (5,1. 21,1. 39,1) and Tring itself was not held by the Count. Its internal boundary is uncertain, because the Count's entry omits Hundred headings. The list includes Redbourn, which is placed in Dacorum (North) in three other entries (6,1; 10,10; 10,14). Langley and Gaddesden were also in Dacorum (10,9; 32,1), and it is not probable that the Count's holdings in these places, in both cases the smaller portion, were in a different Hundred from the larger portion. Since these places surround Hemel Hempstead (with Bovingdon) on three sides and the wording *ipse comes* suggests a new Hundred (see 15,2 note), it is likely that the missing Hundred heading should be placed before Hemel. The eastern border of Tring Hundred was therefore probably the border of Great Berkhamsted (with Nettleden), which follows the well marked natural features of Ashridge and the bottom of the valley that leads to Bourne End and the county boundary.
15,12	EDMER ATOR. The commoner spelling; see Middlesex 8,6 note.
16,2	MUNDEN. With 7½ hides and [1] virgate probably Great Munden; 5 hides and 1 virgate for (Little?) Munden (30,1) giving 13 hides in all.

EARL RALPH. Of Norfolk, who rebelled in 1075. He was quickly defeated, and escaped to Brittany, losing all his possessions in England.

16,5	HARDWIN. Of Scales.
16,8	HARE STREET. See EPNS 179.
16,9	23 ? PLOUGHS. The ploughs listed total 23; there is probably a transcription error.
16,10	1066. TRR, Farley. MS, TRE, confused by a stroke comparable with that in 16,11 below.
17,3	EDWINSTREE HUNDRED. Anstey is in Edwinstree, well removed from the Odsey border. The Hundred heading, apparently an insertion, is placed where there is room, at the end of the entry, as in 23,3, instead of at the beginning, where however no space was available.

THANE. *Homo* (man) in 17,2; 4; 8,9.

17,8	BERKESDEN. See EPNS 171. Ordnance Survey 2½ inch map 'Berkesdon', wrongly.
17,13	COCKHAMSTEAD. On the border between Edwinstree and Braughing Hundred, in later records in Braughing. A Hundred heading is omitted before 17,14, since Hoddesdon could never have been in Edwinstree, and confusion with Hunsdon

(44,1 note) is excluded by an *Inspeximus* (Pat. 1 H 6 p 3 m 4; cited Dugdale *Monasticon Anglicanum* (ed. 1673) 2,26), confirming William I's grants to St. Martin's, including *in Hoddesdona unam hidam.* The placing of both Bozen (17,12, also on the Hundred border and later in Braughing) and Cockhamstead, held by the Count himself, after his men's holdings, would suggest the beginning of a new Hundred, Braughing. But Braughing Hundred is entered after Hoddesdon, and it is therefore probable that 17,12-15 were an addendum, placed at the end of the Count's Edwinstree manors.

19,1 TISCOTT. A deserted village, no longer marked on Ordnance Survey maps.

3½ VILLAGERS. The meaning is not known. Here, as also in, e.g. Cambs. 7,9(192 d), Burwell, 42½ villagers, it might mean that half the land or obligations of one villager lay elsewhere. The wording, and probably the meaning differ from the west country distinction between 'full' *(plenarii* or *integri)* and 'half' *(dimidii) villani,* where the two groups are separately listed (e.g. Shrops. 2,2 (252 b), Onibury, *iiii villani integri et vi dimidii).* The west country meaning is also not known, but there the wording consistently implies a category of inferior status.

19,2 POLEHANGER. In Bedfordshire.

20,2 AYOT. St. Peter's was held by Robert Gernon's heirs, VCH 323.

A. The marginal letter 'A' is placed against a disputed holding; it therefore stands for a relevant word, perhaps some verbal form of *adjudicatio* or *arbitratio,* indicating a decision to be taken.

20,4 AELMER? MS *Aluric homo Aluric,* with *belinton* inserted above the second name. Aelmer of Bennington is mentioned in a score of Hertfordshire entries; and probably intended here, since Chells faces Bennington, on the opposite bank of the river Beane.

20,5 WOOLWICKS. In Stevenage, EPNS 140.

20,6 WYMONDLEY. Probably Little Wymondley, apparently held by Robert's heirs VCH 323.

20,7 SOULBURY. In Buckinghamshire (SP 88 27) between Bletchley and Leighton Buzzard.

20,10 HYDE HALL. So renamed in the 16th century, EPNS 165.

VALUE 6s 8d. So the MS and Farley; a smudged dot after *vi* in the facsimile gives the appearance of *vii sol,* and misled VCH 324.

20,11 *SAPEHAM.* Unidentified. But 15th and 16th century spellings of Sawbridgeworth *(Saebrict's Worth* EPNS 194), include *Sabbisford, Sapsworth.* It is possible that DB *Sapeham* gives an earlier contraction of the same name, and that the place might have been a part of the same original settlement, therefore perhaps to be sought in or about Much Hadham in Edwinstree Hundred, whose lands border on Sawbridgeworth.

21,1 14 HIDES ALWAYS. Here, as sometimes in other counties, see, e.g. Hampshire the text distinguishes between real hides and fiscal hides, upon which tax was assessed. In this instance, the figures for real hides and for the assessment before 1066 coincide; elsewhere they sometimes differ.

21,2 BARWYTHE. Later transferred to Bedfordshire.

23,1 *HAINSTONE.* Unidentified; also so spelt in 33,8. It may be a variant of Hinxworth *(Hainsteworde* 28,7; 36,15. *Haingesteworde* 37,10). Ashwell and *Hainstone* holdings are named together in 33,7-8, with the same holders before 1066 and also in 1086. Hinxworth was an outlier of Ashwell in 36,15, also with the same holders both before 1066 and in 1086. In 37,10 Hinxworth also follows Ashwell, with the same 1086 holder, but different 1066 holders; but one of these Hinxworth holders before 1066 was a man of Archbishop Stigand's, as was the holder of *Hainstone* in 23,1.

LEDMER. MS *Lemar;* Leofmer is a possible alternative.

23,2 [1 PLOUGH THERE]. MS omits *et ibi est 1 car,* probably by accident.

LEDMER. See 23,1 note.

23,3 HALF-HUNDRED OF HITCHIN. The Hundred heading is added at the end of the section, presumably because it had been accidentally omitted at the beginning; see 17,3.

23,4 AMWELL. Essex 1,3 (2b), Hatfield (Broad Oak) (TL 54 16), whose lands bordered on Sawbridgeworth in Hertfordshire, held by Earl Harold before 1066, includes the statement 'attached to this manor before 1066 were three outliers in Hertford-shire, Hertford, Amwell and Hoddesdon, which Ralph of Limesy now holds... value of the three outliers then £12.'

Since Ralph's Amwell holding alone was valued at £18 before 1066, the out-liers attached to Hatfield Broad Oak in Harold's time can only have included a portion of Amwell, and of the other places. Ralph held some land at Hertford, since soon after 1086 he founded Hertford priory and gave it 'one good hide of land at Hertford,' together with lands elsewhere (grant cited Dugdale *Monasticon*

Anglicanum (ed. 1682) 1,331); since he acquired Earl Harold's Hertford outlier, his holding was evidently all or part of the land of Earl Harold's burgesses (B 6), probably including the 24 acres 'which Ilbert took from Hertford and placed in Hailey', (see 34,13 note) which Ralph claimed. Ralph also claimed from Hailey woodland 'which belongs to 3 hides of Amwell', also transferred by Ilbert, formerly held by one of Earl Harold's men. Since Hailey adjoins Hoddesdon and Hertford Heath, these three hides may be the outlier described in the Essex return as Hoddesdon. The Amwell outlier might be Little Amwell. But since Little Amwell formed part of the parish of All Saints, Hertford, until 1864, alternative localisations of Earl Harold's outliers are possible. See also 33,13.

25,2   17 HIDES. The details appear to total 18 hides and ½ virgate.

BURGESSES. See B 11 note.

[10 HIDES..]. The '11th hide' implies the omission, after *Rannulfo*, of *x hid et dim virg*.

NIECE. 'Grand-daughter' is also grammatically possible.

11th HIDE. See 44,1.

[1]4 FREEMEN. */x/iiii*, since they include 10 and 4 listed thereafter.

26,1   5½ PLOUGHS. The details suggest that *et adhuc v car et dim possunt fieri* was omitted.

27,1   1 MILL. The figure is inserted into the MS, and is unclear, It probably intends *.7.1 molin* (1 mill), but might possibly be read as *.7 ii molin* (2 mills).

28,1   ALSTAN OF BOSCOMBE. Possibly Boscombe in Bournemouth, Hampshire, but more probably Boscombe in Wiltshire (SU 20 38), 8 miles north-east of Salisbury. Alstan was a substantial landholder, with land in Gloucestershire and Somerset, as well as in Hertfordshire and Bedfordshire; in Wiltshire (32,2; 71 c) he held 'thaneland' of the Church of Salisbury at Littleton Pannell, 4 miles south of Devizes and 15 miles north-west of Boscombe.

28,7   HINXWORTH. *Hainsteuuorde* MS; Farley misprints *Hamsteuuorde*.

½ VIRGATE. The details of before 1066 make 2 hides 1½ virgates; the text should perhaps be amended to *ii hid et 1 virg et dim*, but the Sheriff's dues better match 2 hides and ½ virgate, see note below.

DUES. 8½d, as elsewhere in Herts., probably represents payment in lieu of *avera* (cartage), at 4d a hide, or 1d a virgate. It should therefore correspond to 2 hides and ½ virgate; it is however possible that the virgate of Alstan's man was exempt from *avera*.

29,1   9 VILLAGERS. *viiii*, with *(no)vem* interlined above it, corrected from viii. 'Nine' is more commonly written *ix* in DB.

30,1   MUNDEN. Probably Little Munden, see 16,2 note.

31,1   EUDO..HUMPHREY. Eudo, the King's Steward. Humphrey of Anneville, who also held from Eudo in Cambridgeshire; he may or may not be identical with the Humphrey who held from other Hertfordshire landholders.

5d. The commutation was assessed on the land, at more than 1 *avera*, though the single *avera* was due if the cart was actually provided.

31,4   NEWSELLS. The entry duplicates Aldred's holding in 31,7.

31,6   SACKVILLE. See OEB 111.

31,7   21 SLAVES. *xxi servus;* singular after twenty-one is normal.

1d A YEAR. *u* placed above the figure *i* probably means *unum*.

31,8   HUMPHREY. Of Anneville, see 31,1 note.

HOLDS ½ HIDE. A short space is left in the MS, perhaps for the missing place name.

32,1   HIDE..IN TRING HUNDRED. Possibly Nettleden, adjoining Berkhamsted.

33,2   2 MILLS. There is a gap in the MS between *ii* and *molin*.

33,7   GERMUND. Of St. Ouen, see Appendix.

33,8   *HAINSTONE*. See 23,1 note.

GERMUND. See 33,7 note.

VALUE...3s. *iii sol* is perhaps an error for *iii lib* (£3).

33,9   PLOUGHSHARES. Reckoned among dues elsewhere; here accusative, with no subject or verb preceding; *habet* (he has) is to be understood.

33,11   40s. MS *val (uit)..xl soch (emannos)* (Value 40 Freemen), in error for *xl sol* (40s).

33,12   'STETCHWORTH'. Unidentified. There is a village with the same DB spelling, now Stetchworth (TL 64 58) in Cambridgeshire, 3 miles south of Newmarket. In 1086 it was divided between Ely Abbey, Hardwin of Scales, and Count Alan. No part of it is included in Geoffrey's Cambridgeshire holdings, but the recorded hides, less those 'taken away', total 9, one short of a 10 hide unit. It is possible that Geoffrey's one hide refers to Cambridgeshire, and was accidentally included

	in his Hertfordshire return (see 15,2 note); but there may have been a place of the same name, now lost, in Hertford Hundred.
33,13	HODDESDON. See 23,4 note.
33,15	HOWARD. Probably identical with Huart de Noderes (probably Noyers in Calvados, OEB 103), IE see Appendix.
33,17	SAWBRIDGEWORTH. The details of the holdings appear to total 30½ hides and 23 acres, in contrast with the total, given as 24½ hides. Sizes of local holdings are given for Hertfordshire here, and in the Ely Inquiry version of Ely holdings, see notes to ch.8. This small sample, of about 260 persons, gives very similar averages to those of Middlesex (see Middlesex, Appendix); the Hertfordshire averages, with the Middlesex averages given in brackets, are, in acres, villagers 21 (30); smallholders 7 (7½); cottagers with land 1½ (1). Four 'men', two priests and a reeve held a hide or half hide each. 'Their payments' refers to pasture and woodland.
33,18	VILLAGERS. Read *Ibi v villani cum quodam milite.*
34,4	GODE AND HER SON. The name Gode, Goda can be either male or female. Joint holdings by a widow and her son (e.g. 36,19) are more probable than by a father and son. In Huntingdonshire Gode and her son Wulfric (19,21; spelt Golde in 29,5) held 3½ hides at Woolley before 1066, and retained 3 of them in 1086. Gode kept none of her 7 hides and 33 acres in Hertfordshire. Three of these holdings she held from Queen Edith, and she is therefore probably also identical with Gode, King Edward's 'man', in 17,4. She was probably not the same woman as Godith, who was consistently Asgar the Constable's 'man' in Hertfordshire, but might possibly be identical, since a Hertfordshire Wulfric was also Asgar's man (33,8).
34,5	LANGLEY. In Broadwater, on the borders of Hitchin Half-Hundred, to which it was later transferred; EPNS wrongly attributes all DB *Langelei* spellings to King's and Abbot's Langley.
34,7	WILLIAN. *Wilie* in Broadwater (EPNS 147) is distinct from *Welei* (Wain in Hitchin, EPNS 14), and from *Welle* (Wellbury in Hitchin, EPNS 20), as also from *Wilge,* etc. (Welwyn, see 7,4 note).
34,8	'RODHANGER'. Its bounds are given in Crawford Charters (*Anecdota Oxoniensia* 7,1895) no. xi, p. 24. It lay between Norton and the 'Street', the Roman road, either northward or westward from the then deserted site of Baldock, see 42,13. The words of the charter bounds, *aet Bradan waetere of smethan hleawe,* might be understood as 'At (the boundary of) Broadwater (Hundred), from the smooth mound (? barrow)'. The place lay on the border between Broadwater and Odsey Hundreds.
34,9	FROM GEOFFREY. A Farley misprint omits *de* (from).
34,13	HERTFORD. For the translation, see *quas sumpsit comes Morit de Tredunga* (15,6 etc.). 'Ilbert of Hertford' (as 1,11; Cambs. 33,10) is a possible alternative.
35,3	EARL RALPH. See 16,2 note.
36	PETER OF VALOGNES. Sheriff of Hertfordshire in 1086.
36,4	ALWIN DOD[SON]. See 42,6.
36,6	HIS OWN PLOUGHS. Included in the estimate for 36,7.
36,8	LEOFRUN..MAN..SHE. *Homo* here includes 'woman'.
36,9	VALUE. Possibly 'Value of this land 2s; before 1066 [....] ' At the beginning of the next line, the 'n' of *tenuit* is stretched in an extraordinary manner, to cover the space of three or four normal letters.
36,11	THESE FOUR...MEN. MS *Ipsi;* Farley misprints *Ipse.*
36,17	FLEXMORE. A field in King's Walden preserves the name, EPNS 23.
36,19	RICHARD. King William's second son, killed in youth in a hunting accident in the New Forest about 1081, when he was riding hard and was swept from his horse by a tree branch (Ordericus Vitalis 5,15, and later writers). Haldane's connection with the tragedy is not known. The King's grandson, and his third son, William Rufus, were also killed while hunting in the New Forest, and popular opinion attributed their deaths to a curse brought upon the King in retribution for the destruction caused when he created the Forest.
37	HARDWIN. The Ely Inquiry (see Appendix) includes a summary total of his Hertfordshire holdings (49a 2; p.124). The summary gives separately the lands held by Hardwin himself in lordship, and those held from him by his *milites* (men-at-arms), a normal collective term in DB and associated texts for those who hold from a listed landholder. Modern English 'tenants' differs in meaning from DB *tenentes terras* (landholders), and 'under-tenants' does not well translate *milites* or its alternatives *homines,* and, occasionally (e.g. Exon DB folio 72) *barones,* (men and 'barons'). In 1086, the Latin words described the armed retainers of recent conquerors, maintained by holdings of land,

to hold down a conquered people; fifty years later, the risk of a national rebellion had receded. See Abingdon Chronicle 2,3 and Appendix to Berkshire (forthcoming).

The Ely figures (with an addition of the DB figures given in brackets), group Freemen and priests with villagers, cottagers with smallholders. The figures are

	Hardwin's Lordship		Hardwin's Men-at-arms	
Manors	10* (5)		10 (18)	
Hides	22 h 3½ v	(21 h 3½ v)	18½ (18½)*	
Lordship ploughs	8½	(8½)	6* (2)	
Villagers	42	(39)	17 (17)	
Smallholders	28	(27)	72 (71)	
Slaves	14	(4)*	10 (10)	
Villagers' ploughs	16½ (16½)		13* (16)	
Value*	£23 8s	(£23 8s)	£16 5s (£16 5s)	emended from £15 by Hardwin

(in all) land for 53 ploughs (53).

*MANORS. MS B has xvii, with x inserted above.
*SLAVES. iiii. evidently for xiiii.
*VALUE. pretium.
*18 HIDES. DB, 18 hides 1 virgate 28½ acres; 1½ acres short of 18½ hides.
*LORDSHIP PLOUGHS. v MS C; the discrepancy probably originates from ii miscopied as v, a common MS error.
*VILLAGERS' PLOUGHS. xiii is probably a misreading of xvi.

37,19	ALGAR..GYRTH. Earls, as in 37,11
	VIRGATE. Virga is a normal variant of virgata.
37,21	WARDEN. OEB 275.
37,22	4 HIDES. So MS. Farley misprints iii hidae.
38	PRINCE EDGAR. Aetheling, prince. Great-nephew of Edward the Confessor, and formally heir to his throne. A child in 1066, London acclaimed him as King during the few weeks resistance after Harold's death at Hastings. He lived until 1125 or later, pardoned by William after participating in the rebellion of 1069, and after periods as a refugee in Scotland and in Flanders.
40,1	MEPPERSHALL. See Bedfordshire 48,1, (216 d), Gilbert's lands, 'Meppershall ...answers for 4 hides in Bedfordshire. In Hertfordshire this village answers for 3 hides and 1 virgate.'
41,1	10s. Probably either 110s or £10, miscopied in the MS.
42,7	GODE. See 34,4 note.
42,13	'RODHANGER'. See 34,8 note. Perhaps Norton Bury, beneath a 'hanger', a (wooded) slope.
42a,1	£33. So the MS. In the facsimile the dot after the figure is smeared, giving the appearance of xxxiiii instead of xxxiii; the error is repeated in VCH 343.
43,1	MEADOW 6s. Possibly an unusual valuation; but perhaps vi sol is a transcription error for vi car (6 ploughs).
44,1	HUNSDON. MS Hodesdone, evidently Honesdone, see 25,2.
EB 1	HOLWELL was transferred to Hertfordshire in 1894, but Holwellbury remains in Bedfordshire. The entries refer to both.
EB 3	WARE. Presumably exchanged with Hugh of Grandmesnil, who held Ware, at 24 hides, in 1086. Ralph is named as the predecessor of Hugh of Beauchamp, explicitly in Beds. 17,2 (Tilbrook, now in Huntingdonshire), implicitly at Little Staughton (Beds. 17,5 and 4) and at Stotfold (Beds. 23,12 and 55,9). Askell of Ware was the predecessor of both (explicitly so called in Beds.17,4) in many holdings in Hertfordshire and Bedfordshire. The notices of Ralph's heirs, his daughter, his widow, his niece's husband Ranulf, and Hugh of Beauchamp,

indicate that the original holdings of Ralph and of Askell before him, included a strategic concentration in the region where the Lea is crossed by the north road and is joined by the Stort, another straddling the north road beyond its junction with the Icknield Way at Baldock, and a third in the Dunstable area, where the Icknield Way crosses Watling Street. The lands exchanged for Ware lie on both banks of the Ouse east of Bedford. Together, they were assessed at 22 hides and 3 virgates, nearly as much as Ware, but their combined value is only about half the value of Ware.

EC 1   EYNESBURY. In Huntingdonshire.

The Hundreds changed little after 1086 (5,1-5,3 notes). But DB suggests earlier changes. Odsey (TL 29 38, in Cambridgeshire) must originally have lain well within its own Hundred, perhaps bounded by the river Cam and the Roman road north-west from Royston. The deeply indented NW border excludes places exceptionally described as both in Herts and Beds, where boundary changes were still easily effected after 1066 (Beds. 1,4-5) and where Edward the Elder had purchased strategic pagan sites (BCS 659). The Shire emerged from the territory of Edward's army of Hertford, whose border is likely to have followed recognisable features, perhaps a more or less regular line along and between the rivers Cam, Flit and Thame to Tring.

APPENDIX

The Ely Inquiry *Inquisitio Eliensis* (IE) is a draft of the returns that concern the Abbey's holdings. It survives in three transcripts, probably made two or three generations after the Survey, edited and published with the 'Cambridgeshire Inquiry' *Inquisitio Comitatus Cantabrigiensis* (ICC) by N.E.S.A. Hamilton in 1876. The principal manuscript (British Museum, Cottonian, Tiberius A vi) was also published by Ellis in DB 4,497 ff., but without ICC. References are here given to the column of the Cottonian MS and to the page of Hamilton's edition.

Variant readings, and information that normally falls within the scope of DB, are given above in the notes to chapter 8. Additional information, chiefly concerned with livestock and with the representatives who gave evidence on oath on behalf of each Hundred, is given below.

The **representatives** of the three Hertfordshire Hundreds in which Ely had holdings are given in columns 39 a 1-2 (p. 100), four Frenchmen, named first (here printed in the left hand column), and four Englishmen from each Hundred. Places and landholders in Hertfordshire are printed in capitals; DB references to the persons are given in round brackets. References in other Hundreds are marked by the appropriate abbreviation.

In HERTFORD[SHIRE]
In EDWINSTREE Hundred (these) men swore, namely

RALPH BAYNARD (24)	GODWIN of HORMEAD (38,2)
RICULF the BISHOP of LONDON'S man (4,19)	Leofsi* the ABBESS of CHATTERIS' man
RODHERE the BISHOP (of LONDON'S man (4,5)	Seric* COUNT EUSTACE'S man
Howard of Noyers (33,15 Hf) [GEOFFREY de MANDEVILLE'S man]	Siward of HORMEAD

and all the other Frenchmen and Englishmen of this Hundred swore.

In the Two Hundreds* of BROADWATER (these) men swore, namely

LETARD the ABBOT [of ELY'S] man	ALFWARD of MARDLEY (42,13)
GOSBERT of BEAUVAIS (35)	HALDANE of TEWIN (36,19)
WILLIAM of LETCHWORTH (20,7)	THORKELL of DIGSWELL(33,5)
Leofgeat G[EOFFREY] of BEC's ? * man (34)	Aelfric of WYMONDLEY
Ralph of SHEPHALL (?) *	Alfwin of WAIN ? (Hc ?) *
Humphrey of KINSBOURNE (? D)*	Aelmer of WESTON
Geoffrey of CHESFIELD	Alfward Froward
Geoffrey of WESTBROOK (? D)*	Alfward of MUNDEN

and all the other Frenchmen and Englishmen of these two Hundreds swore.

In ODSEY Hundred (these) men swore, namely
Hugh* the BISHOP of BAYEUX'S man
FULK (35,3) GOSBERT of BEAUVAIS' man
GERMUND of ST. OUEN (33,7; 8)
Alwin of RUSHDEN*

Boia the BISHOP'S man
Wulfsi of THERFIELD
Albert of SANDON (?) *
WITHGAR* of ORWELL*

and all the other Frenchmen and Englishmen of this Hundred swore.

Alfward Froward (MS *Framward;* see OEB 346) is unlocated and otherwise unknown. The
other 31 representatives either came from places in the Hundreds they represented, or
else held from landholders in those Hundreds, with a few possible exceptions in Broadwater,
noted below, all of whom, however, may have been among the unnamed men who held
from Landholders with Broadwater holdings.

* **Edwinstree**
LEOFSI. MS *Lexius; Leofsi* MS C.
SERIC. MSS *Siriz;* Sired is a possible alternative.
Broadwater
TWO HUNDREDS. As in most records, Broadwater was a double hundred.
GEOFFREY of BEC. MSS *G. de berc (berch* MSS BC). A possible alternative is G(odwin) of
Bark(way), in Edwinstree, who held from Prince Edgar (38,1), and might have been identical
with Godwin who held Watton in Broadwater from Count Alan (16,1). Godwin is less likely
to have been listed among the French, but, in fourth place, might have been so placed,
as in Odsey, below.
SHEPHALL. MSS *Stepehal(l)a,* probably for *Scepehalla.*

KINSBOURNE. MSS *Cheneberna,* probably Kinsbourne Green (TL 10 16, three miles south
of Luton, also commonly *-berne* rather than *-burna,* see EPNS 38); in Dacorum Hundred,
not Kilburn in Middlesex, as OEB 39.
WESTBROOK. MSS *Westbroc.* Probably Westbrook (Hay) (TL 02 05) in Bovingdon,
contrasted with Eastbrook Hay in Hemel Hempstead, both attested in the 13th century,
EPNS 30, see also 42; in Dacorum Hundred.
WAIN? MSS *de werlaio,* which also occurs (*Werleia* ICC 105 b 1 p. 68 and later), as an
abbreviation of *Wedrelai,* **Wederlai,** 'Wetherley', near Barrington, which named a
Cambridgeshire Hundred EPNS Cambs 69. But since no other place outside Hertfordshire
is listed, IE may have intended *Wedlaio* for Wain, *Welei,* or *Wedelee,* EPNS Herts 14; in
Hitchin Half-Hundred.
Odsey
HUGH. Probably distinct from Hugh of Grandmesnil, who held Thundridge in Braughing
Hundred from the Bishop of Bayeux (5,26).
ALWIN of RUSHDEN. Listed in fourth place, but from his name, English; perhaps
a man of Sigar of Chocques, who held Rushden (41,1).
SANDON. MS *Samsona; Sansona,* B,C. Since, in seventh place, he should be English, the
place is hardly a St. Samson in France, as OEB 113, or Samson, near Namur, in Belgium.
Perhaps a copyist's error for Sandon in Hertfordshire, called *Sandona* in a 12th century
verson of an early 10th century charter, BCS 737.
WITHGAR of ORWELL. Orwell(bury) in Kelshall (5,15; 37,6) rather than Orwell in
Cambridgeshire. Before 1066 Algar, Withgar's man, held Barley and Cokenach in
Edwinstree Hundred, four miles east of Kelshall (34,9; 10).

The livestock listed by Ely in Hertfordshire (49 b 1-2, pp. 124-5) are 'idle cattle' (*animalia
ociosa),* beef and dairy cattle in contrast with working oxen; sheep; and pigs: DB 31,8
also lists livestock on an unnamed holding in Hertford Hundred. The figures are

	Cattle	Sheep	Pigs	Woodland Pig Capacity
Hatfield	26	360	60	2,000
Kelshall	2	308	18	-----
Hadham	12	50	50	100
DB 31,8	68	350	150	50

with 50 goats and 1 mare.

INDEX OF PERSONS

Familiar modern spellings are given when they exist. Unfamiliar names are usually given in an approximate late 11th century form, avoiding variants that were already obsolescent or pedantic. Spellings that mislead the modern eye are avoided where possible. Two, however, cannot be avoided; they are combined in the name 'Leofgeat', pronounced 'Leffyet', or 'Levyet'. The definite article is omitted before bynames, except where there is reason to suppose that they described the individual. The chapter numbers of listed landholders are printed in italics. Persons of the same name are not necessarily identical, nor are those who held as men of different lords necessarily different individuals (see, e.g. 2,1).

Edmer Ator 15,12. 19,1.
Edmer 15,1
Edmund 1,14. 5,5
Edred 33,6
Edric 4,7. 35,3. 37,18.
Edsi 4,23
Edward of Pirton 1,10
Edward of Salisbury, the Sheriff 32
Elaf 34,16
Engelric 15,4-6;9. 17,1. 39,1
Eudo the Steward, son of Hubert 31. B 3;5
Count Eustace 17. 24,2. App.
Fair, see Edeva
Fran, see Oswulf
Froward, see Alfward
Fulcwold 15,6
Fulk 35,3. App.
Gauti 17,13
Geoffrey of Bec 34. B 4. 1,9;13. 10,12-13;17;19
Geoffrey of Chesfield App.
Geoffrey de Mandeville 33. B 8. 9,3;9-10
Geoffrey of Runeville 34,22;23
Geoffrey of Westbrook App.
Germund of St. Ouen 33,7;8;12. App.
Gernon, see Robert
Count Gilbert , see Richard
Gilbert son of Solomon 40
Gilbert 4,15
Gode 17,4. 18,1. 32,2. 34,4. 42,7
Godfrey 36,3;4
Goding 10,12
Godith 4,23. 17,6;7;10;14. 33,13;18;19
Godiva 33,7
Godmund 42,15
Godric 10,11. 20,8.
Godwin of Benfield 4,14;18-19. 20,3; 11-12
Godwin of Hormead 38,1-2. App.
Godwin of Letchworth 34,7
Godwin of Soulbury 20,7
Godwin son of Wulfstan 20,9
Godwin 1,13. 15,5. 16,1. 34,20-21.
Gosbert of Beauvais 35. App.
Grutt, see Alnoth
Guy the Priest 34,21
Earl Gyrth 24,1. 26,1. 37,11; 19
Haldane of Tewin 36,19. App.
Hardwin of Scales 37. B 10;16,5
Earl Harold B6. 1,1-15;17. 5,5;23;25. 15,1. 17,2-4;8-9;13. 20,13. 23,4. 24,3. 30,1. 33,17. 34,5; 12-13;24. 35,1;2. 36,11.37,8;11. 14;22.44,1
Herbert son of Ivo 10,9
Horne, see Alwin

Howard of Noyers 33,15. App.
Hubert, see Adam, Eudo
Hugh of Beauchamp 27. 44,1
Hugh of Grandmesnil (see Adelaide) 26. 5,26. 43,1
Hugh 33,9. App.
Humphrey of Anneville B 5
Humphrey of Anneville 31,1;8
Humphrey of Kinsbourne App.
Humphrey 4,1;24. 15,5;12. 36,12
Hunter, see Alwin
Ilbert 1,6;8;9;11;12;13. 34,13. 38,2
Ilger, see Ranulf
Isambard 34,14
Ivo, see Herbert
Kip 33,17
Archbishop Lanfranc 2. 16,1
Ledmer 7,3. 23,1;2. 36,3
Leofeva 1,6;12. 34,12. 37,21
Leofmer, see Ledmer
Leofgeat 16,3. App.
Leofing the Priest 16,5
Leofled 5,19
Leofric 15,5. 34,7
Leofrun 34,14. 36,8
Leofsi 28,1. 31,8. 34,17. App.
Leofwara 4,8
Earl Leofwin B 6. 5,1;9-10;20. 6,1. 15,2;10-11. 34,1;7. 42,14.
Young Leofwin 13,1
Leofwin 13,2. 15,8. 20,12. 29,1. 30,1-3. 33,2. 36,11. 40,1. 44,1 App.
Letard
Little, see Aelfric
Lovett 34,2;8
Mainou the Breton 39
Martell 19,2
Earl Morcar 5,24
Count of Mortain 15. 10,6;9. 39,1
Ordmer 37,13
Osbern 4,9. 5,7;13-16;20-23. 10,12
Osbert 34,5;25
Osgot 16,3
Osmund of Vaubadon 1,13
Oswy 33,14
Oswulf son of Fran 15,7. 17,1. 19,1. 21,1;2
Oswulf (son of Fran) 15,5
Payne 4,13;17. 37,20
Peter of Valognes, the Sheriff 36. B7;11;1,9;12-13;19 9,10. 28,1. 36,9;13. 37,19
Peter, a burgess 42,7
Peter 1,12. 5,9;25. 28,1;5. 37,19
Picot EC 1-2
Earl Ralph 16,2. 35,3
Ralph Bassett 19,1

Ralph Baynard | 24. B,9. App.
Ralph of Limesy | 23. 34,13
Ralph of Shephall(?) | App.
Ralph Tallboys | 1,9;12. 25,2
Ralph Tallboys' daughter | 44
Ralph of Tosny | 22
Ralph | 4,11;12. 5,24. 15,7; 11. 16,7. 21,1. 33,1;13. 34,1;11
Ranulf brother of Ilger | 25
Ranulf | 4,14;15;20. 15,1; 2;13
Rayner | 7,1
Reginald | 34,24
Richard son of King William | 36,19
Richard of Sackville | 31,6
Richard of Tonbridge, son of Count Gilbert, see Rothais
Riculf | 4,19. App.
Bishop Robert of Chester | 7
Robert Gernon | 20
Robert d'Oilly | 19
Robert of Pont-Chardon | 20,8
Robert of Tosny | 22
Robert son of Rozelin | 17,2
Robert (son of Rozelin) | 17,4;8-9
Robert son of Wymarc | 4,6. 5,6. 20,6. 37,9
Robert | 36,1
Robert, see Adam
Rodhere | 4,5;23. App.
Earl Roger | 18
Roger of Mussegross | 16,2
Roger, Peter of Valognes' officer | 28,1
Roger | 5,1. 16,8. 22,2. 34,4;18;25. 36,2; 5;16
Rothais wife of Richard (of Tonbridge) | 42a
Rozelin, see Robert
Rumold | 17,5;6;10
Saehild | 5,20
Saemer the Priest | 37,21
Saemer | 5,7
Saeward | 33,10
Saxi | 22,2
Scova | 5,10
Scova, see Aelfric
Seric | 15,11. App.
Sigar of Chocques | 41 EC 2
Sinoth | 31,2. 37,8
Sired | 37,8;14. App.
Siward of Hormead | App.
Siward | 4,11. 15,13. 33,6. 37,4. 42,12
Snerri | 16,12
Solomon, see Gilbert

Archbishop Stigand | 1,10. 2,1;3;5.4,4; 6;11;17. 5,8;10; 12-19;21;23;26. 7,2-4. 10,10-11. 16,8. 17,5. 23,1-3. 34,14. 37,3;5-6;10; 16. 38,2. 41,1-2. 42a,1. 43,1 5,25. 34,5-6. 35,1-2.
Swein
Tallboys, see Ralph
Theodbald | 37,2-3;5;9-11;15-19
Theodbert | 4,4
Thorbern | 16,6. 25,1
Thorbert, the Priest | 37,3
Thorir | 15,11
Thorkell of Digswell | 30,2. 33,5;15. App.
Thorold | 33,4;11
Thurstan | 5,11
Toki | 31,3
Topi | 36,2
Earl Tosti | 1,18
Uhtred | 37,9
Walcra | 34,17
Bishop Walkelin of Winchester | 3
Walter the Fleming | 30
Walter | 31,5. 33,14
Earl Waltheof | 19,2
Warden, see Wulfric
Wicga | 15,7
Wigot | 6,1
Wigot | 19,1
Bishop William of London | 4. 33,18
William Black | 42,11
William Delamere | 28,3;8
William of Auberville | 29
William of Eu | 28
William of Letchworth | 20,7. App.
William (of Letchworth) | 20,2-6;9-12
William | 4,6-8;20. 24,1-2. 25,1
William, see Adam
Wimund | 16,4;11
Withgar of Orwell | 34,9-10. 37,6-7. App.
Wulfmer of Eton | B3
Wulfmer | 37,4
Wulfric Warden | 37,21
Wulfric | 33,8
Wulfric | 34,4*
Wulfsi of Therfield | App.
Wulfstan, see Godwin
Wulfward | 17,11. 24,2. 42,6
Wulfwen | 32,1
Wulfwin of Eastwick | 34,23-24
Wulfwin | 34,13. 38,2
Wulfwy of Hatfield | B 7
Wulfwy | 4,19-20
Wymarc, see Robert

Churches and Clergy

Archbishop of Canterbury *2*
see Lanfranc, Stigand
Bishop of Bayeux *5.* 10,9. 31,8. 37,19. 42,11
of Chester *7*
of Lisieux *6*
of London *4.* 33,18. App.
of Winchester *3*
Abbess of St. Mary's,
Chatteris *12.*1,1.31,2.37,8.App.

Abbot of Ely *8.* 4,15;21. App.
of Ramsey *11.* 17,1. 37,7;13
of St. Albans *10.* 1,17. 2,3.5,2.32,1. 33,1. 34,2
of Westminster *9.* 2,1-2. 16,1. 28,1
Canons
of St. Martin's, London *17,14*
of St. Paul's, London *13*
of Holy Cross, Waltham *14.*34,13
Monastery of Hitchin *1,3*

Monk, see Osbern. Nun, see Edeva. Priests, see Aelfric, Guy, Leofing, Saemer, Thorbert.

Secular Titles and Occupational Names

Constable *(stalre)* ...Asgar. Count *(comes)* ...Alan, Eustace, Gilbert, of Mortain. Earl *(comes)* ...Algar, Gyrth, Harold, Leofwin, Morcar, Ralph, Tosti, Waltheof. Hunter *(venator)* ...Alwin. Prince *(Adeling)* ...Edgar. Queen *(regina)* ...Edith. Reeve *(prefectus, prepositus)* B 5. 1,18. 9,4. 26,1. 36,13. 43,1 ...Leofsi. Servant *(serviens)* ...*Regis* 42,8; *Comitis* 15,1. Sheriff *(vicecomes)* 4,1;6;23. 5,4;11. 25,2. 28,1;7. 31,7. 34,6;8;18-19;25. 36,11. 37,1;14;19. 42,13 ...Edward of Salisbury, Ilbert, Peter of Valognes. Steward *(dapifer)* ...Eudo. Young *(cilt)* ...Leofwin.

INDEX OF PLACES

The name of each place is followed by (i) the initial of its Hundred and its location on the Map in this volume; (ii) its National Grid reference; (iii) chapter and section references in DB. Bracketed figures denote mention in sections dealing with a different place. Unless otherwise stated, the identifications of EPNS and the spellings of the Ordnance Survey are followed for places in England; of OEB for places abroad. The National Grid reference system is explained on all Ordnance Survey maps, and in the Automobile Association Handbooks; the figures reading from left to right are given before those reading from bottom to top of the map. Places marked with a(*) are in the 100 kilometre grid square lettered SP; those marked with a (†) in square TQ; all others are in square TL. The Hertfordshire Hundreds are Braughing (Bg); Broadwater (Bw); Cashio (C); Dacorum (D); Edwinstree (E); Hertford (Hf); Hitchin (Hc); Odsey (O); Tring (T). Places mentioned only in the Appendix are indexed, but not mapped. Unidentified places are shown in Domesday Book spelling, in italics.

Place				References
Albury	E 30	43	24	4,11
Aldbury	T 10	*96	12	15,3
Aldenham	C 6	†14	00	10,17
Aldenham	D 16	†13	98	9,4
Almshoe	Bw8	20	25	5,5
Alswick	E 15	37	29	24,1
Amwell	Hf 9	37	12	23,4. (34,13)
Anstey	E 8	40	32	17,3. 37,20
Ardeley	O 18	30	27	13,3
Ashwell	O 2	26	39	9,10. 33,7. 36,14. 37,9. (36,15)
Aspenden	E 23	35	28	31,6
Aston	Bw17	27	22	5,8
Ayot St. Lawrence	Bw28	19	16	9,9. 42,12
Ayot St. Peter	Bw29	21	15	20,2
Barkway	E 4	38	35	31,4. 33,9 37,12. 38,1
Barley	E 1	40	38	5,18. 12,1. 29,1. 31,3. 34,9. 37,11
Bayford	Hf 14	31	08	1,18
Beauchamps	E 11	38	31	17,10
Bendish	Hc 18	16	21	10,20
Bengeo	Hf 4	32	13	16,12. 27,1. 33,15. 34,15-19. 36,18
Bennington	Bw 18	29	23	36,7; (6). see Aelmer
Berkhamsted	T 11	*99	08	15,1; (5;12)
Little Berkhamsted	Hf 13	29	07	37,21
Berkesden	E 22	33	28	17,8. 37,19
Boarscroft	T 2	*87	17	15,8
Box	Bw12	27	26	5.7. 28,5. 36,6
Bozen	E 26	41	27	17,12. 20,12. 33,11
Bramfield	Hf 2	29	15	37,22
Braughing	Bg 2	39	25	17,15
Bricewolde	Hf			37,23. 42,9
Brickendon	Hf 11	33	10	14,2. 33,14. 34,14. 42,8
Broadfield	O 15	32	31	7,3. 18,1. 37,5. 41,2
Broxbourne	Hf 16	36	07	43,1
Buckland	E 7	35	33	5,20
Buntingford	E 14	36	29	5,23. 17,6-7. 31,5. 36,12. 37,17
Bushey	D 17	†13	95	33,2. (33,4)
Bygrave	O 6	26	36	7,2;4
Caldecote	O 3	23	38	23,2
Cassio	C 7	10	96	10,16. 33,4
Chaldean	E 32	42	20	4,5
Charlton	Hc 10	17	28	1,8
Chells	Bw11	26	25	20,4. 34,6. 36,4
Chesfield	Bw -	24	27	App.
Cheshunt	Hf 18	35	02	16,9;(16,10-11)
Clothall	O 13	27	31	5,14. 16,3. 28,6. 37,3
Cockhampstead	E 28	41	25	17,13
Codicote	Bw24	21	18	10,6
Cokenach	E 3	39	36	34,10. see Algar
Corney(bury)	E 13	35	30	17,4
Cottered	O 17	31	29	3,1
Datchworth	Bw23	26	19	2,1. 9,7. 34,3. 36,1
Digswell	Bw32	23	14	33,5. 36,2. App.
Temple Dinsley	Hc 14	18	24	1,9
Dunsley	T 7	*93	11	15,9. 39,1
Eastwick	Bg 12	43	11	34,24 see Wulfwin
Epcombs	Hf 5	30	12	42,10
Flamstead	D 4	07	14	22,1
Flexmore	Hc 16	15	22	1,15. 36,17
Great Gaddesden	D 6	02	11	32,1
Little Gaddesden	D 5	*99	13	†5,12
'Gotton'				10,6 note
Graveley	Bw7	23	27	5,4. 20,3.28,1. 35,2. 36,3
Gubblecote	T 4	*90	15	15,6
Little Hadham	E 31	43	22	4,6. 8,3
Much Hadham	E 33	42	19	4,2;7;9.·(4,21)
Hailey	Hf 12	37	10	34,13
Hainstone	O			23,1. 33,8
Hanstead	C 4	14	01	10,1
Hare Street	E 16	39	29	16,8. 33,10
Hatfield	Bw33	23	08	8,1. see Wulfwy
'Hazelhanger'	E			5,19. 37,13
Hemel Hempstead	D 9	05	06	15,10
Hertford	Hf 8	32	12	B. 34,13. see Ilber
Hertingfordbury	Hf 6	30	11	24,3
Hexton	Hc 5	10	30	1,17. 10,19. 34,11
Hinxworth	O 1	23	40	28,7. 36,15. 37,10

Place	Code			Reference
Hitchin	Hc 7	18	29	1,3;19. (1,1-2;4-17. 34,11-12. 36,17)
Hixham Hall	E 27	45	26	4,20
Hoddesdon	Hf 15	37	08	16,10. 17,14. 32,2 33,13, 42,7
Hodenhoe	E 6	34	33	5,21. 37,15
Holwell	.	16	33	EB 1-2
Great Hormead	E 17	40	29)	17,11. 24,2.
Little Hormead	E 18	40	29)	38,2. App.
Hunsdon	Bg 9	41	14	44,1. (25,2)
Hyde (Hall)	E 5	34	32	20,10
Kelshall	O 7	32	36	8,2
Kimpton	Hc 21	17	18	5,24
Kinsbourne	O --	10	16	App.
Knebworth	Bw 22	23	20	31,1
Lampeth	C -			5,3
Langley	Bw 15	21	22	34,5
Abbot's Langley	D 12	09	02	10,9
King's Langley	D 11	07	02	15,11
Layston, see Buntingford				
Letchworth	Bw 2	21	31	20,7. App. see Godwin
Leverage	E 34	43	16	4,8
Ley Green	Hc 13	15	24	1,16
Libury	Bw 19	33	23	2,4. 5,9-12. 30,2-3. 36, 8-10. 42,3-4. (37,19)
Lilley	Hc 11	11	26	34,12. (1,12)
Luffenhall	O 16	29	28	5,13. 13,4. 37,2
Mardley(bury)	Bw 25	26	18	20,1. App. see Alfward
Meesden	E 9	43	32	4,17
North Mimms	D 14	22	04	7,1
Minsden	Bw 14	19	24	1,2
Miswell	T 5	*91	12	15,7. 21,1
Great Munden	Bw 20	35	23	16,2. (16,3). App.
Little Munden	Bw 21	33	21	30,1. (30,2)
Napsbury	D 13	16	04	10,11
Newnham	O 4	24	37	10,18
Newsells	E 2	38	37	31,4;7. (31,3)
Norton	Bw 1	23	34	10,7
Great Offley	Hc 9	14	27	1,10. 28,8. (1,11)
Little Offley	Hc 8	13	28	1,11
Orwell	O 8	32	36	5,15. 37,6. App. 10,6
'Oxwick'	Bw -			34,22
Panshanger	Hf 3	29	13	
Patmore	E 29	45	25	4,10
Brent Pelham	E 19	43	30)	
Furneaux Pelham	E 21	43	27)	4,12-16;18-19
Stocking Pelham	E 20	44	29)	
Pendley	T 9	*94	11	15,4
Pirton	Hc 4	14	31	23,3. see Edward
Puttenham	T 3	*88	14	5,1
Radwell	O 5	23	35	5,17. 36,16
Redbourn	D 7	10	12	6,1. 10,10;14. 15,13
Reed	O 10	36	36	5,16. 16,5-6. 17,2. 31,2. 37,8
Rickmansworth	C 8	†05	93	10,15
'Rodhanger'	Bw 1	23	34	34,8. 42,13
Roxford	Hf 10	30	10	34,21
Rushden	O 14	30	31	41,1. EC 1-2 App.
Rye (House)	Bg 13	38	09	5,25
Sacombe	Bw 27	33	19	2,5. 36,11. 37,1. 42,5;14
St. Albans	C 3	14	07	10,5
Sandon	O 12	32	34	13,5. App.
Sandridge	C 2	17	10	10,3
Sapeham	E -			20,11
Sawbridgeworth	Bg 10	48	14	33,17
Sele (House)	Hf 7	31	12	34,20
Shenley	D 5	19	00	15,2. 33,3
Shenley	C 25	18	01	10,2
Shephall	Bw 16	25	22	2,3. 10,8. App.
Stagenhoe	Hc 17	18	22	25,1
Standon	Bg 3	39	22	42a,1
Stanstead Abbots	Bg 11	38	11	25,2. 33,16. 34,23. 42,15. (44,1)
'Stetchworth'	Hf			33,12
Stevenage	Bw 10	24	26	9,5. (9,6. 28,1)
Stone(bury)	E 25	38	28	36,13
Bishop's Stortford	Bg 5	49	21	4,22
Tewin (Queen's Hoo)	Bw 31	27	16	9,6
Tewin	Hf 1	27	14	36,19. App.
Theobald Street	D 18	18	97	5,2. 9,2-3. 10,13. 33,1 34,2
Therfield	O 9	33	17	11,1. 37,7. App.
Thorley	Bg 6	47	19	4,23. 33,18. (33,19)
Throcking	E 12	33	30	4,1. 5,22. 17,5. 37,16
Thundridge	Bg 7	36	17	5,26
Tiscott	T 1	*88	18	19,1
Tring	T 6	*92	11	17,1. (15,4-6; 9. 39,1)
Wain (Wood)	Hc 12	17	25	1,4;13-14. App.
Wakeley	E 24	34	26	16,7. 17,9. 37,18
King's Walden	Hc 15	16	23	1,6
St. Paul's Walden	C 1	19	22	10,4
Walkern	Bw 13	28	26	42,2
Wallington	O 11	29	33	16,4. 20,9. 33,6. 35,3. 37,4
Wandon (End)	Hc 19	14	20	1,7
Ware	Bg 8	35	14	26,1. EB 3. see Askell
Watton	Bw 26	30	18	2,2. 9,8. 16,1. 42,1. (42,3)
Well(bury)	Hc 6	13	29	1,12
Welwyn	Bw 30	23	16	7,4. 20,8. 28,2-3. 34,4. 42,11. (36,4)
Westbrook	D --	02	05	App.
Westmill	Bg 1	36	27	20,13. 22,2
Weston	Bw 4	25	30	28,4. (28,1-3;6). App.
Wheathampstead	D 8	17	14	9,1
Wickham	Bg 4	47	23	4,24-25. 33, 19-20. 34,25
Widford	E 35	41	15	4,3-4
Wigginton	T 8	*93	10	15,5
Willian	Bw 3	22	30	34,7

						In BEDFORDSHIRE					
Windridge	D 10	12	05	10,12. 34,1		Barwythe	D 3	02	14	21,2
'Woolwicks'	Bw 9	22	25	20,5. 36,5		Caddington	D 2	06	19	13,2
Wormley	Hf 17	36	05	14,1. 16,11. 42,6		Kensworth	D 1	03	19	13,1
Wyddial	E 10	37	31	37,14		Meppershall	Hc 2	13	36	40,1
Great Wymondley	Bw 5	21	28	1,1. 5.6. 35,1. App.		Polehanger	Hc 1	13	37	19,2
Little Wymondley	Bw 6	21	27	20,6		Westoning	Hc 3	02	32	1,5
						Manshead Hundred				1,5

Places not in Hertfordshire

References are to entries in the Indices of Persons and of Places.

Elsewhere in Britain.

BUCKINGHAMSHIRE Eton?, see Wulfmer. Soulbury, see Godwin. CAMBRIDGESHIRE Chatteris, see Abbess. Ely, see Abbot. Stetchworth? Wetherley?, see Wain (App.). CHESHIRE Chester, see Bishop. ESSEX Benfield, see Godwin. Waltham, see Canons. HAMPSHIRE Winchester, see Bishop. KENT Canterbury, see Archbishop. Tonbridge, see Rothais. MIDDLESEX London, see Bishop,Canons. Westminster, see Abbot. WILTSHIRE Boscombe, see Alstan. Salisbury, see Edward.

Outside Britain.

Anneville, see Humphrey. Auberville, see William. Bayeux, see Bishop. Beauchamp, see Hugh. Beauvais, see Gosbert. Bec, see Geoffrey. Chocques, see Sigar. Eu, see William. Gernon, see Robert. Grandmesnil, see Adelaide, Hugh. Limesy, see Ralph. Lisieux, see Bishop. Mandeville, see Geoffrey. Mortain, see Count. Mussegross, see Roger. Noyers, see Howard. Oilly, see Robert. Pont-Chardon, see Robert. Rots, see Ansketel. 'Runeville', see Geoffrey. Sackville, see Richard. St. Ouen, see Germund. 'Samson'?, see Albert (App.). Scales, see Hardwin. Tosny, see Ralph, Robert. Valognes, see Peter. Vaubadon, see Osmund.

SYSTEMS OF REFERENCE TO DOMESDAY BOOK

The manuscript is divided into numbered chapters, and the chapters into sections, usually marked by large initials and red ink. Farley however did not number the sections. References in the past have therefore been to the page or column. Several different ways of referring to the same column have been in use. The commonest are:

(i)	(ii)	(iii)	(iv)	(v)
152a	152	152a	152	152ai
152b	152	152a	152.2	152a2
152c	152b	152b	152b	152bi
152d	152b	152b	152b.2	152b2

The relation between Vinogradoff's notation (i), here followed, and the sections is

132 a	B1 - 11	136 a	10,14 - 10,20	140 a	33,17 - 34,5
b	Landholders 1,1 - 1,2	b	11,1 - 13,5	b	34,6 - 34,13
c	1,3 - 1,7	c	14,1 - 15,5	c	34,13 - 34,21
d	1,7 - 1,11	d	15,5 - 16,1	d	34,22 - 36,1
133 a	1,11 - 1,18	137 a	16,1 - 16,11	141 a	36,2 - 36,11
b	1,18 - 3,1	b	16,12 - 17,8	b	36,11 - 36,19
c	4,1 - 4,8	c	17,8 - 18,1	c	36,19 - 37,9
d	4,8 - 4,17	d	19,1 - 20,7	d	37,10 - 37,19
134 a	4,17 - 4,25	138 a	20,7 - 22,1	142 a	37,19 - 41,1
b	5,1 - 5.10	b	22,1 - 24,1	b	41,1 - 42,11
c	5,10 - 5,18	c	24,2 - 26,1	c	42,11 - 42,15
d	5,18 - 6,1	d	26,1 - 28,7	d	42[a],1 - 44,1
135 a	7,1 - 8,3	139 a	28,8 - 31,6		
b	9,1 - 9,10	b	31,6 - 33,1		
c	9,10 - 10,6	c	33,1 - 33,8		
d	10,6 - 10,13	d	33,9 - 33,17		

TECHNICAL TERMS

Many words meaning measurements have to be transliterated. But translation may not dodge other problems by the use of obsolete or made-up words which do not exist in modern English. The translations here used are given in italics. They cannot be exact; they aim at the nearest modern equivalent.

ARPENT. A measure of extent, usually of vineyards. *arpent*

AVERA. Provision of a cart for the King's use (1,6 note). *cartage*

BEREWIC. An outlying place, attached to a manor. *outlier*

BORDARIUS. Cultivator of inferior status, usually with a little land. *smallholder*

CARUCA. A plough, with the oxen who pulled it, usually reckoned as 8. *plough*

CARUCATA. Normally the equivalent of a *hide*, in former Danish areas. *carucate*

COTARIUS. Inhabitant of a *cote*, cottage, often without land. *cottager*

DOMINICUS. Belonging to a lord or lordship. *the lord's* or *household*

DOMINIUM. The mastery or dominion of a lord *(dominus);* including ploughs, land, men, villages, etc., reserved for the lord's use; often concentrated in a *home farm* or *demesne*, a 'Manor Farm' or 'Lordship Farm'. *lordship*

FEUDUM. Continental variant of *feuum*, not used in England before 1066; either a landholder's total holding, or land held by special grant. *Holding*

FEUUM. Old English *feoh*, cattle, money, possessions in general, compare Latin *pecunia* and German *Vieh*; in later centuries, *feoff*, 'fief' or 'fee'. *holding*

FIRMA. Old English *feorm*, provisions due to the King or lord; a fixed sum paid in place of these and of other miscellaneous dues. *revenue*

GELDUM. The principal royal tax, originally levied during the Danish wars, normally at an equal number of pence on each *hide* of land. *tax*

HIDE. A unit of land measurement, reckoned at 120 acres. *hide*

HONOR. (24,2) equivalent to *feudum*, holding. *Honour*

HUNDRED. A district within a shire, whose assembly of notables and village representatives usually met about once a month. *Hundred*

INWARD. Provision of a mounted man for the King's use (1,6 note). *escort*

M. Marginal abbreviation for *manerium*, manor. *M.*

PRAEPOSITUS, PRAEFECTUS. Old English *gerefa*, a royal officer. *reeve*

SOCA. 'Soke', from *socn*, to seek, comparable with Latin *quaestio*. Jurisdiction, with the right to receive fines and a multiplicity of other dues. District in which such *soca* is exercised; a place in a *soca. jurisdiction*

SOCMANNUS. *'Soke man'*, liable to attend the court of a *soca* and serve its lords; free from many villagers' burdens; before 1066 often with more land and higher status than villagers (see, e.g., Middlesex, Appendix); bracketed in the Commissioners' brief with the *liber homo* (free man). *Freeman*

TAINUS, TEGNUS. Person holding land from the King by special grant; formerly used of the King's ministers and military companions. *thane*

T.R.E. *tempore regis Edwardi*, in King Edward's time. *before 1066*

VILLA. Translating Old English *tun*, town. The later distinction between a small *village* and a large *town* was not yet in use in 1086. *village* or *town*

VILLANUS. Member of a *villa*, usully with more land than a *bordarius. villager*

VIRGATA. A quarter of a hide, reckoned at 30 acres. *virgate*

WARA. 1,5. Literally 'defence'; liability for military or other service, or payment in lieu thereof. *obligations*

Braughing
1. Westmill
2. Braughing
3. Standon
4. Wickham
5. Bishop's Stortford
6. Thorley
7. Thundridge
8. Ware
9. Hunsdon
10. Sawbridgeworth
11. Stanstead Abbots
12. Eastwick
13. Rye (House)

Broadwater
1. Norton, 'Rodhanger'
2. Letchworth
3. Willian
4. Weston
5. Great Wymondley
6. Little Wymondley
7. Graveley
8. Almshoe
9. 'Woolwicks'
10. Stevenage
11. Chells
12. Box
13. Walkern
14. Minsden
15. Langley
16. Shephall
17. Aston
18. Bennington
19. Libury
20. Great Munden
21. Little Munden
22. Knebworth
23. Datchworth
24. Codicote
25. Mardley(bury)
26. Watton
27. Sacombe
28. Ayot St. Lawrence
29. Ayot St. Peter
30. Welwyn
31. Tewin (Queen's Hoo)
32. Digswell
33. Hatfield

Cashio
1. St. Paul's Walden
2. Sandridge
3. St. Albans
4. Hanstead (House)
5. Shenley
6. Aldenham
7. Cassio
8. Rickmansworth

Dacorum

(North)
1. Kensworth
2. Caddington
3. Barwythe
4. Flamstead
5. Little Gaddesden
6. Great Gaddesden
7. Redbourn
8. Wheathampstead
9. Hemel Hempstead
10. Windridge
11. King's Langley
12. Abbot's Langley

(South)
13. Napsbury
14. North Mimms
15. Shenley
16. Aldenham
17. Bushey
18. Theobald Street

Edwinstree
1. Barley
2. Newsells
3. Cokenach
4. Barkway
5. Hyde Hall
6. Hodenhoe
7. Buckland
8. Anstey
9. Meesden
10. Wyddial
11. Beauchamps
12. Throcking
13. Corney(bury)
14. Buntingford
15. Alswick
16. Hare Street
17. Great Hormead
18. Little Hormead
19. Brent Pelham
20. Stocking Pelham

Edwinstree
21. Furneaux Pelham
22. Berkesden
23. Aspenden
24. Wakeley
25. Stoney(bury)
26. Bozen
27. Hixham Hall
28. Cockhampstead
29. Patmore
30. Albury
31. Little Hadham
32. Chaldean
33. Much Hadham
34. Leverage
35. Widford

Hertford
1. Tewin
2. Bramfield
3. Panshanger
4. Bengeo
5. Epcombs
6. Hertingfordbury
7. Sele (House)
8. Hertford
9. Amwell
10. Roxford
11. Brickendon
12. Hailey
13. Little Berkhamsted
14. Bayford
15. Hoddesdon
16. Broxbourne
17. Wormley
18. Cheshunt

NOT MAPPED

Broadwater
'Oxwick'

Cashio
Lampeth

Edwinstree
'Hazelhanger'
Sapeham

Hertford
Bricewolde
'Stetchworth'

Odsey
Hainstone
(see Hinxworth)

Hitchin
1. Polehanger
2. Meppershall
3. Westoning
4. Pirton
5. Hexton
6. Wellbury
7. Hitchin
8. Little Offley
9. Great Offley
10. Charlton
11. Lilley
12. Wain (Wood)
13. Ley Green
14. Temple Dinsley
15. King's Walden
16. Flexmore
17. Stagenhoe
18. Bendish
19. Wandon (End)
20. Kimpton

Odsey
1. Hinxworth
2. Ashwell
3. Caldecote
4. Newnham
5. Radwell
6. Bygrave
7. Kelshall
8. Orwell(bury)
9. Therfield
10. Reed
11. Wallington
12. Sandon
13. Clothall
14. Rushden
15. Broadfield
16. Luffenhall
17. Cottered
18. Ardeley

Tring
1. Tiscott
2. Boarscroft
3. Puttenham
4. Gubblecote
5. Miswell
6. Tring
7. Dunsley
8. Wigginton
9. Pendley
10. Aldbury
11. Berkhamsted

National Grid figures are shown on the map border

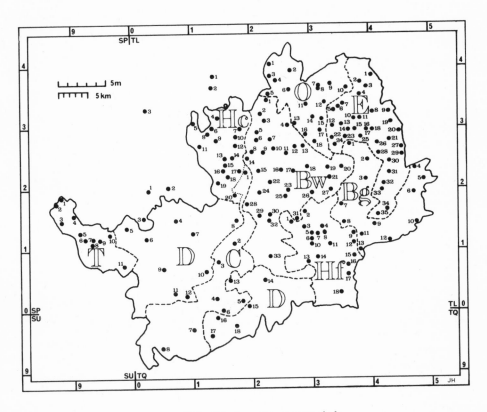

Holwell is shown by an open circle

National Grid figures are shown on the map border

ADDITIONS AND CORRECTIONS *to earlier volumes will be printed as and when necessary. Corrections to Hunts. appear in the Staffs. volume. The text is set under the supervision of the editor, not by the printer. The introduction warned that errors were likely to be most frequent in the first three experimental volumes.*

References are to chapter, section, and line. Words and figures here printed in *italics* are to be *deleted*, those in roman type to be added or retained.

MIDDLESEX

TEXT 2,2,5 *delete star (*)* // 3,9,4 *in 1066* before 1066// 3,12,9 *of the* // 3,26,1 *as 3 hides* for 3 hides // 7,6,5 *Frenchmen with* Frenchmen, // 8,5,9; 10,1,13; 10,2,9 *Wulfward Wight* Wulfward White // 9,8,7-8 *smallholders with* smallholders, // 11,3,6 *priest with* priest, // 11,3,9 *Brictmer... manor* Brictmer held 4 hides of this manor; he was Earl Harold's man; // 11,3,10 *4 hides,*4 hides; // 13,1,9 *woodland, 1200 pigs* woodland for 1200 pigs // 14,1,2 *Land for 2* // 15,1,8 *manor before 1066; he* manor; before 1066 he

NOTES para. 3 (MIDDLESEX) AFTER both ADD columns // ADD 4,5 STAINES. See also Bucks. 7,2 (145 d) (Westminster) 'in EAST BURNHAM..3 thanes..before 1066.. paid 5 ora a year in customary dues to the monastery of Staines'. // BURGESSES. King Edward granted to Westminster 'Stana mid tham lande Staeningahaga withinnon Lundone' (KCD 855; Harmer, Writs, 98). The Staines burgesses probably lived in and about Staining Lane (E.C.2.)// 13,1 WOODLAND. MS 'Sillva' for 'Silva' // 15,1,4 *mean, the* mean the.

APPENDIX Table, line 1,*270* 260 // line 4,*5,5* 4,5 // para. 4, lines 3-4 *from 240...11,2* from 300 to 60 acres (9,6; 11,2) // ADD (at end.) DB usually gives only the taxed hides. It sometimes also gives the total of hides 'which are (or were) there' (e.g. Surrey 1,12, Shere). The Middlesex detail measures cultivated hides to the nearest acre. They are usually near to the number taxed, sometimes very different, but identical in the Westminster manors, all recently granted. Taxed hides may relate to the date of the grant, or to the most recent revision, often long out of date in 1086.

INDEX OF PLACES Hatton *2,1* 7,1 // Holborn *1,1* 1,3 // London ADD 4,5 note; see also Devon, Essex, Surrey.

MAP KEY 0 6 *Harlesdon* Harlesden. TECHNICAL TERMS. HIDE *defferent* different.

SURREY

TEXT 1,1a,3-4 *they paid..they are..they pay* it paid..it is..it pays //1,4,8 *burgessess* burgesses // 2,6,2 *clothing* supplies // 5,4,6 and 5,5,5 *afterwards* later // 5,26,2 *their the* // 5,28,6-7 *that Bishop* that the Bishop // 5,30 *These ... enumerated* It is enumerated and assessed // 6,1 last line *the manor* this manor // 6,3,5; 8,2,4; 15,2,5; 19,21,5; 19,39,5; 36,4,7 *woodland for* woodland at // 8,28,1 *In GODLEY Hundred* [In GODLEY Hundred] // 8,28,7 *fisheries of* fisheries at // 8,28,9 *Value* [Value] // 10,1,7 *Sant* Saint // 13,1,1 *London hold* London, hold // 14,1,3 *sister held* sister, held // 17,4,1 *also holds HAM* holds HAM himself // 19,21,2 *land, and* land and // 19,27,2 *Watton* Walton // 19,35,5 *for*// 19,45,7;22,5,7 *woodland,* woodland at // 29,1,3 *Wulf* Ulf.

NOTES
1,12 DOES NOT NOW. '(Tunc et) modo non dedit' was perhaps intended.
5,17 5,15
5,30 ... 'berewica' 5,29 IT IS. b & a correct and reverse the word order.
18,2 BEFORE 1066. Or 'in which was the hall before 1066. It belongs to this manor'.
19,35 *2 HIDES* 3 HIDES
19,36 ACRE. 'Ibi (habet) .. car(ucam) .. villanum ..servum. Et (ibi est) una acra'.
21,1 HELD. 'tenuit' is repeated, in error.
21,3 THEY DID NOT PAY. Possibly, but not probably, 'He (Walter) did not pay'.
25,1,3 *left ro right* left to right.
27,5 27,3 *the second indented.*

INDEX OF PERSONS. *Alnoth of London* Alnoth // ADD Alnoth of London 6,4 // Ansfrid ADD 5,23 // Geoffrey *4,1* // Hamo *22-25* 23-25 // (Earl) Harold *6,4* // *Herwulf* Herewulf // Ralph *45* 46 // Stigand ADD 2,3 // *Walkerin* Walkelin // Wulfward *26* 24 // Canons of Bayeux ADD 5,2 Reeve ADD 1,1b.

INDEX OF PLACES Addington ADD 36,7 // Beddington *19,15;* 19,15. // Bramley *3;30* 3,29 // Chessington *19,24;* 19,24. // Chilworth *51b* 5,1b // (East) Clandon *829* 8,29 // London ADD 15,2 // Ockley *45* 46 // Southwark *19,1-2.* 19,1-2; // Walton-on-Thames *27-30* 27;30 // Places not named ADD Blackheath 5,1g. Kingston 22,4. Tandridge 5,5. *Godalming 1,14* // Places outside Britain ADD Feugeres .. Ralph.

TECHNICAL TERMS. HUNDRED *who* whose.